Mathematical Models and Simulations, 2nd Edition

Mathematical Models and Simulations, 2nd Edition

Guest Editor

Giovanni Nastasi

MDPI

Basel • Beijing • Wuhan • Barcelona • Belgrade • Novi Sad • Cluj • Manchester

Guest Editor
Giovanni Nastasi
Department of Engineering
and Architecture
University of Enna "Kore"
Enna
Italy

Editorial Office
MDPI AG
Grosspeteranlage 5
4052 Basel, Switzerland

This is a reprint of the Special Issue, published open access by the journal *Axioms* (ISSN 2075-1680), freely accessible at: https://www.mdpi.com/journal/axioms/special_issues/30O36889AY.

For citation purposes, cite each article independently as indicated on the article page online and as indicated below:

Lastname, A.A.; Lastname, B.B. Article Title. *Journal Name* **Year**, *Volume Number*, Page Range.

ISBN 978-3-7258-6151-4 (Hbk)
ISBN 978-3-7258-6152-1 (PDF)
https://doi.org/10.3390/books978-3-7258-6152-1

Contents

axioms

MDPI

Editorial

Mathematical Models and Simulations, 2nd Edition

Giovanni Nastasi

Department of Engineering and Architecture, University of Enna "Kore", Plesso E-Cittadella Universitaria, 94100 Enna, Italy; giovanni.nastasi@unikore.it

1. Introduction

In this Editorial, we are pleased to introduce a Special Issue of the scientific journal *Axioms*, entitled "Mathematical Models and Simulations, 2nd Edition". This is a continuation of a previous Special Issue, entitled "Mathematical Models and Simulations", published in Contribution 1.

Mathematical modeling is a cornerstone of scientific inquiry, providing essential tools for understanding and predicting the behavior of complex systems in physics, biology, finance, and engineering. Alongside theoretical developments, numerical simulations play a crucial role in practical applications, enabling researchers to explore and forecast the dynamics of quantities of interest.

This Special Issue brings together a collection of papers in the field of mathematical physics and applied mathematics, showcasing a diverse range of modeling approaches. These include the development of new analytical frameworks and numerical schemes, as well as innovative applications in fluid dynamics, electrodynamics, decision-making, and data-driven modeling.

The contributions encompass a broad range of mathematical and computational approaches. Several papers address deterministic systems governed by ordinary or partial differential equations, focusing on stability, convergence, and solution behavior. Others explore stochastic, fuzzy, or hybrid modeling techniques that capture uncertainty and complexity in real-world contexts. A variety of computational methods are featured, including finite-difference, finite-element, Galerkin, spline-based, and network simulation techniques, each tailored to the mathematical structure of the problem under study.

Beyond methodological innovation, many works bridge theory and application. Examples include modeling optical fusion effects via equivalent electrical networks, simulating two-dimensional viscous flows with high boundary accuracy, and developing fuzzy decision frameworks for complex business environments. Other studies extend classical analysis through modern theoretical tools such as C-pseudoresolvent families, generalized electrodynamics, and penalized likelihood estimation in spatial statistics.

This Special Issue reflects the dynamic interplay between mathematical theory and computational practice, offering valuable insights and methodologies for researchers engaged in modeling and simulation across scientific disciplines.

2. Overview of the Published Papers

This Special Issue brings together eight high-quality contributions that reflect the diversity and depth of current research in mathematical modeling and simulation. Each paper underwent a rigorous peer-review process and presents original approaches to theoretical analysis, numerical methods, and applied modeling across various domains. The selected works span topics such as differential equations, fluid dynamics, fuzzy decision-making, electrodynamics, statistical modeling, and computational schemes, offering valuable insights and methodologies for both academic and practical applications.

In Contribution 2, M. Alotaibi presents an implicit finite difference scheme for a wave equation with strong damping and discrete delay. Stability is analyzed using the Jury criterion, leading to a condition linking discretization steps with model parameters. A numerical example confirms the scheme's decay behavior and theoretical stability.

In Contribution 3, M. Kostić investigates existence and uniqueness for abstract degenerate non-scalar Volterra equations using the vector-valued Fourier transform and (A,k,B)-regularized C-pseudoresolvent families. The theoretical results are supported by remarks and illustrative applications.

In Contribution 4, V. Sobchuk, O. Kurylko, O. Boryseiko, O. Perehuda, I. Lebedyeva, I. Ulitko, and O. Vashchilina investigate a two-dimensional periodic Stokes flow in a rectangular cavity with constant wall velocities. The velocity field is derived analytically via superposition, while particle trajectories are computed numerically. Boundary accuracy is assessed through local integration control, and fluid advection is modeled using cubic spline interpolation. The results align well with experimental data.

In Contribution 5, J. F. Sanchez-Pérez, J. Solano-Ramírez, F. Marín-García, and E. Castro model the fiber optic fusion effect using the Network Simulation Method (NSM), transforming thermal behavior into an equivalent electrical system. Simulations in NGSpice capture temperature dynamics under high-power conditions, with nondimensional analysis revealing the influence of fiber geometry and refractive index. The results confirm NSM's effectiveness for nonlinear thermal problems in optical systems.

In Contribution 6, V. Nikolova Traneva, V. Todorov, S. Tranev Tranev, and I. Dimov introduce a confidence-interval circular intuitionistic fuzzy set (CIC-IFS) framework for franchise selection, applied to Pizza Hut's European operations. By integrating decision-maker competence and modeling uncertainty through fuzzy aggregation scenarios, the method improves selection accuracy and aligns franchise choices with brand values.

In Contribution 7, Y. M. Alawaideh, A. Alb Lupas, B. M. Al-khamiseh, M. A. Yousif, P. Othman Mohammed, and Y. S. Hamed analyze the Hamiltonian formulation for continuous systems with second-order derivatives using Dirac's theory, focusing on Podolsky's generalized electrodynamics. They show that the Hamiltonian and Euler–Lagrange approaches yield equivalent results, highlighting the Hamiltonian method as a powerful alternative for modeling complex second-order systems.

In Contribution 8, G. Ibacache-Pulgar, P. Pacheco, O. Nicolis, and M. A. Uribe-Opazo extend Thin-Plate Spline Generalized Linear Models (TPS-GLMs) to evaluate local influence via maximum penalized likelihood estimators. Using Fisher Scoring and weighted backfitting, they assess sensitivity to data perturbations and detect influential observations. Applications in agronomy and environmental data illustrate the model's flexibility in capturing nonlinear spatial effects.

In Contribution 9, R. Čiegis, O. Suboč, and R. Čiegis analyze the efficiency of finite-difference and finite-element Galerkin schemes for non-stationary hyperbolic and parabolic problems on dynamic grids. They present improved stability and convergence estimates, highlighting the impact of grid movement and recommending projection operators to enhance accuracy. Computational experiments confirm the theoretical findings.

Conflicts of Interest: The authors declare no conflict of interest.

List of Contributions:

1. Nastasi, G. Mathematical Models and Simulations. *Axioms* **2024**, *13*, 149. https://doi.org/10.3390/axioms13030149.

2. Alotaibi, M. Asymptotic Stability of a Finite Difference Scheme for a Wave Equation with Delayed Damping. *Axioms* **2025**, *14*, 497. https://doi.org/10.3390/axioms14070497.
3. Kostić, M. Abstract Degenerate Non-Scalar Volterra Equations on the Line. *Axioms* **2025**, *14*, 266. https://doi.org/10.3390/axioms14040266.
4. Sobchuk, V.; Kurylko, O.; Boryseiko, O.; Perehuda, O.; Lebedyeva, I.; Ulitko, I.; Vashchilina, O. Simulation of the Advection Process of Stokes Flow Inside a Rectangular Cavity Under Constant Velocities. *Axioms* **2025**, *14*, 3. https://doi.org/10.3390/axioms14010003.
5. Sanchez-Pérez, J.F.; Solano-Ramírez, J.; Marín-García, F.; Castro, E. A Study Using the Network Simulation Method and Nondimensionalization of the Fiber Fuse Effect. *Axioms* **2025**, *14*, 2. https://doi.org/10.3390/axioms14010002.
6. Traneva, V.N.; Todorov, V.; Tranev, S.T.; Dimov, I. A Confidence-Interval Circular Intuitionistic Fuzzy Method for Optimal Master and Sub-Franchise Selection: A Case Study of Pizza Hut in Europe. *Axioms* **2024**, *13*, 758. https://doi.org/10.3390/axioms13110758.
7. Alawaideh, Y.M.; Lupas, A.A.; Al-khamiseh, B.M.; Yousif, M.A.; Mohammed, P.O.; Hamed, Y.S. Hamiltonian Formulation for Continuous Systems with Second-Order Derivatives: A Study of Podolsky Generalized Electrodynamics. *Axioms* **2024**, *13*, 665. https://doi.org/10.3390/axioms13100665.
8. Ibacache-Pulgar, G.; Pacheco, P.; Nicolis, O.; Uribe-Opazo, M.A. Local Influence for the Thin-Plate Spline Generalized Linear Model. *Axioms* **2024**, *13*, 346. https://doi.org/10.3390/axioms13060346.
9. Čiegis, R.; Subač, O.; Čiegis, R. On a Stability of Non-Stationary Discrete Schemes with Respect to Interpolation Errors. *Axioms* **2024**, *13*, 244. https://doi.org/10.3390/axioms13040244.

axioms

MDPI

Article

Asymptotic Stability of a Finite Difference Scheme for a Wave Equation with Delayed Damping

Manal Alotaibi [1,2]

[1] Department of Mathematics, King Fahd University of Petroleum & Minerals (KFUPM), Dhahran 31261, Saudi Arabia; manal.alotibi@kfupm.edu.sa

[2] Center for Integrative Petroleum Research (CIPR), King Fahd University of Petroleum & Minerals (KFUPM), Dhahran 31261, Saudi Arabia

Abstract: In this paper, we propose an implicit finite difference scheme for a wave equation with strong damping and a discrete delay term. Although the scheme is implicit, the use of second-order finite difference approximations for the strong damping term in both space and time prevents it from being unconditionally stable. A sufficient condition for the asymptotic stability of the scheme is established by applying the Jury stability criterion to show that all roots of the characteristic polynomial associated with the resulting linear recurrence lie strictly inside the unit disk. This stability condition is derived under an appropriate constraint that links the time and space discretization steps with the damping and delay parameters. A numerical example is provided to illustrate the decay behavior of the scheme and confirm the theoretical findings.

Keywords: partial differential equations with delay; finite difference scheme; jury stability criterion; discrete-time delay; asymptotic stability

MSC: 35L05; 35M06; 65M06; 65M12

1. Introduction

Delays are ubiquitous in many physical and engineering systems, and experimental evidence suggests that they cannot be ignored. They naturally arise in the study of wave propagation, structural vibrations, and signal processing, where time delays play a critical role in transmission and filtering. Moreover, delays are prevalent in diverse scientific disciplines such as control theory and heat transfer in materials with thermal memory (see [1–3] and references therein).

The well-posedness and stability of delayed evolution equations have attracted considerable attention from researchers; see, for example, [4–8]. Likewise, the numerical solution and stabilization of schemes for both ordinary and partial differential equations with delay have been active areas of research for decades. We refer the reader to [9–12] for ODEs, and to [13–16] for PDEs and references therein.

In [13], Garcia et al. considered the diffusion equation with delay

$$\begin{cases} \frac{\partial u}{\partial t}(t,x) = a^2\frac{\partial^2 u}{\partial x^2}(t,x) + a^2c^2\frac{\partial^2 u}{\partial x^2}(t-\tau,x), & t>\tau,\ 0\le x\le l, \\ u(t,x)=\phi(t,x), & 0\le t\le\tau,\ 0\le x\le l, \\ u(t,0)=u(t,l)=0, & t\ge 0, \end{cases} \tag{1}$$

where $\tau > 0$, $a \neq 0$, and $0 < c < 1$ are real constants. They proved the convergence and asymptotic stability of an explicit finite difference scheme for this problem. In [14], the same authors analyzed the convergence of an implicit finite difference scheme applied to the same model.

In [16], Zhang et al. established asymptotic stability results for a compact θ-method applied to a generalized delay diffusion equation. In another related work, Lekomtsev and Pimenov [15] developed a weighted numerical scheme for parabolic equations with delay, specifically addressing the case of variable heat conductivity. They investigated the accuracy, stability, and convergence order of the proposed method.

While the above studies focus primarily on parabolic problems with delay, related efforts have also been directed toward wave equations exhibiting damping and memory behaviors. Several other articles have proposed and analyzed finite difference schemes for wave equations with various damping and memory effects, notably those in [17–20].

In this paper, we consider a system of wave equations with strong damping and a delayed damping term, given by

$$u_{tt}(x,t) = u_{xx}(x,t) + \mu_1 u_{txx}(x,t) - \mu_2 u_t(x,t-\tau), \quad \text{in } [0,L] \times (0,\infty), \tag{2a}$$
$$u(0,t) = u(L,t) = 0, \tag{2b}$$
$$u(x,0) = u_0(x), \quad u_t(x,0) = u_1(x), \quad \text{in } [0,L], \tag{2c}$$
$$u_t(x,t-\tau) = f_0(x,t-\tau), \quad \text{in } [0,L] \times (0,\tau), \tag{2d}$$

where $\tau > 0$, and μ_1, μ_2 are positive constants. The system (2a)–(2d) features a time-delay term appearing in the *first time derivative* u_t, rather than in the state variable itself—a configuration that introduces significant analytical and numerical challenges. The implicit finite difference scheme constructed to approximate the solution of Problem (2) is based on classical second-order Taylor expansions for the derivatives of $u(x,t)$ (see [21]). These approximations are applied in both space and time and are paired with a consistent initialization of the delay term over the interval $[-\tau, 0]$, as discussed in Section 3.

While delay differential equations and PDEs with delay in the state variable u have been extensively studied, and some works have addressed delays in spatial derivatives such as u_x or u_{xx} in diffusion-type models, the presence of a delay in u_t directly affects the system's temporal dynamics and has received comparatively less attention. This type of delay introduces implicit memory effects and complicates both the discretization process and stability analysis, particularly within finite difference frameworks.

To the best of our knowledge, this specific configuration has not been thoroughly addressed in the literature. In this work, we construct a fully discrete, second-order accurate (in both time and space) implicit finite difference scheme tailored to this structure. Despite the presence of a strong damping term, our stability analysis—based on the Jury criterion—reveals that the scheme is *conditionally stable*, depending on the time step, delay, and damping parameters. These results highlight the subtle interplay between the delay structure and numerical stability, underscoring the need for careful analysis when extending finite difference methods to non-standard delayed PDEs.

In this paper, we focus on constructing a second-order finite difference scheme to approximate the solution of the system (2a)–(2d), building on the work presented in [13,14]. Following the introduction, Section 2 provides essential theoretical results on the continuous system and introduces key definitions that underpin the stability analysis of the discretized model. The finite difference scheme itself is presented in Section 3, with a rigorous stability analysis given in Section 4. Finally, Section 5 illustrates the performance of the proposed scheme through numerical experiments that confirm the theoretical findings. The paper concludes in Section 6.

2. Preliminaries

This section provides the theoretical background necessary for the stability analysis of the proposed finite difference scheme. We begin by recalling an exponential stability result for the continuous Problem (2a)–(2d), which ensures that the system's energy decays under appropriate parameter conditions. We then review the Jury stability criterion, which is instrumental in analyzing the stability of the fully discretized system.

2.1. Exponential Stability of the Continuous System

Before presenting the numerical approximation and its stability analysis, we recall a theoretical result that establishes exponential stability for wave equations with time-delay feedback. In [6], the authors consider a wave equation with frictional (weak) damping and delayed feedback and prove exponential stability under the condition $\mu_2 < \mu_1$. Although their analysis focuses on weak damping, a similar stabilization mechanism applies in the presence of strong damping (i.e., $\mu_1 \Delta u_t$), where the analogous condition becomes

$$\mu_2 < \frac{\mu_1}{C_p}, \tag{3}$$

with C_p denoting the Poincaré constant arising from the use of the Poincaré inequality.

To ensure that the continuous system exhibits exponential stability, we assume throughout our stability analysis of the discrete scheme that the parameters μ_1 and μ_2 satisfy Condition (3).

2.2. Review of the Jury Stability Criterion

Jury's criterion is a classical method used to assess the stability of linear time-invariant discrete-time systems by analyzing their characteristic polynomials in the z-domain. It serves as the discrete-time counterpart to the Routh–Hurwitz criterion used in continuous-time analysis. The method determines whether all roots of the characteristic polynomial lie strictly inside the unit circle in the complex plane. This is achieved by applying a sequence of algebraic tests to the coefficients of the polynomial. For a detailed treatment of the Jury stability criterion and its application to discrete-time systems, we refer the reader to [22,23].

We let $D(z)$ be the characteristic polynomial of the system, given by

$$D(z) = a_0 z^n + a_1 z^{n-1} + \cdots + a_{n-1} z + a_n, \quad \text{with } a_0 > 0.$$

To determine the system's stability, the Jury table is constructed using the coefficients of $D(z)$. The first two rows contain the coefficients in forward and reverse order, respectively. Each subsequent row is computed recursively.

The structure of the Jury table is as follows:

$$\begin{array}{ccccccc}
a_0 & a_1 & a_2 & \cdots & a_{n-2} & a_{n-1} & a_n \\
a_n & a_{n-1} & a_{n-2} & \cdots & a_2 & a_1 & a_0 \\
b_0 & b_1 & b_2 & \cdots & b_{n-2} & b_{n-1} & \\
b_{n-1} & b_{n-2} & \cdots & b_2 & b_1 & b_0 & \\
\vdots & \vdots & & \ddots & & \vdots & \vdots
\end{array}$$

The entries of the third and subsequent rows are computed using the following determinant-based formulas:

$$b_i = \begin{vmatrix} a_n & a_{n-1-i} \\ a_0 & a_{i+1} \end{vmatrix}, \quad c_j = \begin{vmatrix} b_{n-1} & b_{n-2-j} \\ b_0 & b_{j+1} \end{vmatrix}, \quad i = 0, \cdots, n-1, \; j = 0, \cdots, n-2.$$

For the polynomial $D(z)$ to be stable (i.e., all of its roots lie within the unit circle), it must satisfy the following necessary conditions:

$$D(1) > 0, \quad (-1)^n D(-1) > 0.$$

Additionally, the sufficient conditions provided by the Jury test include

$$a_0 > |a_n|, \quad |b_{n-1}| > |b_0|, \quad |c_{n-2}| > |c_0|, \quad \ldots$$

These conditions are applied iteratively through each row of the table. Violation of any one of them indicates that the system is unstable.

2.3. Well-Posedness of the Continuous Problem

Before proceeding with the discretization, we briefly state a standard existence and uniqueness result for the continuous System (2a)–(2d). The well-posedness can be established using semigroup theory combined with energy estimates.

Theorem 1 (Well-posedness of the continuous problem). *We let $\mu_1, \mu_2 > 0$, and assume that the initial data satisfy $u_0, u_1 \in H_0^1(\Omega)$ and $f_0 \in L^2((0,\tau); H_0^1(\Omega))$. Then System* (2a)–(2d) *admits a unique weak solution*

$$u \in C^1([0,T]; H_0^1(\Omega)).$$

For further details and related proofs, we refer the reader to [24,25].

3. Finite Difference Scheme

Building on the foundational work in [13], we begin by discretizing the spatial domain and time interval to construct a finite difference scheme that approximates the solution of System (2a)–(2d). The resulting scheme is then reformulated as a two-level scheme (see [26]), which facilitates the stability analysis presented in the following section.

Spatial discretization: We let $L > 0$ and define $h = \frac{L}{P}$ for some integer P. Then we can divide the interval $[0, L]$ into P intervals of equal size h. We denote by $x_i = ih$ for $i = 0, 1, \cdots, P$ the partition nodes (see Figure 1).

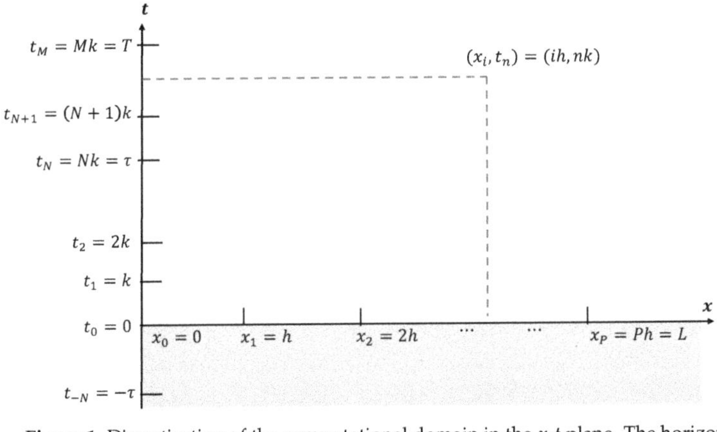

Figure 1. Discretization of the computational domain in the x-t plane. The horizontal axis represents the spatial mesh points $x_i = ih$ for $i = 0, \ldots, P$, and the vertical axis represents the temporal mesh points $t_n = nk$ for $n = 0, \ldots, M$. The shaded region corresponds to the interval $t \in [-\tau, 0]$, used to initialize the delay term $u_t(x, t-\tau)$ through the prescribed data $f_0(x, t-\tau)$. The main finite difference scheme is applied over the interval $t \in [0, T]$.

Time discretization: We can truncate the time interval $(0, \infty)$ to $(0, T]$ for sufficiently large integer $T > \tau$. Then we divide the interval $[0, T]$ into M equal sub-intervals using the time step-size $k = \frac{T}{M}$. We denote by $t_n = nk$, for $n = 0, 1, \cdots, M$ the nodes of the time partitioning. Furthermore, we let $\tau = Nk$, where $N < M$ (see Figure 1).

The discrete solution: Next, we approximate the solution $u(x,t)$ with the discrete solution $u(x_i, t_n) = u(ih, nk)$ for $i = 0, \cdots, P$ and $n = 0, \cdots, M$ and we write $u(x,t) \approx u_i^n = u(ih, nk)$. Similarly, we approximate $u(x, t-\tau) \approx u_i^{n-N} = u(ih, (n-N)k)$.

Remark 1. *The discrete-time domain shown in Figure 1 covers the main computational interval $[0, T]$, while the delayed term $u_t(x, t-\tau)$ requires initialization on the separate interval $[-\tau, 0]$. This distinction is visualized by shading the region $t < 0$. All delay values are initialized via the given function $f_0(x, t-\tau)$ as defined in Equation* (2d).

Finite difference approximations. The partial derivatives in (2) are approximated using second-order central differences as follows:

$$u_{tt}\big|_{(x_i,t_n)} \approx \frac{u_i^{n-1} - 2u_i^n + u_i^{n+1}}{k^2}, \tag{4}$$

$$u_{xx}\big|_{(x_i,t_n)} \approx \frac{u_{i-1}^n - 2u_i^n + u_{i+1}^n}{h^2}, \tag{5}$$

$$u_{txx}\big|_{(x_i,t_n)} \approx \frac{1}{2kh^2}\Big[(u_{i-1}^{n+1} - 2u_i^{n+1} + u_{i+1}^{n+1}) - (u_{i-1}^{n-1} - 2u_i^{n-1} + u_{i+1}^{n-1})\Big], \tag{6}$$

$$u_t\big|_{(x_i,t_n-\tau)} \approx \frac{u_i^{n-N+1} - u_i^{n-N-1}}{2k}, \tag{7}$$

where k and h are the time and space steps, respectively, and $N \in \mathbb{N}$ satisfies $\tau = Nk$.

Substituting the above approximations into the PDE (2), sampled at the grid point (x_i, t_n), yields the discrete equation:

$$\begin{aligned} 2h^2u_i^{n-1} - 4h^2u_i^n + 2h^2u_i^{n+1} = {} & 2k^2(u_{i-1}^n - 2u_i^n + u_{i+1}^n) \\ & + \mu_1 k(u_{i-1}^{n+1} - 2u_i^{n+1} + u_{i+1}^{n+1}) \\ & - \mu_1 k(u_{i-1}^{n-1} - 2u_i^{n-1} + u_{i+1}^{n-1}) \\ & - \mu_2 kh^2 u_i^{n-N+1} + \mu_2 kh^2 u_i^{n-N-1}. \end{aligned}$$

Rearranging terms, we obtain an update formula for u_i^{n+1}:

$$\begin{aligned} -\mu_1 k u_{i-1}^{n+1} + 2(\mu_1 k + h^2)u_i^{n+1} - \mu_1 k u_{i+1}^{n+1} = {} & -\mu_1 k u_{i-1}^{n-1} + 2(\mu_1 k - h^2)u_i^{n-1} - \mu_1 k u_{i+1}^{n-1} \\ & + 2k^2(u_{i-1}^n + u_{i+1}^n) + 4(h^2 - k^2)u_i^n \\ & - \alpha(u_i^{n-N+1} - u_i^{n-N-1}), \end{aligned} \tag{8}$$

where $\alpha = \mu_2 kh^2$.

We define $U^n = [u_1^n, u_2^n, \ldots, u_{P-1}^n]^T \in \mathbb{R}^{P-1}$. Recurrence (8) can be written in compact matrix form as

$$AU^{n+1} = CU^n + BU^{n-1} - \alpha(U^{n-N+1} - U^{n-N-1}), \qquad n \geq 0, \tag{9}$$

where A, B, and C are tridiagonal matrices.

For completeness, their entries are defined as follows:

$$\begin{aligned} A &= \text{tridiag}(-\mu_1 k,\ 2(\mu_1 k + h^2),\ -\mu_1 k), \\ B &= \text{tridiag}(-\mu_1 k,\ 2(\mu_1 k - h^2),\ -\mu_1 k), \\ C &= \text{tridiag}(2k^2,\ 4(h^2 - k^2),\ 2k^2). \end{aligned}$$

Since Scheme (9) is a three-level recurrence, the initial vectors U^0 and U^1 must be computed using the initial and delay data provided in (2c)–(2d).

The finite difference approximations of the initial and boundary conditions:

The initial and boundary conditions in (2) are also approximated by the finite difference approximations as follows:

$$u_0^n = u_P^n = 0, \quad n = 0, \cdots, M \quad \text{boundary condition} \tag{10}$$

$$u_i^0 = u_0(x_i), \quad i = 1, \cdots, P-1 \quad \text{initial condition for } u \tag{11}$$

$$u_i^1 - u_i^{-1} = 2ku_1(x_i), \quad i = 1, \cdots, P-1 \quad \text{initial condition for } u_t \tag{12}$$

$$u_i^{n-N+1} - u_i^{n-N-1} = 2kf_0(x_i, t_n - \tau), \quad i = 1, \cdots, P-1 \text{ and } n = 0, \cdots, N-1 \tag{13}$$

Using (11), we define $U^0 = [u_1^0, u_2^0, \cdots, u_{P-1}^0]^T$. To define the vector U^1, we first rewrite the initial Condition (12) as $u_i^{-1} = u_i^1 - 2ku_1(x_i)$, or in a vector notation as

$$U^{-1} = U^1 + V, \tag{14}$$

where $V = -2k[u_1(x_1), u_1(x_2), \cdots, u_1(x_{P-1})]^T \in \mathbb{R}^{P-1}$.

Next, we write the matrix Equation (9) at $n = 0$ as follows:

$$AU^1 = BU^{-1} + CU^0 - \alpha\Big(U^{-N+1} - U^{-N-1}\Big).$$

After substituting U^{-1} from (14), we can solve for U^1 the following equation:

$$(A - B)U^1 = BV + CU^0 - \alpha\Big(U^{-N+1} - U^{-N-1}\Big). \tag{15}$$

Once the solution of (15) is obtained, we can compute U^{-1} from (14). However, solving (15) requires evaluating $U^{-N+1} - U^{-N-1}$ that can be obtained from (13) with $n = 0$ as follows:

$$U^{-N+1} - U^{-N-1} = F^0,$$

where F^n is a $P - 1$ vector defined as

$$F^n = 2k[f_0(x_1, t_n - \tau), f_0(x_2, t_n - \tau), \cdots, f_0(x_{P-1}, t_n - \tau)]^T, \quad \text{for } n \geq 0 \tag{16}$$

Note that for $n = 1, \cdots, N-1$, the conditions in (13) can be written in vector notation as

$$\begin{array}{ll}
\text{For } n = N-1 \Rightarrow & U^0 - U^{-2} = F^{N-1} \\
\text{For } n = N-2 \Rightarrow & U^{-1} - U^{-3} = F^{N-2} \\
\text{For } n = N-3 \Rightarrow & U^{-2} - U^{-4} = F^{N-3} \\
\vdots & \vdots \\
\text{For } n = 3 \Rightarrow & U^{4-N} - U^{2-N} = F^3 \\
\text{For } n = 2 \Rightarrow & U^{3-N} - U^{1-N} = F^2 \\
\text{For } n = 1 \Rightarrow & U^{2-N} - U^{-N} = F^1
\end{array}$$

Given U^0 and U^{-1} (from (14)), we can solve the first two equations to obtain U^{-2} and U^{-3}, respectively. Subsequently, we can compute $U^{-4}, \ldots, U^{-N}$ in a step-by-step manner.

We let A_* denote the block diagonal matrix $\text{diag}(A, I, I, \cdots, I)$, where I is the identity matrix of size $(P-1) \times (P-1)$, $U_*^n = [U^n, U^{n-1}, \cdots, U^{n-N+1}, U^{n-N}, U^{n-N-1}]^T$ and

$$\Phi_* = \begin{bmatrix} C & B & 0 & \cdots & 0 & -\alpha I & 0 & \alpha I \\ I & 0 & 0 & \cdots & 0 & 0 & 0 & 0 \\ \vdots & \vdots & \vdots & & \vdots & \vdots & \vdots & \vdots \\ 0 & 0 & 0 & \cdots & I & 0 & 0 & 0 \\ 0 & 0 & 0 & \cdots & 0 & I & 0 & 0 \\ 0 & 0 & 0 & \cdots & 0 & 0 & I & 0 \end{bmatrix}. \quad (17)$$

Then, Equation (9) can be rewritten in an equivalent compact form

$$A_* U_*^{n+1} = \Phi_* U_*^n, \; n \geq 0. \quad (18)$$

Since $\mu_1, k, h > 0$, the matrix A is symmetric and positive definite and therefore nonsingular (invertible). The invertibility of the matrix A implies that the block diagonal matrix A_* is also invertible. We let $\Psi_* := A_*^{-1}\Phi_*$. Equation (18) has a unique solution given by

$$U_*^{n+1} = \Psi_* U_*^n, \; n \geq 0. \quad (19)$$

4. Asymptotic Stability of the Fully Discrete Scheme

In this section, we establish conditions on the mesh parameters that ensure the asymptotic stability of the fully discretized System (19). Specifically, we determine sufficient criteria under which all eigenvalues of the associated amplification matrix Ψ_* lie strictly inside the unit disk. This guarantees that the discrete solution decays asymptotically as time progresses, in accordance with the Jury stability criterion.

Given the matrix

$$\mathcal{M} = \begin{bmatrix} -2 & 1 & 0 & \dots & 0 & 0 \\ 1 & -2 & 1 & \cdots & 0 & 0 \\ 0 & 1 & -2 & \cdots & 0 & 0 \\ \vdots & \vdots & \vdots & \ddots & -2 & 1 \\ 0 & 0 & 0 & \cdots & 1 & -2 \end{bmatrix},$$

we can define the matrices A, B and C in terms of the matrix $\mathcal{M}$ as follows:

$$\begin{aligned} A &= 2h^2 I - \mu_1 k \mathcal{M}, \\ B &= -2h^2 I - \mu_1 k \mathcal{M}, \\ C &= 4h^2 I + 2k^2 \mathcal{M}. \end{aligned} \quad (20)$$

The eigenvalues of the matrix $\mathcal{M}$ (see, for example, [21]) are given by

$$\lambda_m = -4\sin^2\left(\frac{\pi m}{2P}\right), \quad m = 1, \ldots, P-1, \quad (21)$$

and decrease strictly as m increases. Moreover, the matrix $\mathcal{M}$ is diagonalizable and can be written as $\mathcal{M} = Q\Lambda Q^{-1}$, where Q is the matrix of eigenvectors and Λ is the diagonal matrix of eigenvalues. Having that the identity matrix can be written as $I = QQ^{-1}$, we reformulate the block matrices Φ_* and A_* as follows:

$$A_* = Q_* \tilde{A}_* Q_*^{-1}, \quad (22)$$

$$\Phi_* = Q_* \tilde{\Phi}_* Q_*^{-1}, \quad (23)$$

where $\tilde{A}_* = \mathrm{diag}(2h^2 I - \mu_1 k\Lambda, I, \cdots, I)$, $Q_* = \mathrm{diag}(Q, Q, \cdots, Q)$ and

$$\tilde{\Phi}_* = \begin{bmatrix} 4h^2 I + 2k^2\Lambda & -2h^2 I - \mu_1 k\Lambda & 0 & \cdots & 0 & -\alpha I & 0 & \alpha I \\ I & 0 & 0 & \cdots & 0 & 0 & 0 & 0 \\ \vdots & \vdots & \vdots & & \vdots & \vdots & \vdots & \vdots \\ 0 & 0 & 0 & \cdots & I & 0 & 0 & 0 \\ 0 & 0 & 0 & \cdots & 0 & I & 0 & 0 \\ 0 & 0 & 0 & \cdots & 0 & 0 & I & 0 \end{bmatrix}. \tag{24}$$

Substituting (22) and (23) into (18), we obtain

$$Q_*\tilde{A}_*(Q_*^{-1}U_*^{n+1}) = Q_*\tilde{\Phi}_*(Q_*^{-1}U_*^n), \quad n \geq 0. \tag{25}$$

We let $\mathcal{U}^n := Q^{-1}U^n = [\varphi_1^n, \varphi_2^n, \dots, \varphi_{P-1}^n]^\top \in \mathbb{R}^{P-1}$, and define the block vector

$$\mathcal{U}_*^n := [\mathcal{U}^n, \mathcal{U}^{n-1}, \dots, \mathcal{U}^{n-N+1}, \mathcal{U}^{n-N}, \mathcal{U}^{n-N-1}]^\top = Q_*^{-1}U_*^n,$$

so that $\mathcal{U}_*^n \in \mathbb{R}^{(P-1)(N+2)}$. Then, the difference Equation (25) simplifies to

$$\mathcal{U}_*^{n+1} = \tilde{\Psi}_*\mathcal{U}_*^n, \quad n \geq 0, \tag{26}$$

where $\tilde{\Psi}_* := \tilde{A}_*^{-1}\tilde{\Phi}_*$. It follows that Ψ_* (from (19)) and $\tilde{\Psi}_*$ (from (26)) are similar matrices and therefore share the same set of eigenvalues.

Equation (26) may be reformulated into an equivalent expression by reordering its components. For $m = 1, \dots, P-1$, we define

$$H_m^n := [\varphi_m^n, \varphi_m^{n-1}, \dots, \varphi_m^{n-N+1}, \varphi_m^{n-N}, \varphi_m^{n-N-1}]^\top,$$

and assemble them into a block vector

$$H_*^n := [H_1^n, H_2^n, \dots, H_{P-1}^n]^\top.$$

In a similar manner, for $m = 1, \dots, P-1$, we define the diagonal matrix

$$D_m := \operatorname{diag}\Big(2h^2 - \mu_1 k\lambda_m, 1, \dots, 1\Big),$$

and the matrix G_m as

$$G_m := \begin{bmatrix} 4h^2 + 2k^2\lambda_m & -(2h^2 + \mu_1 k\lambda_m) & 0 & \cdots & 0 & -\alpha & 0 & \alpha \\ 1 & 0 & 0 & \cdots & 0 & 0 & 0 & 0 \\ 0 & 1 & 0 & \cdots & 0 & 0 & 0 & 0 \\ \vdots & \vdots & \vdots & \ddots & \vdots & \vdots & \vdots & \vdots \\ 0 & 0 & 0 & \cdots & 1 & 0 & 0 & 0 \\ 0 & 0 & 0 & \cdots & 0 & 1 & 0 & 0 \\ 0 & 0 & 0 & \cdots & 0 & 0 & 1 & 0 \end{bmatrix},$$

We then define $D_* := \operatorname{diag}(D_1, \dots, D_{P-1})$ and $G_* := \operatorname{diag}(G_1, \dots, G_{P-1})$. The matrix D_* is invertible, since each D_m is invertible for $m = 1, \dots, P-1$. This allows us to introduce the block matrix

$$\tilde{\tilde{\Psi}}_* := D_*^{-1}G_* = \operatorname{diag}(D_1^{-1}G_1, \cdots, D_{P-1}^{-1}G_{P-1}),$$

and to rewrite the difference Equation (26) in the equivalent form:

$$H_*^{n+1} = \tilde{\tilde{\Psi}}_* H_*^n, \quad n \geq 0. \tag{27}$$

The matrices $\tilde{\Psi}_*$ and $\tilde{\tilde{\Psi}}_*$ are similar and therefore have the same set of eigenvalues.

The matrices

$$D_m^{-1}G_m = \begin{bmatrix} \frac{4h^2+2k^2\lambda_m}{2h^2-\mu_1 k\lambda_m} & \frac{-(2h^2+\mu_1 k\lambda_m)}{2h^2-\mu_1 k\lambda_m} & 0 & \cdots & 0 & \frac{-\alpha}{2h^2-\mu_1 k\lambda_m} & 0 & \frac{\alpha}{2h^2-\mu_1 k\lambda_m} \\ 1 & 0 & 0 & \cdots & 0 & 0 & 0 & 0 \\ 0 & 1 & 0 & \cdots & 0 & 0 & 0 & 0 \\ \vdots & \vdots & \vdots & \ddots & \vdots & \vdots & \vdots & \vdots \\ 0 & 0 & 0 & \cdots & 1 & 0 & 0 & 0 \\ 0 & 0 & 0 & \cdots & 0 & 1 & 0 & 0 \\ 0 & 0 & 0 & \cdots & 0 & 0 & 1 & 0 \end{bmatrix},$$

for $m = 1, \ldots, P-1$, are companion matrices (see [27]) corresponding to the $P-1$ polynomials

$$\pi_m(z) = z^{N+2} - \frac{4h^2 + 2k^2\lambda_m}{2h^2 - \mu_1 k\lambda_m} z^{N+1} + \frac{2h^2 + \mu_1 k\lambda_m}{2h^2 - \mu_1 k\lambda_m} z^N + \frac{\alpha}{2h^2 - \mu_1 k\lambda_m} z^2 - \frac{\alpha}{2h^2 - \mu_1 k\lambda_m}. \tag{28}$$

The $N+2$ roots of each polynomial $\pi_m(z)$ are precisely the eigenvalues of the matrix $D_m^{-1}G_m$. Therefore, verifying that all eigenvalues of the block matrix Ψ_* in (19) lie strictly within the unit disk reduces to showing that all roots of $\pi_m(z)$, for $m = 1, \ldots, P-1$, lie inside the unit disk.

Remark 2. *The index m corresponds to the spectral modes associated with the diagonalization of the spatial discretization matrix $\mathcal{M}$, whose eigenvalues $\lambda_m < 0$ define the modal structure of the semi-discrete system. This decoupling enables mode-by-mode stability analysis via the characteristic polynomials $\pi_m(z)$. Consequently, verifying that all such polynomials have roots strictly inside the unit disk ensures the asymptotic stability of the fully discrete scheme.*

To analyze the stability of discrete dynamical systems or difference schemes—particularly when explicit root-finding is impractical—we often turn to root location criteria tailored to the unit disk. One such result is the Jury stability criterion, a discrete analogue of the Routh–Hurwitz test for continuous systems. It provides a systematic, algebraic procedure to determine whether all the roots of a characteristic polynomial lie strictly inside the unit circle. This criterion is especially well suited for analyzing the stability of linear recurrence relations and finite difference schemes, making it a natural tool in our context. In this work, we apply the Jury test to assess the stability of the proposed second-order scheme by verifying the root conditions of the associated characteristic equation.

To assess the stability of the proposed finite difference scheme, we analyze the location of the roots of its characteristic equation. For this purpose, we employ the Jury stability criterion, presented in Section 2, which is well suited for evaluating whether all roots of $\pi_m(z)$ lie within the unit circle.

Proposition 1. *We let $N > 0$ and let λ_m denote the mth eigenvalue of the matrix $\mathcal{M}$ defined in* (21). *Suppose the parameters μ_1, μ_2, k, and h are positive and satisfy the following Courant–Friedrichs–Lewy (CFL) time-step restriction involving the spectral radius $\rho(\mathcal{M}) := \max_m |\lambda_m|$:*

$$0 < k < k_{CFL} := \min\left\{ \frac{2h^2}{\mu_2 h^2 + (\mu_1 + 4\mu_2)\rho(\mathcal{M})}, \frac{\sqrt{2}h}{\sqrt{\rho(\mathcal{M})}} \right\}. \tag{29}$$

Then all roots of the polynomial $\pi_m(z)$ defined in (28) *lie strictly inside the unit disk.*

Proof. We analyze the asymptotic stability of the fully discrete scheme by applying the Jury stability criterion to the mode-wise characteristic polynomial

$$\pi_m(z) = z^{N+2} - A_m z^{N+1} + B_m z^N + C_m z^2 - C_m = \sum_{j=0}^{n} a_j z^{n-j}, \quad n = N+2. \tag{30}$$

The coefficients A_m, B_m, C_m are given by

$$A_m = \frac{4h^2 + 2k^2\lambda_m}{2h^2 - \mu_1 k\lambda_m}, \quad B_m = \frac{2h^2 + \mu_1 k\lambda_m}{2h^2 - \mu_1 k\lambda_m}, \quad C_m = \frac{\mu_2 k h^2}{2h^2 - \mu_1 k\lambda_m},$$

where $\lambda_m < 0$ is the mth eigenvalue of $\mathcal{M}$. The coefficients a_j in (A1) are

$$a_0 = 1, \quad a_1 = -A_m, \quad a_2 = B_m, \quad a_{n-2} = C_m, \quad a_{n-1} = 0, \quad a_n = -C_m,$$
$$a_j = 0 \text{ for } 3 \le j \le n-3.$$

Before proceeding, we note that the coefficients $A_m, B_m,$ and C_m share the same denominator $2h^2 - \mu_1 k\lambda_m$, which is positive since $\lambda_m < 0$. Therefore, $C_m > 0$ immediately. The coefficients A_m and B_m are also positive provided that

$$k^2 < \frac{2h^2}{|\lambda_m|} \quad \text{and} \quad k < \frac{2h^2}{\mu_1|\lambda_m|}.$$

These inequalities are both implied by the CFL condition (29). Hence, we conclude that all three coefficients $A_m, B_m,$ and C_m are positive under the CFL restriction.

Step 1: Necessary conditions. We first verify the necessary Jury conditions:

$$\text{NC1:} \quad \pi_m(1) = 1 - A_m + B_m = \frac{-2k^2\lambda_m}{2h^2 - \mu_1 k\lambda_m} > 0, \quad \text{since } \lambda_m < 0.$$
$$\text{NC2:} \quad (-1)^n \pi_m(-1) = 1 + A_m + B_m > 0, \quad \text{since } A_m, B_m > 0.$$

Step 2: First sufficient condition. The condition $|a_0| > |a_n|$ becomes

$$\text{SC1:} \quad 1 > |-C_m| = C_m,$$

which leads to

$$C_m < 1 \quad \Leftrightarrow \quad \frac{\mu_2 k h^2}{2h^2 - \mu_1 k\lambda_m} < 1. \tag{31}$$

Since $\lambda_m < 0$, the denominator is positive. Multiplying both sides and solving gives

$$k < \frac{2h^2}{\mu_2 h^2 + \mu_1 \lambda_m}. \tag{32}$$

Although $\lambda_m < 0$, the right-hand side remains positive because

$$\mu_2 h^2 + \mu_1\lambda_m < \mu_2 h^2 + \mu_1|\lambda_m| < \mu_2 h^2 + \mu_1 \rho(\mathcal{M}),$$

which implies

$$\frac{2h^2}{\mu_2 h^2 + \mu_1\lambda_m} > \frac{2h^2}{\mu_2 h^2 + \mu_1\rho(\mathcal{M})}.$$

Under the CFL condition (29), we have

$$k < \frac{2h^2}{\mu_2 h^2 + (\mu_1 + 4\mu_2)\rho(\mathcal{M})} < \frac{2h^2}{\mu_2 h^2 + \mu_1 \rho(\mathcal{M})},$$

which ensures Inequality (32) holds. Hence, $C_m < 1$ and the first necessary condition (SC1) is satisfied.

Step 3: Second sufficient condition. The next Jury condition involves

$$b_0 = a_n a_1 - a_0 a_{n-1} = (-C_m)(-A_m) = A_m C_m, \quad b_{n-1} = a_n^2 - a_0^2 = C_m^2 - 1.$$

Note. The quantity $b_0 = A_m C_m$ is positive under the CFL condition (29). Also, Step 2 guarantees that $b_{n-1} = C_m^2 - 1 < 0$. The Jury condition reads

$$\text{SC2:} \qquad |b_{n-1}| > |b_0| \quad \Rightarrow \quad 1 - C_m^2 > A_m C_m.$$

To verify this inequality rigorously, we consider the difference

$$1 - C_m^2 - A_m C_m = \frac{(2h^2 - \mu_1 k \lambda_m)^2 - \left[h^4 k^2 \mu_2^2 + 2h^2 k \mu_2 (2h^2 + k^2 \lambda_m)\right]}{(2h^2 - \mu_1 k \lambda_m)^2}.$$

We let $D(k) := 2h^2 - \mu_1 k \lambda_m$ and define the polynomial

$$\chi(k) := D(k)^2 - h^4 k^2 \mu_2^2 - 2h^2 k \mu_2 (2h^2 + k^2 \lambda_m).$$

Thus, Condition $1 - C_m^2 > A_m C_m$ is equivalent to $\chi(k) > 0$.
Since $\chi(0) = D(0)^2 = 4h^4 > 0$, it suffices to show $\chi(k)$ is non-decreasing. Direct differentiating gives

$$\chi'(k) = -4\mu_2 h^4 - 2\mu_2^2 k h^4 + 4\mu_1 |\lambda_m| h^2 + 6\mu_2 |\lambda_m| k^2 h^2 + 2\mu_1 \lambda_m^2 k.$$

Each term in $\chi'(k)$ is nonnegative except the first two, which are of size $O(h^4)$. The positive terms scale like $O(h^2)$ or $O(k)$. Then, under the CFL restriction (29), we have

$$k < \min\left\{ \frac{2h^2}{(\mu_1 + 4\mu_2)|\lambda_m|}, \frac{\sqrt{2}h}{\sqrt{|\lambda_m|}} \right\}.$$

This ensures the positive terms dominate. Hence, $\chi'(k) \geq 0$, and $\chi(k) \geq \chi(0) > 0$ for all $0 \leq k \leq k_{\text{CFL}}$. We conclude that SC2 is satisfied.

Step 4: Higher-order conditions. Due to the sparsity of $\pi_m(z)$, all higher-order determinants in the Jury table involve only the nonzero coefficients $a_0, a_1, a_2, a_{n-2}, a_n$. This structure allows the higher-order Jury inequalities to be expressed in a simplified form:

$$(1 - \theta_1 C_m)(1 - \theta_2 C_m) > \theta_3 C_m, \quad \text{with } \theta_i > 0.$$

A detailed verification of this form and the derivation of representative cases, including the third sufficient condition SC3, is provided in Appendix A. That appendix shows how these inequalities follow from the previously established conditions SC1 and SC2, and are thus guaranteed by the CFL restriction (29).

Therefore, under the CFL condition (29), all Jury conditions are satisfied for each mode m, and all roots of $\pi_m(z)$ lie strictly inside the unit disk. □

Remark 3. *If the damping and delay parameters μ_1 and μ_2 are sufficiently large, then the first term in the CFL condition* (29) *becomes more restrictive than the second, and the condition simplifies to*

$$k < \frac{2h^2}{\mu_2 h^2 + (\mu_1 + 4\mu_2)\rho(\mathcal{M})}.$$

However, for generality and mathematical precision, we retain the full minimum expression in (29).

Remark 4. *While the proposed scheme discretizes a wave equation with delay, the Jury criterion is not applied to the PDE directly but to the characteristic polynomial $\pi_m(z)$ derived from the recurrence relation* (A1). *The coefficients depend on delay parameters (e.g., μ_2) but remain constant for each mode. Thus, the standard Jury test is applicable. See [28] for more general validation.*

Since the roots of $\pi_m(z)$ are the eigenvalues of the matrix $\tilde{\tilde{\Psi}}_*$, and hence are also eigenvalues of Ψ_*, we arrive at the following result.

Proposition 2. *We let $k, h > 0$. If the CFL-type condition* (29) *is satisfied, then all eigenvalues of the matrix Ψ_* in* (19) *lie strictly inside the unit disk.*

The following theorem then follows immediately from Proposition 2 and ([29] Theorem 4.13).

Theorem 2 (Stability of the Discrete Scheme)**.** *We let $k, h > 0$. If Inequality* (29) *is satisfied, then the finite difference scheme* (19) *is asymptotically stable.*

Remark 5. *In [13], the authors consider the delayed diffusion equation stated in our Introduction as Equation* (1). *Their stability condition for the explicit scheme is given in Theorem 5 (page 863) and reads*

$$\Delta t < \frac{\Delta x^2}{2a^2(1 + c^2)},$$

where a is the diffusion coefficient and c is the delay strength. The condition reflects a CFL-type restriction that involves the time step Δt, space step Δx, and delay-related constant.

In [14], the same delay model is treated using implicit schemes, and unconditional stability is shown in Proposition 4 (page 1284) through spectral norm estimates of a block companion matrix.

In contrast, the present work considers a delayed wave equation with strong damping and delay in the derivative $u_t(t - \tau)$. The resulting discrete scheme leads to a higher-order recurrence relation, and the stability condition derived in Proposition 1 implies

$$0 < k < \frac{2h^2}{\mu_2 h^2 + (\mu_1 + 4\mu_2)\rho(\mathcal{M})},$$

where μ_1 and μ_2 are the damping and the delay parameters, respectively, and $\rho(\mathcal{M})$ is the spectral radius of the spatial discretization matrix.

This condition shares the CFL-type structure with [13], but reflects the more complex dynamics introduced by the wave operator and delay in the derivative term. As the associated characteristic polynomial has higher degree and five nonzero terms, we apply the Jury stability criterion rather than relying on spectral radius estimates or root formulas. This approach offers a general framework to verify asymptotic stability in delayed wave systems.

Remark 6. *The exponential stability of the continuous system is ensured under certain assumptions on the delay and damping parameters presented in Condition* (3). *In contrast, the CFL-type condition* (29) *arises purely from the discrete stability analysis and is not inherited from the* *continuous model. This condition ensures that the roots of the characteristic polynomial lie strictly inside the unit disk, thereby guaranteeing asymptotic stability of the numerical scheme.*

5. Numerical Examples

We now illustrate the performance of the proposed finite difference scheme by solving System (2a)–(2d) in a one-dimensional spatial domain. The domain is discretized uniformly with spatial step size h, and time integration is carried out using the second-order implicit scheme derived in Section 3.

To investigate the stability of the numerical scheme, we consider parameter values μ_1 and μ_2 that satisfy the exponential stability Condition (3) of the continuous system. This ensures that any observed instability is due to the discretization and not the underlying PDE. We also examine the role of the CFL-type restriction (29), which governs the asymptotic stability of the discrete scheme. As μ_2 increases, both conditions become more restrictive, emphasizing the need for careful parameter selection.

The initial data for all test cases are given by

$$u_0(x) = 2x(x-L), \quad u_1(x) = 0, \quad f_0(x, t-\tau) = \sin(x). \tag{33}$$

We compare two test cases where the continuous system is exponentially stable, but the numerical scheme may or may not be stable depending on whether the CFL condition is satisfied. These cases are summarized in Table 1, where we denote the continuous stability Condition (3) as Condition I and the CFL-type condition (29) as Condition II.

Table 1. Satisfaction of stability conditions in each test case.

Case	Condition I: $\mu_2 < \frac{\mu_1}{C_p}, \quad C_p = \frac{L}{\pi}$	Condition II: $k < k_{CFL}$
1	Satisfied	Satisfied
2	Satisfied	Not satisfied

We fix the spatial domain to the interval $[0,5]$ and the time interval to $[0,200]$. The scheme parameters h, k, τ, μ_1, μ_2 are listed in Table 2.

Table 2. Parameter values used for each test case.

Case	h	k	τ	μ_1	μ_2	k_{CFL}
1	0.5	0.01036	1.03	3.0	1.69646	0.01295
2	0.5	0.01554	1.55	3.0	1.69646	0.01295

Figure 2 shows the evolution of the energy norm

$$\|E\| = \frac{1}{2}\left[\|u_t\|^2 + \|\nabla u\|^2\right] \tag{34}$$

over time on a logarithmic scale. In Case 1, where both stability conditions are satisfied, the energy decays exponentially, indicating that the discrete scheme faithfully reproduces the decay behavior of the continuous system. In Case 2, although the continuous system is exponentially stable, the CFL condition is violated. As a result, the numerical solution becomes unstable over time. These results highlight the necessity of the discrete stability condition for maintaining asymptotic stability in practice, even when the continuous model is well behaved.

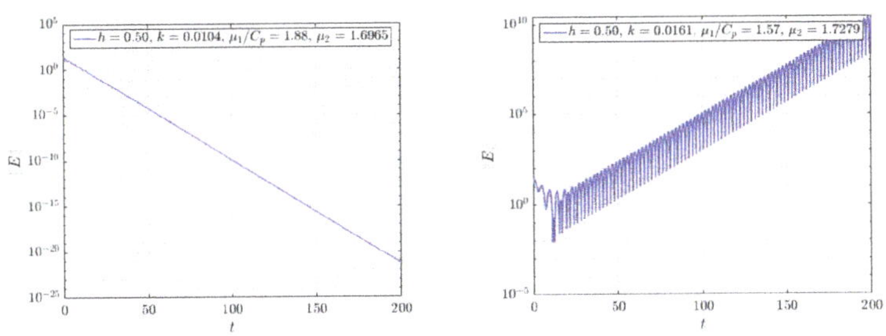

(**a**) (**b**)

Figure 2. Log plots of the energy norm $\|E\|$ versus time for two test cases listed in Table 1. Each case demonstrates the influence of the CFL-type condition on the asymptotic stability of the numerical scheme, assuming the continuous system is exponentially stable. (**a**) Case 1: Both conditions satisfied. Condition I: $\mu_2 < \mu_1/C_p$. Condition II: CFL condition satisfied. (**b**) Case 2: Only Condition I satisfied. Condition I: $\mu_2 < \mu_1/C_p$. Condition II: CFL condition not satisfied.

To complement the energy norm analysis, we present the numerical solution $u(x,t)$ under the parameter values used in Case 1. As shown in Figure 3, the solution profiles at selected time levels exhibit a clear decrease in amplitude over time. This indicates that the solution decays across the spatial domain. Figure 4 provides a 3D surface plot of $u(x,t)$, highlighting the smooth decay of the solution. These plots visually confirm the behavior predicted by the theoretical analysis: the solution vanishes gradually as time progresses, in accordance with the exponential decay of the energy norm.

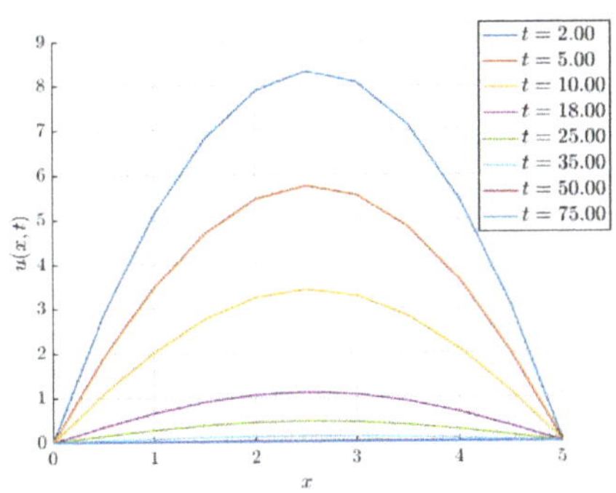

Figure 3. Solution $u(x,t)$ at selected time levels under the parameter settings of Case 1 (see Table 2). The amplitude decreases as time progresses, indicating uniform temporal decay across the spatial domain.

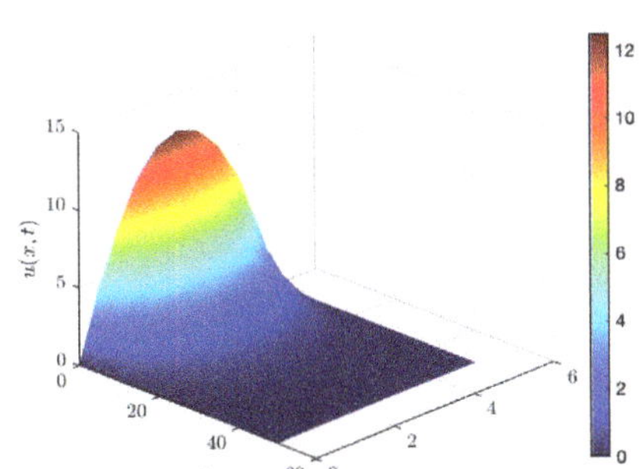

Figure 4. Three-dimensional surface plot of the solution $u(x,t)$ for $x \in [0,5]$ and $t \in [0,50]$.

Remark 7. *The parameter sets in Tables 2 and 3 are designed to test the stability of the scheme under different theoretical scenarios. Specifically, we vary μ_1, μ_2, τ, and k to create cases that either satisfy or violate the derived stability conditions (Condition I and Condition II). These parameters are not chosen to reflect a specific physical application, but rather to support a structured numerical investigation of the proposed scheme's stability behavior.*

Table 3. Parameter values for the simulations in Figure 5. All configurations satisfy the CFL-type stability condition.

h	k	τ	μ_1	μ_2	k_{CFL}
0.50	0.0155	0.1554	1.1310	3.9021	0.019425
0.50	0.0052	0.0518	3.3929	3.9021	0.006475
0.50	0.0031	0.0311	5.6549	3.9021	0.003885

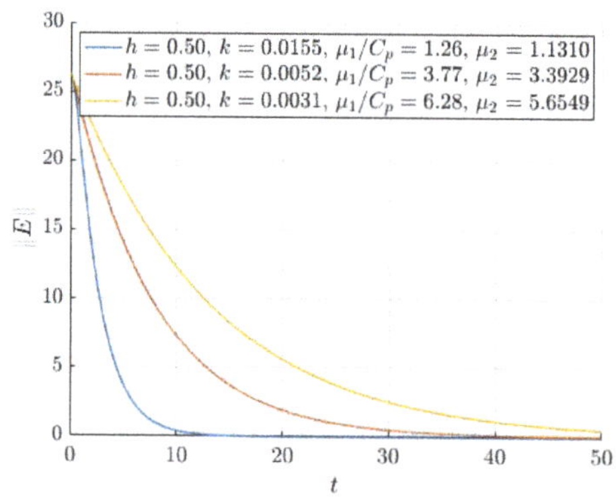

Figure 5. Energy decay over time for three configurations of Case 1 with increasing μ_1, plotted on a linear scale. All cases satisfy the continuous and discrete stability conditions. As μ_1 increases, the required time step k decreases due to the CFL condition, resulting in slower observed decay per unit time.

5.1. *Effect of Damping Strength and CFL Restriction on Decay Rate*

To explore the effect of increasing the damping parameter μ_1 on the energy decay rate, we simulate three configurations of Case 1, keeping μ_2 fixed and adjusting k to satisfy the CFL-type stability condition (29) in each case. The corresponding parameter values are listed in Table 3. The results are presented in Figure 5, plotted on a linear scale, with time restricted to the interval $[0, 30]$ to highlight differences in the early-stage decay behavior.

All three simulations satisfy both stability conditions, yet the observed decay rate varies. The case with the smallest μ_1 exhibits the fastest decay. As μ_1 increases, the CFL restriction imposes a smaller time step k, which leads to slower decay. This observation illustrates the practical trade-off: stronger damping does not necessarily accelerate decay in simulations due to the more restrictive CFL condition it entails.

5.2. *Effect of the CFL Condition When Continuous Stability Fails*

We also consider a case where the exponential stability condition for the continuous system is not satisfied (i.e., $\mu_2 \geq \mu_1/C_p$), while the CFL-type condition remains enforced. As illustrated in Figure 6a, the numerical solution in this case still exhibits asymptotic decay, confirming the stabilizing influence of the CFL condition on the discrete scheme. This result suggests that the CFL restriction plays a central role in maintaining numerical stability, even when the continuous system lies near or beyond the exponential stability threshold.

By contrast, when both the continuous and discrete stability conditions are violated, as shown in Figure 6b, the solution becomes numerically unstable. This reinforces the necessity of satisfying at least the CFL condition for obtaining stable numerical results.

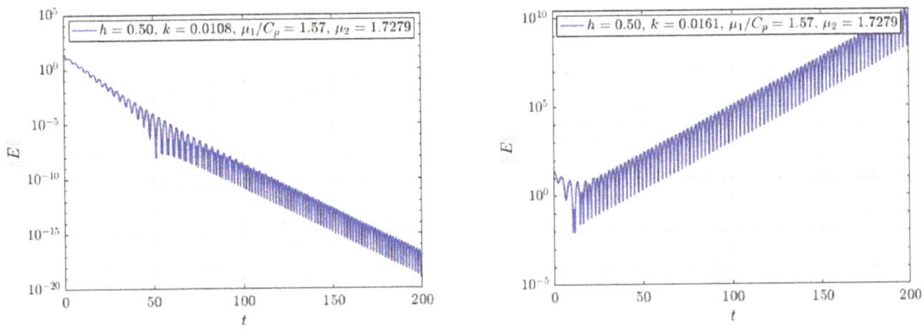

(a) (b)

Figure 6. Log plots of the energy norm $\|E\|$ versus time for two test cases where the continuous exponential stability condition is not satisfied. In (**a**), the CFL condition ensures asymptotic decay. In (**b**), the absence of both stability conditions leads to numerical instability. (**a**) $\mu_2 \geq \mu_1/C_p$, CFL condition satisfied. The numerical solution remains asymptotically stable, despite the continuous system lacking exponential stability. (**b**) $\mu_2 \geq \mu_1/C_p$, CFL condition not satisfied. The numerical solution becomes unstable, confirming the necessity of the CFL restriction.

6. Conclusions and Future Work

In this paper, we analyzed a wave equation with strong damping and a delay term. We developed a fully discrete second-order finite difference scheme for the spatial and temporal discretization of the problem. The stability of the discrete scheme was rigorously analyzed using the Jury stability criterion. A CFL-type condition on the time step was derived to guarantee that the roots of the characteristic polynomials associated with each mode lie strictly within the unit disk, ensuring asymptotic stability of the scheme.

Numerical experiments confirmed the theoretical results and demonstrated that the discrete solution exhibits exponential-like decay in practice, consistent with the behavior of the continuous system. These results highlight the effectiveness of the proposed method and emphasize the importance of careful parameter selection in the presence of time delay.

The proposed scheme can in principle be extended to higher spatial dimensions such as (1 + 2)D or (1 + 3)D. The finite difference formulation and stability framework are generalizable, but such an extension would lead to significantly larger discrete systems, increasing both computational cost and implementation complexity. Efficient implementation in higher dimensions remains an open direction for future study.

Beyond dimensionality, extending the scheme to non-uniform grids in space or time is another important challenge. Non-uniform discretization would require the reformulation of the stability analysis, likely leading to mesh-dependent conditions. This direction is particularly relevant for adaptive methods or problems with localized features.

Another promising direction for future work is the development of higher-order accurate difference schemes for delayed wave equations. While standard finite difference techniques can be extended to achieve greater accuracy, doing so may significantly increase the complexity of both implementation and stability analysis. Extending the Jury-based framework to handle such cases remains an open challenge.

Finally, incorporating nonlinearities—such as a nonlinear source term—into the delayed wave model is a natural next step. While the finite difference scheme could be modified to handle such terms, the linear stability tools used in this paper would not directly apply. A new analysis framework would be needed, possibly based on energy methods or nonlinear stability theory.

Funding: This research received no external funding.

Data Availability Statement: No new data were created or analyzed in this study.

Acknowledgments: The author gratefully acknowledges the support of King Fahd University of Petroleum and Minerals (KFUPM), particularly the Department of Mathematics and the Center for Integrative Petroleum Research (CIPR), for providing the academic and research environment that made this work possible. Special thanks are extended to Nasser-Eddine Tatar and Salah Eddine Kabbaj from the Department of Mathematics at KFUPM for their valuable guidance and encouragement throughout the development of this work. The author also wishes to thank the anonymous reviewers for their constructive and insightful comments, which significantly improved the quality and clarity of the manuscript.

Conflicts of Interest: The author declares no conflicts of interest.

Appendix A. Higher-Order Conditions in the Jury Stability Criterion

In this appendix, we provide a detailed construction of the components of the Jury table introduced in Section 2 and verify the higher-order stability conditions referenced in Step 4 of the proof of Proposition 1.

We apply the Jury stability criterion to the following real polynomial of degree $N+2$:

$$\pi_m(z) = z^{N+2} - A_m z^{N+1} + B_m z^N + C_m z^2 - C_m = \sum_{j=0}^{n} a_j z^{n-j}, \quad n = N+2. \tag{A1}$$

The coefficients A_m, B_m, C_m are defined by

$$A_m = \frac{4h^2 + 2k^2\lambda_m}{2h^2 - \mu_1 k\lambda_m}, \quad B_m = \frac{2h^2 + \mu_1 k\lambda_m}{2h^2 - \mu_1 k\lambda_m}, \quad C_m = \frac{\mu_2 k h^2}{2h^2 - \mu_1 k\lambda_m},$$

where $\lambda_m < 0$ is the mth eigenvalue of the matrix $\mathcal{M}$. The nonzero coefficients a_j are

$$a_0 = 1, \quad a_1 = -A_m, \quad a_2 = B_m, \quad a_{n-2} = C_m, \quad a_{n-1} = 0, \quad a_n = -C_m,$$
$$a_j = 0 \quad \text{for } 3 \le j \le n-3.$$

The first-level Jury components b_j and the second-level components c_j are computed using

$$b_j = \begin{vmatrix} -C_m & a_{n-1-j} \\ 1 & a_{j+1} \end{vmatrix}, \qquad j = 0, \ldots, n-1, \tag{A2}$$

$$c_j = \begin{vmatrix} C_m^2 - 1 & b_{n-2-j} \\ A_m C_m & b_{j+1} \end{vmatrix}, \qquad j = 0, \ldots, n-2. \tag{A3}$$

These values are summarized in Table A1.

We recall from Proposition 1 that the first two sufficient Jury conditions are

$$\text{SC1:} \quad |a_0| > |a_n| \Rightarrow C_m < 1,$$
$$\text{SC2:} \quad |b_{n-1}| > |b_0| \Rightarrow 1 - C_m^2 > A_m C_m.$$

Under the CFL condition (29), both SC1 and SC2 are satisfied. We now verify the third sufficient condition:

$$\text{SC3:} \qquad |c_{n-2}| > |c_0|.$$

From Table A1, we find

$$|c_{n-2}| = (C_m^2 - 1)^2 - C_m^2 A_m^2 > 0, \quad \text{from SC2,}$$

and

$$|c_0| = \left|(1 - C_m^2)(1 + B_m) - A_m^2\right| C_m.$$

Then, SC3 reads

$$(C_m^2 - 1)^2 - C_m^2 A_m^2 > \left|(1 - C_m^2)(1 + B_m) - A_m^2\right| C_m. \tag{A4}$$

A sufficient condition for (A4) to hold is

$$(C_m^2 - 1)^2 > \left|(1 - C_m^2)(1 + B_m) - A_m^2\right| C_m,$$

which can be rewritten in the form

$$(1 - \theta_1 C_m)(1 - \theta_2 C_m) > \theta_3 C_m,$$

with $\theta_1 = \theta_2 = C_m > 0$, and $\theta_3 = |(1 - C_m^2)(1 + B_m) - A_m^2| > 0$.

Given that $C_m < 1$ (from SC1) and $A_m C_m < 1 - C_m^2$ (from SC2), both A_m and C_m are sufficiently small under the CFL condition (29), ensuring the right-hand side of (A4) is smaller than the left-hand side. This reasoning can be extended recursively.

In fact, all higher-order conditions (involving $c_j, d_j, \ldots$) preserve the same structure: the left-hand side is a product of terms like $(1 - \theta_i C_m)$, while the right-hand side involves a small multiple of C_m. Consequently, the CFL restriction, together with SC1 and SC2, guarantees that all sufficient conditions in the Jury table are satisfied.

Table A1. Jury table components for the polynomial $\pi_m(z)$, showing the values of a_j, b_j, and c_j computed using determinant formulas.

j	a_j	b_j	c_j
0	1	$A_m C_m$	$C_m[(1 - C_m^2)(1 + B_m) - A_m^2]$
1	$-A_m$	$-C_m(1 + B_m)$	$A_m C_m (C_m^2 + B_m)$
2	B_m	0	0
3	0	0	0
$\vdots$	$\vdots$	$\vdots$	$\vdots$
$n-3$	0	$-C_m^2 - B_m$	$2A_m C_m^2 - A_m + A_m B_m C_m^2$
$n-2$	C_m	A_m	$(C_m^2 - 1)^2 - C_m^2 A_m^2$
$n-1$	0	$C_m^2 - 1$	—
n	$-C_m$	—	—

References

1. Gou, Y.; Shi, X.; Qiu, X.; Huo, X.; Yu, Z. Assessment of induced vibrations derived from the wave superposition in time-delay blasts. *Int. J. Rock Mech. Min. Sci.* **2021**, *144*, 104814. [CrossRef]
2. Zhong, Q.C. *Robust Control of Time-Delay Systems*; Springer Science & Business Media: Berlin/Heidelberg, Germany, 2006.
3. Nunziato, J.W. On heat conduction in materials with memory. *Q. Appl. Math.* **1971**, *29*, 187–204. [CrossRef]

4. Ning, Z.H.; Yan, Q.X. Stabilization of the wave equation with variable coefficients and a delay in dissipative boundary feedback. *J. Math. Anal. Appl.* **2010**, *367*, 167–173. [CrossRef]
5. Nicaise, S.; Pignotti, C. Stabilization of the wave equation with boundary or internal distributed delay. *Differ. Integral Equ.* **2008**, *21*, 935–958. [CrossRef]
6. Nicaise, S.; Pignotti, C. Stability and Instability Results of the Wave Equation with a Delay Term in the Boundary or Internal Feedbacks. *SIAM J. Control Optim.* **2006**, *45*, 1561–1585. [CrossRef]
7. Al-Khulaifi, W.; Alotaibi, M.; Tatar, N.E. Exponential decay in a delayed wave equation with variable coefficients. *AIMS Math.* **2024**, *9*, 27770–27783. [CrossRef]
8. Alotaibi, M.; Tatar, N.E.; Al-Khulaifi, W. Exponential stability for a wave equation with time-varying delay. *Carpathian J. Math.* **2025**, *41*, 837–848.
9. Bellen, A.; Zennaro, M. Numerical solution of delay differential equations by uniform corrections to an implicit Runge-Kutta method. *Numer. Math.* **1985**, *47*, 301–316. [CrossRef]
10. Bellen, A.; Guglielmi, N.; Zennaro, M. Numerical stability of nonlinear delay differential equations of neutral type. *J. Comput. Appl. Math.* **2000**, *125*, 251–263. [CrossRef]
11. Bocharov, G.A.; Rihan, F.A. Numerical modelling in biosciences using delay differential equations. *J. Comput. Appl. Math.* **2000**, *125*, 183–199. [CrossRef]
12. Chocholaty, P.; Slahor, L. A numerical method to boundary value problems for second order delay differential equations. *Numer. Math.* **1979**, *33*, 69–75. [CrossRef]
13. Garcia, P.; Castro, M.; Martín, J.A.; Sirvent, A. Numerical solutions of diffusion mathematical models with delay. *Math. Comput. Model.* **2009**, *50*, 860–868. [CrossRef]
14. Garcia, P.; Castro, M.; Martín, J.A.; Sirvent, A. Convergence of two implicit numerical schemes for diffusion mathematical models with delay. *Math. Comput. Model.* **2010**, *52*, 1279–1287. [CrossRef]
15. Lekomtsev, A.; Pimenov, V. Convergence of the scheme with weights for the numerical solution of a heat conduction equation with delay for the case of variable coefficient of heat conductivity. *Appl. Math. Comput.* **2015**, *256*, 83–93. [CrossRef]
16. Zhang, Q.; Chen, M.; Xu, Y.; Xu, D. Compact θ-method for the generalized delay diffusion equation. *Appl. Math. Comput.* **2018**, *316*, 357–369. [CrossRef]
17. Cui, M.; Ji, C.C.; Dai, W. A Finite Difference Method for Solving the Wave Equation with Fractional Damping. *Math. Comput. Appl.* **2024**, *29*, 2. [CrossRef]
18. Gao, J.; Bai, Q.; He, S.; Buh, E. New Two-Level Time-Mesh Difference Scheme for the Symmetric Regularized Long Wave Equation. *Axioms* **2023**, *12*, 1057. [CrossRef]
19. Gao, J.; He, S.; Bai, Q.; Liu, J. A Time Two-Mesh Finite Difference Numerical Scheme for the Symmetric Regularized Long Wave Equation. *Fractal Fract.* **2023**, *7*, 487. [CrossRef]
20. Wang, X.; Wang, S.; Qiao, X.; Zheng, F. Semi-Discretized Approximation of Stability of Sine-Gordon System with Average-Central Finite Difference Scheme. *Mathematics* **2024**, *12*, 2592. [CrossRef]
21. Thomas, J.W. *Numerical Partial Differential Equations: Finite Difference Methods*; Springer: New York, NY, USA, 1995. [CrossRef]
22. Ogata, K. *Discrete-Time Control Systems*, 2nd ed.; Prentice Hall: Hoboken, NJ, USA, 1995.
23. Kuo, B.C. *Automatic Control Systems*, 7th ed.; Prentice Hall: Hoboken, NJ, USA, 1995.
24. Guesmia, A. Well-posedness and exponential stability of an abstract evolution equation with infinite memory and time delay. *IMA J. Math. Control Inf.* **2013**, *30*, 507–526. [CrossRef]
25. Messaoudi, S.A.; Fareh, A.; Doudi, N. Well posedness and exponential stability in a wave equation with a strong damping and a strong delay. *J. Math. Phys.* **2016**, *57*, 111501. [CrossRef]
26. Richtmyer, R.; Morton, K.W. *Differential Methods for Initial-Value Problems*; John Wiley & Sons Inc.: New York, NY, USA, 1967.
27. LaSalle, J.P. *The Stability and Control of Discrete Processes*; Springer: New York, NY, USA, 1986.
28. Choo, Y. An elementary proof of the Jury test for real polynomials. *Automatica* **2011**, *47*, 249–252. [CrossRef]
29. Elaydi, S. *An Introduction to Difference Equations*, 3rd ed.; Undergraduate Texts in Mathematics; Springer: New York, NY, USA, 2005. [CrossRef]

axioms

MDPI

Article

Abstract Degenerate Non-Scalar Volterra Equations on the Line

Marko Kostić

Faculty of Technical Sciences, University of Novi Sad, Trg D. Obradovića 6, 21125 Novi Sad, Serbia; marco.s@verat.net

Abstract: The main aim of this paper is to investigate the existence and uniqueness of solutions for some classes of abstract degenerate non-scalar Volterra equations on the line. In order to achieve our aims, we essentially apply the vector-valued Fourier transform. We use the class of (A, k, B)-regularized C-pseudoresolvent families in our analysis as well, and present several useful remarks and illustrative applications of the established results.

Keywords: abstract degenerate non-scalar Volterra equations on the line; (A, k, B)-regularized C-pseudoresolvent families; Fourier transform

MSC: 45D05; 42A38; 47D99

1. Introduction and Preliminaries

In ([1], Section 11, Section 12), J. Prüss investigated the solvability of the following problem on the line:

$$u(t) = f(t) + \int_0^{+\infty} A(s)u(t-s)\,ds, \quad t \in \mathbb{R}, \tag{1}$$

where X and Y are complex Banach spaces such that Y is densely embedded into X, $A \in L^1_{loc}([0,+\infty) : L(Y,X))$ and $f \in L^1_{loc}(\mathbb{R} : X)$. The author introduced the notion of a vector-valued homogeneous space $\mathcal{H}(X)$ and analyzed the well-posedness of the equation

$$u'(t) = \int_0^{+\infty} A_0(s)u'(t-s)\,ds + \int_0^{+\infty} dA_1(s)u(t-s)\,ds + f(t), \quad t \in \mathbb{R}, \tag{2}$$

where $A_0 \in L^1([0,+\infty) : L(Y,X))$ and $A_1 \in BV([0,+\infty) : L(Y,X))$. The existence of strong solutions to (2) has been proved in the case that the forcing term $f(\cdot)$ belongs to a subspace $\mathcal{H}^{\sigma}_{\Lambda}(X)$ of $\mathcal{H}(X)$. In particular, for such inhomogeneities $f(\cdot)$, the Fourier–Carleman spectrum $\sigma(f) \subseteq \Lambda$ is compact (cf. ([1], Subsection 0.5, Subsection 0.6) for more details on the subject), where the real spectrum of (2) is defined through

$$\Lambda := \Big\{\xi \in \mathbb{R} : i\xi - i\xi\widehat{A_0}(i\xi) - \widehat{dA_1}(i\xi) \in L(Y,X) \text{ is not invertible}\Big\},$$

and $\mathcal{H}^{\sigma}_{\Lambda}(X)$ is a proper subspace of the space consisting of all functions $f(\cdot)$, which admits an extension to an entire function of exponential growth (the strong solution $u(\cdot)$ of (2) also enjoys this feature; see ([1], Theorem 11.1). For some other references concerning the abstract Volterra integro-differential equations on the line, one may refer, e.g., to the paper [2] by V. E. Fedorov and N. M. Skripka and [3] by R. Ponce. The abstract Volterra integro-differential inclusions on the real line with generalized Weyl fractional derivatives have recently been investigated in [4]; cf. also [5,6] for some other important references worth mentioning.

https://doi.org/10.3390/axioms14040266

Here, we briefly analyze the following extension of problem (1):

$$Bu(t) = Cf(t) + \int_0^{+\infty} A(s)u(t-s)\,ds, \quad t \in \mathbb{R}, \tag{3}$$

where X and Y are complex Banach spaces, Y is embedded into X, B is a closed linear operator with a domain and range contained in X, $Y \subseteq D(B)$, $A \in L^1_{loc}([0,+\infty) : L(Y,X))$, $f \in L^1_{loc}(\mathbb{R} : X)$ and the operator $C \in L(X)$ is injective. For simplicity, we will not consider the perturbations of term $A(\cdot)$ which are bounded in variation, and we will apply the usually considered Fourier transform in place of the Fourier–Carleman transform considered in [1].

The structure of this paper is as follows: We first explain the basic notation and terminology used throughout the paper. After that, we recall the basic definitions and results on (A,k,B)-regularized C-pseudoresolvent families (Section 1.1) and generalized Weyl integro-differential operators (Section 1.2).

In Section 2, we investigate the well-posedness of abstract degenerate non-scalar Volterra integral Equation (3) on the line. The first structural result of Section 2 is Proposition 2, where we consider the situation in which $(S(t))_{t\geq 0} \subseteq L(X,[D(B)])$ is a global (A,k,B)-regularized C-pseudoresolvent family. Here, we prove the existence of solutions to the Cauchy problem

$$Bu(t) = \int_{-\infty}^{t} k(t-s)Cf(s)\,ds + \int_{-\infty}^{t} A(t-s)u(s)\,ds, \quad t \in \mathbb{R}.$$

In Proposition 3, we clarify a uniqueness result for the above problem, where we assume the existence of a global (A,k,B)-regularized C-uniqueness family $(V(t))_{t\geq 0} \subseteq L(X)$ for (3); cf. [7] for the notion and more details in this direction. In Theorem 1, we apply the Fourier transform in the space of tempered vector-valued distributions in order to analyze the existence and uniqueness of solutions to Problem (3); cf. also Example 1, where we provide some applications to the kernels

$$A(t) := a_1(t)A_1 + ... + a_m(t)A_m, \quad t \geq 0,$$

where $m \in \mathbb{N}$, $a_j \in L^1([0,+\infty))$, A_j is a closed linear operator on X $(1 \leq j \leq m)$ and the vector space $Y := D(B) \cap D(A_1) \cap ... \cap D(A_m)$ is equipped with the graph norm $\|y\|_Y := \|y\| + \|By\| + \|A_1 y\| + ... + \|A_m y\|$, $y \in Y$. In Theorem 2, we consider the differential and analytical properties of mapping

$$\xi \mapsto \left(B - \int_0^{+\infty} e^{-i\xi s} A(s)\,ds\right)^{-1} C \in L(X,Y), \quad \xi \in \mathbb{R},$$

which is incredibly important in our analysis. After that, we are ready to apply the operator-valued version of Mikhlin's theorem ([8], Proposition 8.2.3) in the analysis of the existence of a solution $u(\cdot)$ of (3) which satisfies $u \in L^1(\mathbb{R} : Y)$ and $Bu \in L^1(\mathbb{R} : X)$; cf. Theorem 3 for more details. The existence and uniqueness of almost-periodic-type solutions to (3) are briefly considered in Section Almost-Periodic-Type Solutions to (3).

For convenience, we will work in the setting of complex Banach spaces. We will reconsider the results established by J. Prüss in ([1], Section 11, Section 12) for a degenerate abstract Cauchy problem on the line (3) somewhere else. We will not consider here the abstract semilinear Volterra integral equations of non-scalar type on the line as well.

Before explaining the notation and terminology used throughout the paper, we feel it is our duty to emphasize that we have not been able to find any practical applications of the established results in physical or engineering models and also that our theoretical findings are not accompanied here by any numerical illustrations or concrete examples. Although some notations probably could be refined, we have done our best to increase the clarity and readability of this paper as well as the exposition of the material.

Notation and preliminaries. If $\zeta > 0$, then we set $g_\zeta(t) := t^{\zeta-1}/\Gamma(\zeta)$, $t > 0$, where $\Gamma(\cdot)$ denotes the Euler Gamma function and $g_0(t) :=$the Dirac delta distribution. If $z \in \mathbb{C}$ and $r > 0$, then we set $L(z,r) := \{w \in \mathbb{C} : |z-w| < r\}$.

Unless specified otherwise, we assume henceforward that $(X, \|\cdot\|)$ and $(Y, \|\cdot\|_Y)$ are complex Banach spaces such that Y is embedded into X as well as that $A \in L^1_{loc}([0,\tau) : L(Y,X))$, where $L(Y,X)$ denotes the space consisting of all continuous linear mappings from Y into X and $L(X) \equiv L(X,X)$. We assume that the operator $C \in L(X)$ is injective and B is a closed linear operator in X such that $Y \subseteq D(B)$, by $[D(B)]$. We denote the Banach space $(D(B), \|\cdot\|_B)$, where the graph norm $\|\cdot\|_B$ is defined by $\|x\|_B := \|x\| + \|Bx\|$, $x \in D(B)$. The symbol I stands for the identity operator on X. For more details about the integration of functions with values in Banach spaces, we refer the reader to [7,8]. We will use the same notion and notation as in [7]. Finally, let us recall that the Fourier transform on the real line and its inverse transform are defined by

$$(\mathcal{F}f)(\xi) := \int_{-\infty}^{+\infty} e^{-i\xi t} f(t)\, dt \text{ and } (\mathcal{F}^{-1}f)(t) := \frac{1}{2\pi}\int_{-\infty}^{+\infty} e^{i\xi t} f(\xi)\, d\xi \ \ (t,\, \xi \in \mathbb{R}),$$

respectively; see [8–12] and the references quoted therein.

1.1. (A,k,B)-Regularized C-Pseudoresolvent Families

We need the following notion (cf. ([7], Definition 2.9.2)):

Definition 1. *Let $\tau \in (0,\infty]$, $k \in C([0,\tau))$, $k \neq 0$ and $A \in L^1_{loc}([0,\tau) : L(Y,X))$. A family $(S(t))_{t\in[0,\tau)}$ in $L(X,[D(B)])$ is called an (A,k,B)-regularized C-pseudoresolvent family if the following holds:*

(S1) The mappings $t \mapsto S(t)x$, $t \in [0,\tau)$ and $t \mapsto BS(t)x$, $t \in [0,\tau)$ are continuous in X for every fixed $x \in X$, $BS(0) = k(0)C$ and $S(t)C = CS(t)$, $t \in [0,\tau)$.

(S2) Put $U(t)x := \int_0^t S(s)x\, ds$, $x \in X$, $t \in [0,\tau)$. Then (S2) means $U(t)Y \subseteq Y$, $U(t)_{|Y} \in L(Y)$, $t \in [0,\tau)$ and $(U(t)_{|Y})_{t\in[0,\tau)}$ is locally Lipschitz continuous in $L(Y)$.

(S3) The resolvent equations

$$BS(t)y = k(t)Cy + \int_0^t A(t-s)dU(s)y, \quad t \in [0,\tau),\ y \in Y, \tag{4}$$

$$BS(t)y = k(t)Cy + \int_0^t S(t-s)A(s)y\, ds, \quad t \in [0,\tau),\ y \in Y, \tag{5}$$

hold, and (4), resp. (5), is called the first resolvent equation, resp. the second resolvent equation.

Let us recall that (S3) can be equivalently written as

$$\text{(S3)}' \qquad \begin{aligned} BU(t)y &= \Theta(t)Cy + \int_0^t A(t-s)U(s)y\, ds, \quad t \in [0,\tau),\ y \in Y, \\ BU(t)y &= \Theta(t)Cy + \int_0^t U(t-s)A(s)y\, ds, \quad t \in [0,\tau),\ y \in Y, \end{aligned}$$

where $\Theta(t) := \int_0^t k(s)\, ds$, $t \in [0,\tau)$; cf. also ([1], p. 153).

By continuity, we mean continuity in X. We need to recall the notion from ([7], Definition 2.9.3):

Definition 2. *Let $\tau \in (0,\infty]$, $k \in C([0,\tau))$, $k \neq 0$ and $A \in L^1_{loc}([0,\tau) : L(Y,X))$. A strongly continuous operator family $(V(t))_{t\in[0,\tau)} \subseteq L(X)$ is said to be an (A,k,B)-regularized C-uniqueness family if*

$$V(t)By = k(t)Cy + \int_0^t V(t-s)A(s)y\,ds, \quad t \in [0,\tau),\ y \in Y.$$

For further information, the reader may consult [7] and the references quoted therein.

1.2. Generalized Weyl Fractional Derivatives

For Weyl fractional calculus, we refer to the research monographs [13] by K. S. Miller and B. Ross and [14] by S. G. Samko, A. A. Kilbas and O. I. Marichev; cf. also the research articles quoted in [4]. In ([15], Definition 3), we recently introduced the notion of a generalized Weyl (α,a)-fractional derivative $D_W^{\alpha,a}u$ of a locally integrable function $u : \mathbb{R} \to X$, where X is a complex Banach space. A special case of $D_W^{\alpha,a}u$ is the usually considered Weyl fractional derivative $D_W^{\alpha}u$:

Definition 3. *Suppose that $a \in L^1_{loc}([0,\infty))$, $u : \mathbb{R} \to X$ is a locally integrable function, $\alpha > 0$ and $m = \lceil\alpha\rceil$. The generalized Weyl fractional derivative $D_W^{\alpha,a}u$ of function $u(\cdot)$ is well defined if the mapping $t \mapsto \int_{-\infty}^t a(t-s)u(s)\,ds$, $t \in \mathbb{R}$ is well defined and m-times continuously differentiable by*

$$\left[D_W^{\alpha,a}u\right](t) := \frac{d^m}{dt^m}\int_{-\infty}^t a(t-s)u(s)\,ds, \quad t \in \mathbb{R}.$$

The function $t \mapsto I_{W,a}(t) := \int_{-\infty}^t a(t-s)u(s)\,ds$, $t \in \mathbb{R}$ is said to be a generalized Weyl a-integral of function $u(\cdot)$. If $a(t) = g_\zeta(t)$ for some $\zeta \in (0,1)$, then the class of functions for which the above integral absolutely converges was first considered by M. J. Lighthill in [16].

We need the following auxiliary results from [4]:

Lemma 1. *(i) Suppose that $a,\ b \in L^1_{loc}([0,+\infty))$, $u \in L^1_{loc}(\mathbb{R} : X)$ and $t \in \mathbb{R}$. If*

$$\int_{-t}^{+\infty} \left|(a *_0 b)(s-t)\right| \cdot \|u(-s)\|\,ds < +\infty, \tag{6}$$

then the term $(I_{W,a}I_{W,b}u)(t)$ is well defined, the term $(I_{W,a*_0b}u)(t)$ is well defined and we have $(I_{W,a}I_{W,b}u)(t) = (I_{W,a*_0b}u)(t)$.

(ii) Suppose that $a \in L^1_{loc}([0,+\infty))$, Z is a complex Banach space, the operator family $(R(t))_{t>0} \subseteq L(Z,X)$ is strongly continuous, for each $x \in Z$ we have $\int_0^1 \|R(t)x\|\,dt < +\infty$, $u \in L^1_{loc}(\mathbb{R} : Z)$ and $t \in \mathbb{R}$. If

$$\int_{-t}^{+\infty} \left\|(a *_0 R)(s-t)u(-s)\right\|\,ds < +\infty,$$

then the term $(I_{W,a}I_{W,R}u)(t)$ is well defined, the term $(I_{W,a*_0R}u)(t)$ is well defined and we have $(I_{W,a}I_{W,R}u)(t) = (I_{W,a*_0R}u)(t)$.

We can similarly prove the next proposition:

Proposition 1. *Suppose that* $A \in L^1_{loc}([0,+\infty) : L(Y,X))$, *Z is a complex Banach space, the operator family* $(R(t))_{t>0} \subseteq L(Z,Y)$ *is strongly continuous,* $\int_0^1 \|R(t)\|_{L(Z,Y)}\,dt < +\infty$, $u \in L^1_{loc}(\mathbb{R} : Z)$ *and* $t \in \mathbb{R}$. *If*

$$\int_{-t}^{+\infty} \Big\| (A *_0 R)(s-t)u(-s) \Big\| \,ds < +\infty,$$

then the term $(I_{W,A} I_{W,R} u)(t)$ *is well defined, the term* $(I_{W,A*_0 R} u)(t)$ *is well defined and we have* $(I_{W,A} I_{W,R} u)(t) = (I_{W,A*_0 R} u)(t)$.

2. Well-Posedness of Abstract Degenerate Non-Scalar Volterra Integral Equations on the Line

In the following proposition, all considered integrals are taken with respect to the topology of space X (cf. also ([7], Proposition 11.4)):

Proposition 2. *Assume that* $k \in C([0,\infty))$, $k \neq 0$, $A \in L^1_{loc}([0,\infty) : L(Y,X))$, $f \in L^1_{loc}(\mathbb{R} : Y)$ *and* $(S(t))_{t\geq 0} \subseteq L(X,[D(B)])$ *is a global* (A,k,B)*-regularized C-pseudoresolvent family. Suppose that the functions*

$$u(t) := \int_{-\infty}^{t} S(t-s)f(s)\,ds, \quad t \in \mathbb{R} \quad \text{and} \quad v(t) := \int_{-\infty}^{t} U(t-s)f(s)\,ds, \quad t \in \mathbb{R}$$

are well defined and Lebesgue measurable on the real line, the integrals $\int_{-\infty}^{t} BU(t-s)f(s)\,ds$ *and* $\int_{-\infty}^{t} \Theta(t-s)Cf(s)\,ds$ *are convergent and*

$$\int_0^{+\infty} \Big\| (A *_0 U)(s)f(t-s) \Big\| \,ds < +\infty, \quad t \in \mathbb{R}.$$

Then, we have

$$Bv(t) = \int_{-\infty}^{t} \Theta(t-s)Cf(s)\,ds + \int_{-\infty}^{t} A(t-s)v(s)\,ds, \quad t \in \mathbb{R}. \tag{7}$$

Furthermore, if the function $u(\cdot)$ *is continuous, the functions* $\int_{-\infty}^{\cdot} k(\cdot - s)Cf(s)\,ds$ *and* $\int_{-\infty}^{\cdot} A(\cdot - s)u(s)\,ds$ *are well defined and continuous on the real line and the integrals defining the functions* $v(\cdot)$ *and* $\int_{-\infty}^{\cdot} \Theta(\cdot - s)Cf(s)\,ds$ *are absolutely convergent, then the function* $Bu(\cdot)$ *is also continuous on the real line and we have*

$$Bu(t) = \int_{-\infty}^{t} k(t-s)Cf(s)\,ds + \int_{-\infty}^{t} A(t-s)u(s)\,ds, \quad t \in \mathbb{R}. \tag{8}$$

Proof. It is clear that $v(t) = \int_0^{+\infty} U(s)f(t-s)\,ds$, $t \in \mathbb{R}$. The prescribed assumptions imply, together with ([7], Theorem 1.2.3), Proposition 1 and (S3)′, that

$$\begin{aligned} Bv(t) &= \int_0^{+\infty} BU(s)f(t-s)\,ds = \int_0^{+\infty} \Big[\Theta(s)C + (A *_0 U)(s)\Big] f(t-s)\,ds \\ &= \int_{-\infty}^{t} \Theta(t-s)Cf(s)\,ds + \int_{-\infty}^{t} A(t-s)v(s)\,ds, \quad t \in \mathbb{R}, \end{aligned}$$

as claimed. Suppose now that the requirements in the second part of the proposition hold. To show that $Bu(\cdot)$ is continuous on the real line and (8) holds, observe first that the integral which defines the function $v(\cdot)$ is absolutely continuous and the function $u(\cdot)$ is continuous. It can be simply proved by means of Lemma 1(ii) that

$$v(t) = \int_{-\infty}^{t} (g_1 *_0 S)(t-s)f(s)\, ds = \int_{-\infty}^{t}\int_{-\infty}^{s} S(s-r)f(r)\, dr\, ds, \quad t \in \mathbb{R},$$

so that $v'(t) = u(t)$, $t \in \mathbb{R}$. Since the functions $\int_{-\infty}^{\cdot} k(\cdot - s)Cf(s)\, ds$ and $\int_{-\infty}^{\cdot} A(\cdot - s)u(s)\, ds$ are continuous on the real line and the integral which defines the function $v(\cdot) = \int_{-\infty}^{\cdot}(g_1 *_0 A)(\cdot - s)u(s)\, ds$ is absolutely convergent, we can similarly prove with the help of Lemma 1(ii) that

$$\frac{d}{dt}\int_{-\infty}^{t} \Theta(t-s)Cf(s)\, ds = \int_{-\infty}^{t} k(t-s)Cf(s)\, ds, \quad t \in \mathbb{R}$$

and

$$\frac{d}{dt}\int_{-\infty}^{t} A(t-s)v(s)\, ds = \int_{-\infty}^{t} A(t-s)u(s)\, ds, \quad t \in \mathbb{R}.$$

This simply implies the desired assertion by differentiation of (7). □

In the commonly considered case $k(\cdot) \equiv 1$, the integral $\int_{-\infty}^{t} Cf(s)\, ds$ must be defined for all $t \in \mathbb{R}$ so that the boundedness of function $Cf(\cdot)$ is not sufficient enough for applications of Proposition 2.

The uniqueness of solutions to Problem (8) with $f \equiv 0$ is examined in the following result:

Proposition 3. *Assume that $k \in C([0,\infty))$, $k \neq 0$ and $(V(t))_{t\geq 0} \subseteq L(X)$ is an (A,k,B)-regularized C-uniqueness family for (3). Suppose, further, that $u : \mathbb{R} \to X$ is a continuous function, $u(t) \in Y$ for a.e. $t \in \mathbb{R}$, there exist $b \in L^1_{loc}([0,\infty))$ and $m \in \mathbb{N}$ such that $k *_0 b = g_m$, the integral $\int_{-\infty}^{t} g_m(t-s)Cu(s)\, ds$ is absolutely convergent in X for each $t \in \mathbb{R}$, the integral $\int_{-\infty}^{t}(V *_0 A)(t-s)Cu(s)\, ds$ is absolutely convergent in X for each $t \in \mathbb{R}$ and*

$$Bu(t) = \int_{-\infty}^{t} A(t-s)u(s)\, ds, \quad t \in \mathbb{R}. \tag{9}$$

Then, $u(t) = 0$ for all $t \in \mathbb{R}$.

Proof. Since we have assumed that the integral $\int_{-\infty}^{t}(V *_0 A)(t-s)Cu(s)\, ds$ is absolutely convergent in X, Proposition 1 and (9) together imply that the integral $\int_{-\infty}^{t} V(t-s)Bu(s)\, ds$ is convergent in X for each $t \in \mathbb{R}$ and

$$\begin{aligned}\int_{-\infty}^{t} V(t-s)Bu(s)\, ds &= \int_{-\infty}^{t} V(t-s)\int_{-\infty}^{s} A(s-r)u(r)\, dr\, ds \\ &= \int_{-\infty}^{t} (V *_0 A)(t-s)u(s)\, ds, \quad t \in \mathbb{R}.\end{aligned}$$

Using the functional equality of $(V(t))_{t\geq 0}$, the above yields

$$\int_{-\infty}^{t} V(t-s)Bu(s)\, ds = \int_{-\infty}^{t}\Big[V(t-s)Bu(s) - k(t-s)Cu(s)\Big] ds, \quad t \in \mathbb{R},$$

so that $\int_{-\infty}^{t} k(t-s)Cu(s)\, ds = 0$, $t \in \mathbb{R}$. Since $k *_0 b = g_m$ and the integral $\int_{-\infty}^{t} g_m(t-s)Cu(s)\, ds$ is absolutely convergent in X for each $t \in \mathbb{R}$, Lemma 1(i) implies $\int_{-\infty}^{t} g_m(t-s)Cu(s)\, ds = 0$, $t \in \mathbb{R}$. Keeping in mind that the function $u(\cdot)$ is continuous, we can differentiate m-times the last equality to show that $Cu(t) = 0$, $t \in \mathbb{R}$. By the injectiveness of regularizing operator C, we finally obtain $u(t) = 0$, $t \in \mathbb{R}$. □

Concerning possible applications of Proposition 2 and Proposition 3 with $C \neq I$, we would like to say that these results can be successfully applied to the $(A,1)$-regularized C-pseudoresolvent families constructed in ([17], Theorem A.12, Corollary A.13) and $(A,1,B)$-regularized C-pseudoresolvent families constructed in ([7], Theorem 2.9.7). In a degenerate setting, possible applications can be given to the abstract degenerate fractional integro-differential equations considered on p. 221 in [7].

Suppose now that, for every $\xi \in \mathbb{R}$ and $x \in X$, there is a unique continuous function $u : \mathbb{R} \to X$ such that (3) holds with $f(t) = e^{i\xi t}Cx$, $t \in \mathbb{R}$, the function $Bu(\cdot)$ is differentiable and $(d/dt)\int_0^{+\infty} A(s)u(t-s)\,ds = \int_0^{+\infty} A(s)u'(t-s)\,ds$, $t \in \mathbb{R}$. Then, the closedness of B implies $(d/dt)Bu(t) = Bu'(t)$, $t \in \mathbb{R}$, and we have

$$Bu'(t) = \int_0^{+\infty} A(s)u'(t-s)\,ds + i\xi e^{i\xi t}Cx, \quad t \in \mathbb{R}.$$

Multiplying (3) with $i\xi$ and using the uniqueness of the solutions, it follows that $u'(t) = i\xi u(t)$, $t \in \mathbb{R}$ so that there is a unique element $y \in Y$ s.t. $u(t) = e^{i\xi t}y$, $t \in \mathbb{R}$. Coming back to (3), we obtain

$$Be^{i\xi t}y = \int_0^{+\infty} A(s)e^{i\xi(t-s)}y\,ds + e^{i\xi t}Cx, \quad t \in \mathbb{R}.$$

Therefore, the integral $\int_0^{+\infty} e^{-i\xi s}A(s)y\,ds$ is convergent for every $\xi \in \mathbb{R}$ and $(B - \int_0^{+\infty} e^{-i\xi s}A(s)\,ds)y = Cx$. Consequently, we have

$$\left(B - \int_0^{+\infty} e^{-i\xi s}A(s)\,ds\right)^{-1} C \in L(X,Y), \quad \xi \in \mathbb{R}. \tag{10}$$

If $h(\cdot)$ is a vector-valued function and the integral

$$\int_{-\infty}^{+\infty} e^{-i\xi t}h(t)\,dt := \lim_{T \to +\infty} \int_{-T}^{T} e^{-i\xi t}h(t)\,dt$$

is convergent for some $\xi \in \mathbb{R}$, then we tacitly assume henceforth that $h(\cdot)$ is locally integrable. By a Fourier-transformable function, we mean any locally integrable function $h(\cdot)$ such that the integral $\int_{-\infty}^{+\infty} e^{-i\xi t}h(t)\,dt$ is convergent for all $\xi \in \mathbb{R}$.

The condition (10) has an important role in the formulation of the subsequent theorem, which seems to be new even for the equations of scalar type, with $B = I$:

Theorem 1. *(i)* *Suppose that the operator $B - \int_0^{+\infty} e^{-i\xi s}A(s)\,ds$ is well defined and injective for all $\xi \in \mathbb{R}$. Then, there exists a unique function $u \in L^1(\mathbb{R} : Y)$ such that the integral $\int_{-\infty}^{+\infty} e^{-i\xi t}Bu(t)\,dt$ is convergent in X for every $\xi \in \mathbb{R}$,* (3) *holds with $f \equiv 0$ and $\int_{-\infty}^{+\infty}\int_0^{+\infty} \|A(s)u(t-s)\|\,ds\,dt < +\infty$.*

(ii) *Suppose that* (10) *holds, $f \in L^1(\mathbb{R} : X)$, the function*

$$\xi \mapsto G(\xi) := \left(B - \int_0^{+\infty} e^{-i\xi s}A(s)\,ds\right)^{-1} C \cdot \int_{-\infty}^{+\infty} e^{-i\xi t}f(t)\,dt, \quad \xi \in \mathbb{R} \tag{11}$$

is locally integrable in Y and the regular distribution determined by $G(\cdot)$ belongs to the space of tempered Y-valued distributions. If $u := \mathcal{F}^{-1}G \in u \in L^1(\mathbb{R} : Y)$, then $u(\cdot)$ is a solution of (3) *for a.e. $t \in \mathbb{R}$, provided that $Bu \in L^1(\mathbb{R} : X)$ and $\int_{-\infty}^{+\infty}\int_0^{+\infty} \|A(s)u(t-s)\|\,ds\,dt < +\infty$.*

Proof. Suppose that the function $Bu(\cdot)$ is Fourier transformable, (3) holds with $f \equiv 0$ and $\int_{-\infty}^{+\infty} \int_0^{+\infty} \|A(s)u(t-s)\| \, ds \, dt < +\infty$. Since B is closed, it follows that

$$B \int_{-\infty}^{+\infty} e^{-i\xi t} u(t) \, dt = \int_{-\infty}^{+\infty} e^{-i\xi t} Bu(t) \, dt, \quad \xi \in \mathbb{R};$$

Furthermore, the Fubini theorem yields that the function $t \mapsto \int_0^{+\infty} A(s)u(t-s) \, ds$, $t \in \mathbb{R}$ is Fourier transformable and

$$\begin{aligned} B \int_{-\infty}^{+\infty} e^{-i\xi t} u(t) \, dt &= \int_{-\infty}^{+\infty} e^{-i\xi t} \int_0^{+\infty} A(s)u(t-s) \, ds \, dt \\ &= \int_0^{+\infty} e^{-i\xi s} A(s) \int_{-\infty}^{+\infty} e^{-i\xi (t-s)} u(t-s) \, dt \, ds \\ &= \left(\int_0^{+\infty} e^{-i\xi s} A(s) \, ds \right) \cdot \int_{-\infty}^{+\infty} e^{-i\xi t} u(t) \, dt, \quad \xi \in \mathbb{R}, \end{aligned}$$

so that

$$\left(B - \int_0^{+\infty} e^{-i\xi s} A(s) \, ds \right) \cdot \int_{-\infty}^{+\infty} e^{-i\xi t} u(t) \, dt = 0, \quad \xi \in \mathbb{R}.$$

The injectivity of operator $B - \int_0^{+\infty} e^{-i\xi s} A(s) \, ds$ implies $\int_{-\infty}^{+\infty} e^{-i\xi t} u(t) \, dt = 0$, $\xi \in \mathbb{R}$. Since $u \in L^1(\mathbb{R} : Y)$, the Fourier inversion formula ([8], Theorem 1.8.1 d) yields that $u(t) = 0$ for a.e. $t \in \mathbb{R}$, which completes the proof of (i). The proof of (ii) is quite similar. First of all, it is clear that

$$(\mathcal{F}u)(\xi) = \left(B - \int_0^{+\infty} e^{-i\xi s} A(s) \, ds \right)^{-1} C \cdot \int_{-\infty}^{+\infty} e^{-i\xi t} f(t) \, dt, \quad \xi \in \mathbb{R}.$$

Taking into account the prescribed assumptions, the above simply implies by the reverse procedure that

$$\int_{-\infty}^{+\infty} e^{-i\xi t} Bu(t) \, dt = \int_{-\infty}^{+\infty} e^{-i\xi t} \int_0^{+\infty} A(s)u(t-s) \, ds \, dt + \int_{-\infty}^{+\infty} e^{-i\xi t} Cf(t) \, dt,$$

for any $\xi \in \mathbb{R}$. Since $Bu(\cdot) \in L^1(\mathbb{R} : X)$, $\int_0^{+\infty} A(s)u(\cdot - s) \, ds \in L^1(\mathbb{R} : X)$ and $Cf(\cdot) \in L^1(\mathbb{R} : X)$, the Fourier inversion formula ([8], Theorem 1.8.1 d) yields that (3) holds for a.e. $t \in \mathbb{R}$. $\square$

Unfortunately, we cannot expect that there exists a function $H \in L^1(\mathbb{R} : L(X,Y))$ such that

$$(\mathcal{F}H)(\xi) = G(\xi) = \left(B - \int_0^{+\infty} e^{-i\xi s} A(s) \, ds \right)^{-1} C \in L(X,Y), \quad \xi \in \mathbb{R}, \tag{12}$$

so the solution $u \in L^p(\mathbb{R} : Y)$ of (3), where $1 \le p \le \infty$, cannot be found in the form $u = H * f$ with $H \in L^1(\mathbb{R} : L(X,Y))$ and $f \in L^p(\mathbb{R} : X)$. More precisely, the following holds:

Proposition 4. *Suppose that $A \in L^1([0,\infty) : L(Y,X))$, $H \in L^1(\mathbb{R} : L(X,Y))$ and (12) holds. Then, $X = Y = \{0\}$.*

Proof. Suppose the contrary. Take any $x \in X$ such that $x \neq 0$. Then, $Cx \neq 0$ and

$$\left(B - \int_0^{+\infty} e^{-i\xi s} A(s)\, ds\right)(\mathcal{F}H)(\xi)x = Cx, \quad \xi \in \mathbb{R}. \tag{13}$$

Define $\tilde{A} : \mathbb{R} \to L(Y, X)$ by $\tilde{A}(t) := A(t)$, $t \geq 0$ and $\tilde{A}(t) := 0$, $t < 0$. By ([8], Theorem 1.8.1 a), the equality (13) implies

$$B(\mathcal{F}H)(\xi)x = \left(\mathcal{F}(\tilde{A} * H)\right)(\xi)x + Cx. \tag{14}$$

It is clear that $\tilde{A} * H \in L^1(\mathbb{R} : L(X))$ so that the Riemann–Lebesgue lemma ([8], Theorem 1.8.1 c) yields that $\lim_{|\xi| \to +\infty}(\mathcal{F}H)(\xi)x = 0$ and $\lim_{|\xi| \to +\infty}(\mathcal{F}(\tilde{A} * H))(\xi)x = 0$. Keeping in mind these facts, the closedness of B and (14) together imply $0 = B0 = Cx$, which is a contradiction. □

Now we will illustrate Theorem 1(ii) with the following example:

Example 1. *The most symptomatic case for applications to multi-term problems is the case in which we have*

$$A(t) := a_1(t)A_1 + ... + a_m(t)A_m, \quad t \geq 0,$$

where $m \in \mathbb{N}$, $a_j \in L^1([0, +\infty))$ and A_j is a closed linear operator on X ($1 \leq j \leq m$). We endow the vector space $Y := D(B) \cap D(A_1) \cap ... \cap D(A_m)$ with the graph norm $\|y\|_Y := \|y\| + \|By\| + \|A_1 y\| + ... + \|A_m y\|$, $y \in Y$, under which Y is complete. In our concrete situation, we have

$$\left(B - \int_0^{+\infty} e^{-i\xi s} A(s)\, ds\right)^{-1} C$$
$$= \left(B - \int_0^{+\infty} e^{-i\xi s} a_1(s)\, ds \cdot A_1 - ... - \int_0^{+\infty} e^{-i\xi s} a_m(s)\, ds \cdot A_m\right)^{-1} C, \quad \xi \in \mathbb{R}.$$

Assume now that there exist closed linear operator A on X and complex polynomials $P_j(\cdot)$, where $0 \leq j \leq m$, such that $B := P_0(A)$ and $A_j := P_j(A)$ for $1 \leq j \leq m$; cf. [7] for the notion and more details. Despite the negative result established in Proposition 4, the requirements necessary for applications of Theorem 1 are satisfied in many concrete situations, especially in those situations where the forcing term $f(\cdot)$ belongs to the Schwartz space of rapidly decreasing functions $\mathcal{S}(X)$, and the functions $\xi \mapsto (B - \int_0^{+\infty} e^{-i\xi s} A(s)\, ds)^{-1} C \in L(X, Y)$, $\xi \in \mathbb{R}$ and $\xi \mapsto \int_0^{+\infty} e^{-i\xi s} A(s)\, ds \in L(Y, X)$, $\xi \in \mathbb{R}$ admit polynomially bounded holomorphic extensions to the strip $\{z \in \mathbb{C} : |\Im z| < \epsilon\}$, where a sufficiently small number $\epsilon > 0$. Take, for instance, $a_j(t) = \exp(-\epsilon_j t) g_{\alpha_j}(t)$, $t > 0$, where $\epsilon_j > 0$ and $\alpha_j > 0$ for $1 \leq j \leq m$. Then, the functions $\xi \mapsto (B - \int_0^{+\infty} e^{-i\xi s} A(s)\, ds)^{-1} C \in L(X, Y)$, $\xi \in \mathbb{R}$ and $\xi \mapsto B(B - \int_0^{+\infty} e^{-i\xi s} A(s)\, ds)^{-1} C \in L(X)$, $\xi \in \mathbb{R}$ are infinitely differentiable and all their derivatives are polynomially bounded on the real line, which follows by means of the product rule, Cauchy integral theorem and equality

$$B\left(B - \int_0^{+\infty} e^{-i\xi s} A(s)\, ds\right)^{-1} C$$
$$= C + \left[\int_0^{+\infty} e^{-i\xi s} A(s)\, ds\right] \cdot \left(B - \int_0^{+\infty} e^{-i\xi s} A(s)\, ds\right)^{-1} C, \quad \xi \in \mathbb{R},$$

so that the solution $u = \mathcal{F}^{-1}G$ *of* (3) *and the function* $Bu(\cdot)$ *belong to the space* $\mathcal{S}(Y)$. *For some concrete examples, we may refer to ([7], Theorem 1.2.7, Example 2.5.8). We can also provide many illustrative applications of Theorem 1(ii) to the abstract (degenerate) Volterra equations of the scalar type on the line.*

Let us note that Theorem 1(ii) can be also applied to the abstract degenerate non-scalar Volterra equations on the line, provided that the forcing term $f(\cdot)$ *belongs to the space of rapidly decreasing ultra-differentiable functions of Beurling type* $\mathcal{S}^{(M_p)}(X)$ *as well as that the functions* $\xi \mapsto (B - \int_0^{+\infty} e^{-i\xi s}A(s)\,ds)^{-1}C \in L(X,Y)$, $\xi \in \mathbb{R}$ *and* $\xi \mapsto B(B - \int_0^{+\infty} e^{-i\xi s}A(s)\,ds)^{-1}C \in L(X)$, $\xi \in \mathbb{R}$ *admit ultra-polynomially bounded holomorphic extensions to the strip* $\{z \in \mathbb{C} : |\Im z| < \epsilon\}$; *see ([18], Proposition 4.1) and ([7], Example 2.2.18) for more details in this direction.*

For the sequel, we need the next result:

Theorem 2. *Suppose that the mapping* $\xi \mapsto (B - \int_0^{+\infty} e^{-i\xi s}A(s)\,ds)^{-1}C \in L(X,Y)$, $\xi \in \mathbb{R}$ *is continuous and* $\int_0^{+\infty} s\|A(s)\|_{L(Y,X)}\,ds < +\infty$. *Then, the following holds:*

(i) *If the assumption* $x \in D(B)$ *implies* $Cx \in D(B)$ *and* $BCx = CBx$ *and the assumptions* $y \in Y$ *and* $t \geq 0$ *imply* $Cy \in Y$ *and* $A(t)Cy = CA(t)t$ *for* $t \geq 0$, *then the following holds:*

$$\frac{d}{d\xi}\left(B - \int_0^{+\infty} e^{-i\xi s}A(s)\,ds\right)^{-1} C^2 = \left(B - \int_0^{+\infty} e^{-i\xi s}A(s)\,ds\right)^{-1} C \times \left(B - \int_0^{+\infty} e^{-i\xi s}(-is)A(s)\,ds\right)\left(B - \int_0^{+\infty} e^{-i\xi s}A(s)\,ds\right)^{-1} C \in L(X,Y),\ \xi \in \mathbb{R}. \tag{15}$$

Furthermore, if for each $\xi \in \mathbb{R}$ *there exists* $\epsilon > 0$ *such that there exist analytic mappings* $F : L(\xi,\epsilon) \to L(X,Y)$ *and* $G : L(\xi,\epsilon) \to L(X)$ *such that* $F(t) = (B - \int_0^{+\infty} e^{-its}A(s)\,ds)^{-1}C$, $t \in (\xi - \epsilon, \xi + \epsilon)$ *and*

$$G(t) = \left(B - \int_0^{+\infty} e^{-its}(-is)A(s)\,ds\right)\left(B - \int_0^{+\infty} e^{-its}A(s)\,ds\right)^{-1} C,\ t \in (\xi - \epsilon, \xi + \epsilon),$$

then the mapping $F' : L(\xi,\epsilon) \to L(X,Y)$ *is analytic, the mapping* $\lambda \mapsto C^{-1}F(\lambda)G(\lambda) \in L(X,Y)$, $\lambda \in L(\xi,\epsilon)$ *is analytic,* $F'(\lambda)x = C^{-1}F(\lambda)G(\lambda)x$, $\lambda \in L(\xi,\epsilon)$, $x \in X$, $\frac{d}{d\xi}(B - \int_0^{+\infty} e^{-i\xi s}A(s)\,ds)^{-1}C \in L(X,Y)$, $\xi \in \mathbb{R}$,

$$C^{-1}\left(B - \int_0^{+\infty} e^{-i\xi s}A(s)\,ds\right)^{-1} C \times \left(B - \int_0^{+\infty} e^{-i\xi s}(-is)A(s)\,ds\right)\left(B - \int_0^{+\infty} e^{-i\xi s}A(s)\,ds\right)^{-1} C \in L(X,Y),\ \xi \in \mathbb{R}, \tag{16}$$

and

$$\frac{d}{d\xi}\left(B - \int_0^{+\infty} e^{-i\xi s}A(s)\,ds\right)^{-1} C = C^{-1}\left(B - \int_0^{+\infty} e^{-i\xi s}A(s)\,ds\right)^{-1} C \times \left(B - \int_0^{+\infty} e^{-i\xi s}(-is)A(s)\,ds\right)\left(B - \int_0^{+\infty} e^{-i\xi s}A(s)\,ds\right)^{-1} C \in L(X,Y),\ \xi \in \mathbb{R}. \tag{17}$$

(ii) *If* $(B - \int_0^{+\infty} e^{-i\xi s}A(s)\,ds)^{-1} \in L(X,Y)$, $\xi \in \mathbb{R}$, *then the following holds:*

$$\frac{d}{d\xi}\left(B-\int_0^{+\infty}e^{-i\xi s}A(s)\,ds\right)^{-1}C=\left(B-\int_0^{+\infty}e^{-i\xi s}A(s)\,ds\right)^{-1}$$
$$\times\left(B-\int_0^{+\infty}e^{-i\xi s}(-is)A(s)\,ds\right)\left(B-\int_0^{+\infty}e^{-i\xi s}A(s)\,ds\right)^{-1}C\in L(X,Y),\ \xi\in\mathbb{R}. \tag{18}$$

Proof. Denote $I_x := (B-\int_0^{+\infty}e^{-ixs}A(s)\,ds)^{-1}C$, $x\in\mathbb{R}$. Then we have

$$B\Big[I_x-I_y\Big]=\left(B-\int_0^{+\infty}e^{-ixs}A(s)\,ds\right)\Big[I_x-I_y\Big]$$
$$+\left[\int_0^{+\infty}e^{-ixs}A(s)\,ds-\int_0^{+\infty}e^{-iys}A(s)\,ds\right]\cdot I_y,\quad x,\ y\in\mathbb{R}.$$

Let us fix now a number $x\in\mathbb{R}$. Since the operator $B-\int_0^{+\infty}e^{-ixs}A(s)\,ds$ is injective, the above equality implies after a simple computation that

$$\frac{I_x-I_y}{x-y}=\left(B-\int_0^{+\infty}e^{-ixs}A(s)\,ds\right)^{-1}$$
$$\cdot\left[\int_0^{+\infty}\frac{e^{-ixs}-e^{-iys}}{x-y}A(s)\,ds\right]\cdot I_y\in L(X,Y),\quad y\in\mathbb{R}\setminus\{x\}.$$

Since $\int_0^{+\infty}s\|A(s)\|_{L(Y,X)}\,ds<+\infty$, the dominated convergence theorem implies

$$\lim_{y\to x}\int_0^{+\infty}\frac{e^{-ixs}-e^{-iys}}{x-y}A(s)\,ds=\int_0^{+\infty}e^{-ixs}(-is)A(s)\,ds\in L(Y,X).$$

Moreover, the mapping $\xi\mapsto(B-\int_0^{+\infty}e^{-i\xi s}A(s)\,ds)^{-1}C\in L(X,Y)$, $\xi\in\mathbb{R}$ is continuous so that $\lim_{y\to x}I_y=I_x$ in $L(X,Y)$. Taken together with the above equality, we obtain

$$\lim_{y\to x}\left[\int_0^{+\infty}\frac{e^{-ixs}-e^{-iys}}{x-y}A(s)\,ds\right]\cdot I_y=\left[\int_0^{+\infty}e^{-ixs}(-is)A(s)\,ds\right]\cdot I_x\in L(X).$$

This simply yields (15) and (18). The second statement in (i) remains to be proved. Towards this end, observe first that the mapping $F':L(\xi,\epsilon)\to L(X,Y)$ is analytic. Let $x\in X$ be fixed. From the first part of (i) and the identity theorem for holomorphic functions ([8], Proposition A.2), it follows that $F'(\lambda)Cx=F(\lambda)G(\lambda)x$, $\lambda\in L(\xi,\epsilon)$. Using the last equality, prescribed commutativity assumptions and ([8], Proposition A.3), we find that the mapping $\lambda\mapsto C^{-1}F(\lambda)G(\lambda)\in L(X,Y)$, $\lambda\in L(\xi,\epsilon)$ is analytic and $F'(\lambda)=C^{-1}F(\lambda)G(\lambda)\in L(X,Y)$, $\lambda\in L(\xi,\epsilon)$. This simply yields that $(d/d\xi)(B-\int_0^{+\infty}e^{-i\xi s}A(s)\,ds)^{-1}C\in L(X,Y)$, $\xi\in\mathbb{R}$ as well as that (16) and (17) hold true, finishing the proof of the theorem. □

Observe that the statements of Bernstein's lemma ([8], Lemma 8.2.1) and Mikhlin's theorem ([8], Proposition 8.2.3) continue to hold for the vector-valued functions. Using this fact, it readily follows that there exists a function $u\in L^1(\mathbb{R}:Y)$ such that $(\mathcal{F}u)(\xi)=G(\xi)$,

$\xi \in \mathbb{R}$, where $G(\cdot)$ is given by (11), provided that $G \in C^1(\mathbb{R} : Y)$ and there exists a sufficiently small real number $\epsilon > 0$ such that

$$\sup_{\xi\in\mathbb{R}}\Big[(1+|\xi|)^{\epsilon}\|G(\xi)\|_Y + (1+|\xi|)^{1+\epsilon}\|G'(\xi)\|_Y\Big] < +\infty. \tag{19}$$

Now we would like to state the following result:

Theorem 3. *Suppose that* (10) *holds,* $\int_0^{+\infty}\|A(s)\|_{L(Y,X)}\,ds < +\infty$*,* $f \in L^1(\mathbb{R} : X)$*,* $G \in C^1(\mathbb{R} : Y)$*,* $BG \in C^1(\mathbb{R} : X)$ *and there exists* $\epsilon > 0$ *such that* (19) *holds and*

$$\sup_{\xi\in\mathbb{R}}\Big[(1+|\xi|)^{\epsilon}\|BG(\xi)\| + (1+|\xi|)^{1+\epsilon}\|BG'(\xi)\|\Big] < +\infty. \tag{20}$$

Then, there exists a function $u \in L^1(\mathbb{R} : Y)$ *such that* $Bu \in L^1(\mathbb{R} : X)$*,* $(\mathcal{F}u)(\xi) = G(\xi)$*,* $\xi \in \mathbb{R}$ *and* (3) *holds for a.e.* $t \in \mathbb{R}$*.*

Proof. Clearly, there exists a function $u \in L^1(\mathbb{R} : Y)$ such that $(\mathcal{F}u)(\xi) = G(\xi)$, $\xi \in \mathbb{R}$. Since $BG \in C^1(\mathbb{R} : X)$ and (20) holds, we similarly obtain $Bu \in L^1(\mathbb{R} : X)$. Furthermore,

$$\begin{aligned}\int_{-\infty}^{+\infty}\int_0^{+\infty}\|A(s)u(t-s)\|\,ds\,dt &\leq \int_0^{+\infty}\|A(s)\|_{L(Y,X)}\int_{-\infty}^{+\infty}\|u(t-s)\|_Y\,dt\,ds\\ &= \|u\|_{L^1(\mathbb{R}:Y)}\cdot\int_0^{+\infty}\|A(s)\|_{L(Y,X)}\,ds < +\infty.\end{aligned}$$

Now the statement follows Theorem 1(ii). □

Under certain reasonable assumptions, we have the following identity:

$$\begin{aligned}&\frac{d}{d\xi}\left[\left(B-\int_0^{+\infty}e^{-i\xi s}A(s)\,ds\right)^{-1}C\cdot\int_{-\infty}^{+\infty}e^{-i\xi t}f(t)\,dt\right]\\ &=\left[\frac{d}{d\xi}\left(B-\int_0^{+\infty}e^{-i\xi s}A(s)\,ds\right)^{-1}C\right]\cdot\int_{-\infty}^{+\infty}e^{-i\xi t}f(t)\,dt\\ &+\left[\left(B-\int_0^{+\infty}e^{-i\xi s}A(s)\,ds\right)^{-1}C\right]\cdot\int_{-\infty}^{+\infty}e^{-i\xi t}(-i\xi)f(t)\,dt,\quad \xi\in\mathbb{R},\end{aligned}$$

so that Theorem 2 can be used to state a straightforward corollary of Theorem 3. To illustrate this result, let us assume that $C = \mathrm{I}$ and $A(t) = a(t)A$, $t \geq 0$, where $a \in L^1([0, +\infty))$ and A is a closed linear operator on X. Then, we have

$$\begin{aligned}&\frac{d}{d\xi}\left[\left(B-\int_0^{+\infty}e^{-i\xi s}A(s)\,ds\right)^{-1}\cdot\int_{-\infty}^{+\infty}e^{-i\xi t}f(t)\,dt\right]\\ &=\left(B-\left[\int_0^{+\infty}e^{-i\xi s}a(s)\,ds\right]\cdot A\right)^{-1}\cdot\left(B+\left[\int_0^{+\infty}e^{-i\xi s}(i\xi)a(s)\,ds\right]\cdot A\right)\\ &\cdot\left(B-\left[\int_0^{+\infty}e^{-i\xi s}a(s)\,ds\right]\cdot A\right)^{-1}\cdot\int_{-\infty}^{+\infty}e^{-i\xi t}f(t)\,dt\\ &+\left(B-\left[\int_0^{+\infty}e^{-i\xi s}a(s)\,ds\right]\cdot A\right)^{-1}\cdot\int_{-\infty}^{+\infty}e^{-i\xi t}(-i\xi)f(t)\,dt,\quad \xi\in\mathbb{R},\end{aligned}$$

so that Theorem 2 can be applied in many concrete situations in which the terms $\int_{-\infty}^{+\infty} e^{-i\xi t} f(t)\, dt$ and $\int_{-\infty}^{+\infty} e^{-i\xi t} (-i\xi) f(t)\, dt$ decay sufficiently enough as $|\xi| \to +\infty$.

Finally, let us note that it would be very tempting to state some notable results on the existence of L^p-solutions of (3) in the case of $1 < p < \infty$.

Almost-Periodic-Type Solutions to (3)

The notion of almost periodicity was introduced by H. Bohr around 1924–1926 ([19–21]); cf. also [22,23] and the references quoted therein. Suppose that $f : \mathbb{R} \to X$ is continuous. If $\epsilon > 0$, then a number $\tau \in \mathbb{R}$ is said to be an ϵ-period for $f(\cdot)$ if $\|f(t+\tau) - f(t)\| \leq \epsilon$, $t \in \mathbb{R}$. By $\vartheta(f, \epsilon)$, we denote the set consisting of all ϵ-periods for $f(\cdot)$. Let us recall that $f(\cdot)$ is almost periodic if, for each $\epsilon > 0$, the set $\vartheta(f, \epsilon)$ is relatively dense in $\mathbb{R}$, i.e., there exists $l > 0$ such that any subinterval of $\mathbb{R}$ of length l meets $\vartheta(f, \epsilon)$. Any almost-periodic function $f : \mathbb{R} \to X$ is bounded and uniformly continuous, and the set of all almost-periodic functions $f : \mathbb{R} \to X$, denoted by $AP(\mathbb{R} : X)$, is a vector space with the usual operations. Equipped with the sup-norm, $AP(\mathbb{R} : X)$ is a Banach space.

Let $1 \leq p < +\infty$. Then, we say that a function $f \in L^p_{loc}(\mathbb{R} : X)$ is Stepanov p-almost periodic if there is $l > 0$ such that any subinterval of $\mathbb{R}$ of length l contains a point τ such that

$$\int_t^{t+1} \|f(s+\tau) - f(s)\|\, ds < \epsilon, \quad t \in \mathbb{R}.$$

Further on, a function $f \in L^p_{loc}(\mathbb{R} : X)$ is said to be

(i) equi-Weyl-p-almost periodic, if, for each $\epsilon > 0$, we can find $l > 0$ and $L > 0$ such that any interval $I \subseteq \mathbb{R}$ of length L contains a point $\tau \in I$ such that

$$\sup_{x \in \mathbb{R}} \left[\frac{1}{l} \int_x^{x+l} \|f(t+\tau) - f(t)\|^p\, dt \right]^{1/p} \leq \epsilon;$$

(ii) Weyl-p-almost periodic, if, for each $\epsilon > 0$, we can find $L > 0$ such that any interval $I \subseteq \mathbb{R}$ of length L contains a point $\tau \in I$ such that

$$\lim_{l \to \infty} \sup_{x \in \mathbb{R}} \left[\frac{1}{l} \int_x^{x+l} \|f(t+\tau) - f(t)\|^p\, dt \right]^{1/p} \leq \epsilon.$$

Any almost-periodic function $f : \mathbb{R} \to X$ is Stepanov p-almost periodic, any Stepanov-p-almost-periodic function $f : \mathbb{R} \to X$ is equi-Weyl-p-almost periodic and any equi-Weyl-p-almost-periodic function $f : \mathbb{R} \to X$ is Weyl-p-almost periodic. All these inclusions are strict. Let us also note that the set of all Stepanov-p-almost-periodic functions $f : \mathbb{R} \to X$, resp. equi-Weyl-p-almost-periodic functions $f : \mathbb{R} \to X$, is a vector space with the usual operations, which is no longer true for Weyl-p-almost-periodic functions.

We will first observe that the Banach contraction principle can be successfully applied in the analysis of the existence and uniqueness of almost periodic solutions to the Problem (1), provided that $Y = X$, $\int_0^{+\infty} \|A(s)\|_{L(X)}\, ds < 1$ and $f : \mathbb{R} \to X$ is almost periodic. Towards this end, it suffices to observe that the mapping $\Pi : AP(\mathbb{R} : X) \to AP(\mathbb{R} : X)$, given by

$$(\Pi g)(t) := f(t) + \int_0^{+\infty} A(s) g(t-s)\, ds, \quad t \in \mathbb{R}, \quad g \in AP(\mathbb{R} : X),$$

is a well-defined contraction.

Concerning Proposition 2, we will only observe here that the solution $u(\cdot)$ inherits certain Weyl almost-periodic behavior from the forcing term $f(\cdot)$; cf. [22]. It is also worth noting that, for every $\omega \in \mathbb{R}$, the abstract Cauchy problem (3) is equivalent to the problem

$$Bh(t) = e^{-\omega t}Cf(t) + \int_0^{+\infty} \Big[e^{-\omega s}A(s)\Big]h(t-s)\,ds, \quad t \in \mathbb{R},$$

where $h(t) := e^{-\omega t}u(t)$, $t \in \mathbb{R}$, as well as that the problem (8) is equivalent with the problem

$$Bh(t) = \int_{-\infty}^{t} \big[e^{-\omega(t-s)}k(t-s)\big]\big[e^{-\omega s}Cf(s)\big]\,ds + \int_{-\infty}^{t} \big[e^{-\omega(t-s)}A(t-s)\big]h(s)\,ds, \quad t \in \mathbb{R}. \tag{21}$$

This observation allows us to consider the situations in which the kernel $A(\cdot)$ is not uniformly integrable in $L(Y,X)$ but only exponentially bounded. Here, it is worth noting that, if the operator family $(S(t))_{t\geq 0}$ in $L(X,[D(B)])$ is a global (A,k,B)-regularized C-pseudoresolvent family (the operator family $(V(t))_{t\geq 0}$ in $L(X)$ is a global (A,k,B)-regularized C-uniqueness family), then $(e^{-\omega t}S(t))_{t\geq 0}$ is a global $(e^{-\omega\cdot}A, e^{-\omega\cdot}k, B)$-regularized C-pseudoresolvent family ($(e^{-\omega t}V(t))_{t\geq 0}$ is a global $(e^{-\omega\cdot}A, e^{-\omega\cdot}k, B)$-regularized C-uniqueness family). For example, if we assume that the forcing term $e^{-\omega\cdot}Cf(\cdot)$ is almost periodic and the operator family $(e^{-\omega t}S(t))_{t\geq 0}$ is exponentially decaying, then the solution $h(\cdot)$ of (21) will be almost periodic as well ([22]). For many important examples and applications of $(A,1,\mathrm{I})$-regularized I-pseudoresolvent families, we refer the reader to [1].

We close this subsection by stating the next proposition:

Proposition 5. *Let $B \in L(X)$. Then, the following holds:*

(i) Suppose that $A \in L^1([0,+\infty) : L(Y,X))$. If $u : \mathbb{R} \to X$ is almost periodic and (3) *holds, then the function $Cf : \mathbb{R} \to X$ is almost periodic.*

(ii) Suppose that $1 \leq p < \infty$, $1/p + 1/q = 1$ and $\sum_{k=0}^{\infty} \|A(\cdot)\|_{L^q[k,k+1]} < \infty$. If $u : \mathbb{R} \to X$ is Stepanov p-almost periodic and (3) *holds, then the function $Cf : \mathbb{R} \to X$ is Stepanov p-almost periodic.*

(iii) Let $1/p + 1/q = 1$ and let

$$\|A(t)\|_{L(Y,X)} \leq \frac{Mt^{\beta-1}}{1+t^{\gamma}}, \ t > 0 \text{ for some finite constants } \gamma > \beta,\ \beta \in (0,1],\ M > 0.$$

Suppose that $u : \mathbb{R} \to Y$ is equi-Weyl-p-almost periodic, resp. Weyl-p-almost periodic and Weyl p-bounded, $q(\beta-1) > -1$ provided that $p > 1$, resp. $\beta = 1$, provided that $p = 1$, and (3) *holds. Then, the function $Cf : \mathbb{R} \to X$ is equi-Weyl-p-almost periodic, resp. $Cf : \mathbb{R} \to X$ can be represented as the difference of two Weyl-p-almost-periodic functions.*

Proof. We will prove only (iii), because the proofs of (i) and (ii) are quite similar to the proof of (iii); cf. also ([22], Proposition 2.6.11). Using the argumentation given in the proof of ([22], Theorem 2.11.4), we can show that the mapping $t \mapsto \int_0^{+\infty} A(s)u(t-s)\,ds$, $t \in \mathbb{R}$ is equi-Weyl-p-almost periodic, resp. Weyl-p-almost periodic. Since $B \in L(X)$, the function $Bu(\cdot)$ is also equi-Weyl-p-almost periodic, resp. Weyl-p-almost periodic, which simply implies the required conclusion. □

3. Conclusions and Final Remarks

In this paper, we have investigated the existence and uniqueness of solutions for some classes of abstract degenerate non-scalar Volterra equations on the line. We have provided several new results and illustrative applications in this direction considering also the existence and uniqueness of almost-periodic-type solutions.

The admissibility of homogeneous spaces of functions defined on the real line and the Euclidean space $\mathbb{R}^n$, some connections between the abstract Volterra integro-differential equations on the half-line and the abstract Volterra integro-differential equations on the real line and the abstract multi-term Cauchy problems with generalized Weyl integro-differential operators will be analyzed somewhere else.

Funding: This research is partially supported by grant 451-03-68/2020/14/200156 of the Ministry of Science and Technological Development, Republic of Serbia.

Data Availability Statement: Data are contained within the article.

Conflicts of Interest: The author declares no conflicts of interest.

References

1. Prüss, J. *Evolutionary Integral Equations and Applications;* Birkhäuser-Verlag: Basel, Switzerland, 1993.
2. Fedorov, V.E.; Skripka, N.M. Evolution equations with Liouville derivative on $\mathbb{R}$ without initial conditions. *Mathematics* **2024**, *12*, 572. [CrossRef]
3. Ponce, R. Bounded mild solutions to fractional integrodifferential equations in Banach spaces. *Semigroup Forum* **2013**, *87*, 377–392.
4. Kostić, M. Abstract Volterra Integro-Differential Inclusions with Generalized Weyl Fractional Derivatives. Submitted. Available online: https://www.researchgate.net/publication/388819627 (accessed on 2 March 2025).
5. Wani, S.A.; Khan, S.; Naikoo, S.A. Differential and integral equations for the Laguerre–Gould–Hopper-based Appell and related polynomials. *Bol. Soc. Mat. Mex.* **2020**, *26*, 617–646. [CrossRef]
6. Khan, S. Fractional calculus and generalized forms of special polynomials associated with Appell sequences. *Georgian Math. J.* **2021**, *28*, 261–270. [CrossRef]
7. Kostić, M. *Abstract Degenerate Volterra Integro-Differential Equations;* Mathematical Institute SANU: Belgrade, Serbia, 2020.
8. Arendt, W.; Batty, C.J.K.; Hieber, M.; Neubrander, F. *Vector-Valued Laplace Transforms and Cauchy Problems;* Monographs in Mathematics; Birkhäuser: Basel, Switzerland, 2001; Volume 96.
9. Carmichael, R.D. Cauchy integral and boundary value for vector-valued tempered distributions. *Axioms* **2022**, *11*, 392. [CrossRef]
10. Chill, R. Tauberian theorems for vector-valued Fourier and Laplace transforms. *Studia Math.* **1998**, *128*, 55–69. [CrossRef]
11. Kluvánek, I. Fourier transforms of vector-valued functions and measures. *Studia Math.* **1970**, *37*, 1–12.
12. Okada, S. The Fourier transform of vector-valued functions. *Glasgow Mat. J.* **1985**, *26*, 181–186.
13. Miller, K.S.; Ross, B. *An Introduction to the Fractional Calculus and Fractional Differential Equations;* Wiley: New York, NY, USA, 1993.
14. Samko, S.G.; Kilbas, A.A.; Marichev, O.I. *Fractional Integrals and Derivatives: Theory and Applications;* Nauka i Tehnika: Minsk, Belarus, 1987. (In Russian)
15. Kostić, M. Multidimensional fractional calculus: Theory and applications. *Axioms* **2024**, *13*, 623. [CrossRef]
16. Lighthill, M.J. *Introduction to Fourier Transform and Generalised Functions;* Cambridge University Press: Cambrige, UK, 1959.
17. Kostić, M. *Generalized Semigroups and Cosine Functions;* Mathematical Institute SANU: Belgrade, Serbia, 2011.
18. Dimovski, P.; Prangoski, B.; Velinov, D. Multipliers and convolutors in the space of tempered ultradistributions. *Novi Sad J. Math.* **2014**, *44*, 1–18.
19. Bohr, H. Zur theorie der fastperiodischen Funktionen I. *Acta Math.* **1924**, *45*, 29–127. [CrossRef]
20. Bohr, H. Zur theorie der fastperiodischen Funktionen II. *Acta Math.* **1925**, *16*, 101–214. [CrossRef]
21. Bohr, H. Zur theorie der fastperiodischen Funktionen III. *Acta Math.* **1926**, *HT*, 237–281. [CrossRef]
22. Kostić, M. *Almost Periodic and Almost Automorphic Type Solutions to Integro-Differential Equations;* W. de Gruyter: Berlin, Germany, 2019.
23. Kostić, M. *Selected Topics in Almost Periodicity;* W. de Gruyter: Berlin, Germany, 2022.

axioms

MDPI

Article

Simulation of the Advection Process of Stokes Flow Inside a Rectangular Cavity Under Constant Velocities

Valentyn Sobchuk [1,†], Oleksandr Kurylko [1,*,†], Oleksandr Boryseiko [1,†], Oleh Perehuda [1,†], Iryna Lebedyeva [1,†], Igor Ulitko [1,†] and Olena Vashchilina [2,†]

1 Faculty of Mechanics and Mathematics, Taras Shevchenko National University of Kyiv, 4E Academician Glushkov Avenue, 03127 Kyiv, Ukraine

2 Faculty of Information Technology, Taras Shevchenko National University of Kyiv, 24 Bohdana Havrylyshyna Street, 04116 Kyiv, Ukraine

* Correspondence: alexandr.kurylko@knu.ua

† These authors contributed equally to this work.

Abstract: A two-dimensional periodic Stokes flow of viscous incompressible fluid in a rectangular cavity with constant velocities applied to the top and bottom walls is considered. The study of advection regimes is reduced to the sequential solving of two problems. To solve the first problem, the analytical method of superposition, which allows one to obtain any desired accuracy of the velocity field, is used. To solve the second problem, which is associated with obtaining the trajectories of individual fluid particles, numerical calculations of the Cauchy problem were performed. An analysis of the boundary conditions accuracy was performed based on the control of local integration. The advection of the selected volume of fluid in the rectangular cavity under the periodic motion of walls for a finite period time based on piecewise spline cubic interpolation is modeled. The obtained numerical results agree with well-known experimental data.

Keywords: Stokes flow; advection; mixing; rectangular cavity; simulation

MSC: 76D07; 65D07

1. Introduction

The mixing problem of laminar fluid flow is important in microtechnology when developing mixing devices in chemical engineering and microbiology. The interest in the problem arose due to the use of various mixing technologies in industry and technology (aerodynamics, oceanology, biology, chemistry, etc.). Monitoring conditions of unstable chemical reactions requires the creation of special microchemical processes that maintain them in a narrow range of physical parameters. They are capable of mixing high-molecular-weight compounds in a liquid, the molecules of which cannot withstand high stress.

The analysis of various motions allows one to conclude that at the initial stage of flow with different geometric scales, convective mixing mechanisms prevail, and the problem of mixing is reduced to the analysis of the processes of deformation of the volume of liquid in the selected velocity field. This problem is related to the Lagrangian description of motion in hydrodynamics and is reduced to the analysis of the system of motion of Lagrangian particles in the Eulerian velocity field. This type of problem is called the problem of fluid advection.

Fluid advection is associated with the study of the time deformation of selected volumes or regions (in a two-dimensional case) of a fluid that contains a large number of particles. Despite the fact that such systems have infinitely many degrees of freedom, special attention is paid to the consolidation of individual fluid parts in hydrodynamic flows. Reducing the number of degrees of freedom allows one to simplify the analysis of the phenomenon, as well as reveal the main properties and patterns in intensive modes of advection.

The study of advection regimes arising in some areas of the flow is reduced to the sequential decoupling of two problems. The first problem is to determine the velocity field inside a rectangular cavity for a given fluidity at the boundaries. It is necessary to obtain exact solutions because the second problem is to find the movement trajectory of individual particles of the fluid in the selected area and the deformation of the boundaries of the fluid associated with a dynamically unstable fluid of movement inside the rectangle. To solve the first problem, we use the superposition method, which allows one to find the asymptotics of unknown coefficients in a number of general solutions, allowing one in turn to obtain the desired accuracy.

2. Literature Analysis

In the Lagrangian representation, the problem of advection of a passive marker particle by a prescribed flow defines a dynamical system. For two-dimensional incompressible flow, this system is Hamiltonian and has just one degree of freedom. For unsteady flow, the system is non-autonomous and one expects to observe chaotic particle motion. These ideas are developed in [1] and subsequently corroborated through the study of a model that provides an idealization of a stirred tank. In the model, the fluid is assumed incompressible and inviscid and its motion completely two-dimensional.

The heat transfer rate from a solid boundary to a highly viscous fluid can be enhanced significantly by a phenomenon that is called chaotic advection or Lagrangian turbulence. Although the flow is laminar and dominated by viscous forces, some fluid particle trajectories are chaotic due either to a suitable boundary displacement protocol or change in geometry. As in turbulent flow, the heat transfer rate enhancement between the boundary and the fluid is intimately linked to the mixing of fluid in the system. Chaotic advection in real Stokes flows, i.e., flows governed by viscous forces and that can be constructed experimentally, is discussed in [2].

The Stokes flow inside a two-dimensional rectangular cavity is analyzed in [3] for a highly viscous, incompressible fluid flow, driven by a single rotlet. Specifically, a rigorous solution of the governing two-dimensional biharmonic equation for the stream function is constructed analytically by means of the superposition principle. With this solution, multicellular flow patterns can be described for narrow cavities, in which the number of flow cells is directly related to the value of the aspect ratio.

The two-dimensional chaotic mixing of similar Newtonian fluids in the presence of an advected dissimilar minor phase fluid body with specified size, interfacial tension, and viscosity ratio was numerically investigated in [4]. The interfacial tension was sufficiently high to allow only small deformations in the dissimilar minor phase body. Mixing was confined to a rectangular cavity with periodically driven upper and lower surfaces. Regions of regular motion (i.e., islands) of comparable size to the minor phase body were eventually destroyed or replaced by the minor phase body. Islands persisted for longer times when the initial separation distance between the minor phase body and island was large or when the viscosity ratio was small. When interfacial tension was small enough to deform the minor phase body more readily, islands showed little indication of instability. The results suggest opportunities for improving mixing uniformity in real processes and disclose how interactions between dissimilar fluids affect mixing.

The advection of neutrally buoyant discs in two-dimensional chaotic Stokes flow is considered in [5,6]. The goal of the study is to explore a possibility to enhance laminar mixing in batch-flow mixers. The addition of freely moving bodies to periodically driven chaotic flow renders the flowfield nonperiodic [4], i.e., the Lagrangian chaos of the bodies' motion induces the Eulerian chaos of the flow that makes mixing more intensive. Simulations were performed using a new variant of the immersed boundaries method that allows for the direct numerical simulation of fluid–solid flows on a regular rectangular grid without the explicit calculation of the forces that the particles exert on the fluid.

The simultaneous effects of flow pulsation and geometrical perturbation on laminar mixing in curved ducts have been numerically studied in [7] by three different metrics: analysis of the secondary flow patterns, Lyapunov exponents, and vorticity vector analysis.

The authors of [8] present the paradigm of "designing for chaos" as a general framework for enhancing mixing in microfluidic applications. Designing for chaos is based on a fundamental understanding of the kinematics underlying the mixing process. Computational and experimental analyses demonstrate the effectiveness of the resulting design in generating chaos in the flow.

In paper [9], a modified three-dimensional Navier–Stokes system in an unbounded domain, which holds the Poincare inequality, is considered. Unique global solvability is proven. For the corresponding semigroup the existence of the global attractor in strong topology of phase space is ascertained, and the convergence of the obtained attractors to the set of bounded trajectories of the Navier–Stokes 3D-system is shown.

A numerical scheme for approximating the incompressible Navier–Stokes equations based on an auxiliary variable associated with the total system energy was presented in [10]. By introducing a dynamic equation for the auxiliary variable and restating the Navier–Stokes equations into an equivalent system, the scheme satisfies a discrete energy stability property in terms of a modified energy, and it allows for an efficient solution algorithm and implementation.

Based on the analysis of literature sources, it was found that the superposition method is not widely used in the study of fluid advection in bounded domains with a viscous incompressible fluid. This formed the aim of the present study: to analytically define the velocity field inside a rectangular cavity using the method of superposition. The method provides the high accuracy and low computational cost needed to obtain the desired velocity field. It also analytically describes the local structure of the stream function near corners and points of discontinuity of boundary velocities.

The purpose of the work is also to simulate the advection process of the allocated volume of fluid in a rectangular cavity under the action of tangential velocities applied to the top and bottom walls, using the method of piecewise spline interpolation [11]. The use of cubic spline interpolation on smooth contour segments allows one to determine the coordinates of additional points on the boundary of the selected volume with high accuracy. The motion of the walls is set by the law, which was considered in the experimental work of Ottino [12]. The novelty of the present study is that the superposition method and piecewise spline cubic interpolation in such a combination were used for the first time to simulate the experiment described in Ottino's paper.

3. Analytical Determination of the Velocity Field of a Flow of a Viscous Fluid in a Rectangular Cavity

3.1. The Equation of Motion of a Viscous Fluid in the Stokes Approximation

Consider a two-dimensional flow of a viscous incompressible homogeneous fluid whose density is equal to ρ. Inside the cavity of dimensions $2a \times 2b$, where the top and bottom boundaries are movable and the side walls are stationary, the flow moves with constant kinematic viscosity ν. Define the Cartesian coordinate system related to the geometric center of the rectangle (Figure 1). The velocity of the top wall is denoted by $U_{top}(x)$, and the bottom one is $U_{bot}(x)$. The problem is to determine the distribution of the velocity field $\vec{U}(x, y)$ inside the cavity under consideration.

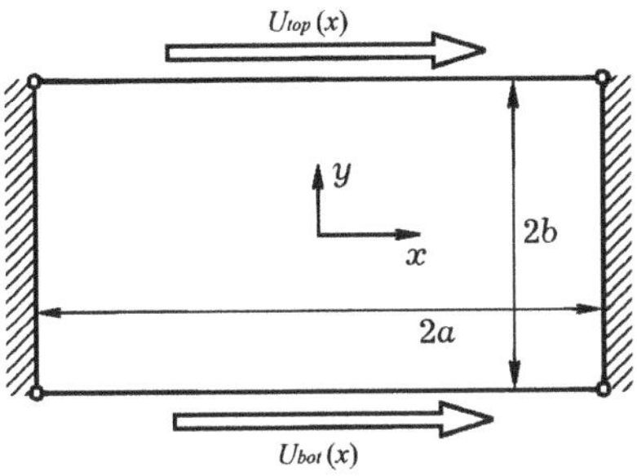

Figure 1. Geometry of a rectangular cavity.

The flow regime is determined by the Reynolds number Re

$$Re = \frac{UL}{\nu}, \tag{1}$$

where U is a characteristic flow rate $U = max\{U_{top}(x), U_{bot}(x)\}$, and L is the geometric scale of the flow, $L = 2a$. For this case, the inertial and viscous terms are proportional to u^2/L and $u\nu/L^2$, respectively. The Reynolds number, given by (1), shows the ratio of inertial forces to viscosity forces [13].

The velocity index for the flow under consideration must be chosen in such a way that the Reynolds number $Re \ll 1$. This approximation in the available sources [14] is called the *Stokes approximation*.

The motion of a viscous incompressible fluid, which has constant physical properties, can be described by the Navier–Stokes equation and the continuity equation

$$\frac{\partial \vec{u}}{\partial t} + \vec{u}\nabla\vec{u} = \vec{F} - \frac{1}{\rho}\nabla p + \nu\Delta\vec{u}, \tag{2}$$

$$\vec{\nabla} \cdot \vec{u} = 0, \tag{3}$$

where $\vec{u}$—velocity vector, $\vec{F}$—the main vector of volume forces, p—pressure, and t—time.

The left part of Equation (2) can be written as

$$\frac{d\vec{u}}{dt} = \frac{\partial \vec{u}}{\partial t} + \vec{u}\nabla\vec{u}. \tag{4}$$

The term in the left-hand side of (2) is called the inertial term; it represents the acceleration of a fluid particle or substantial acceleration. This term corresponds to the force of inertia and shows the rate of formation of the momentum of a fluid element on which external forces act. In the right-hand side of (2), the first term is responsible for the volume forces. The second term is responsible for the pressure and the third for the viscosity force.

For small Reynolds numbers, flows begin to develop under the action of viscosity forces; hence, the inertial properties of the fluid can be neglected. The formation of such flows occurs under the action of an applied pressure gradient, or they are affected by the reaction of the boundaries of the Stokes approximation to an instantaneous change in the velocity field throughout the entire flow region.

In case the inertial components are neglected for an incompressible fluid, when there are no external volume forces and, taking into account all conservative mass pressure forces, the Navier–Stokes equations are simplified to the form:

$$-\frac{1}{\rho}\vec{\nabla}p+\nu\Delta\vec{u}=0, \tag{5}$$

together with the continuity Equation (3), it is called the Stokes equation.

This equation is linear with respect to the flow velocity field and pressure distribution, and the time component is not included. So the Stokes equations describe a stationary flow of a viscous incompressible fluid, with constant boundary conditions and a stationary pressure gradient.

In the Cartesian coordinate system (x,y), the system of Stokes equations can be represented in the form of three differential equations

$$\begin{cases} -\frac{1}{\rho}\frac{\partial p}{\partial x}+\nu(\frac{\partial^2 u}{\partial x^2}+\frac{\partial^2 u}{\partial y^2})=0, \\ -\frac{1}{\rho}\frac{\partial p}{\partial y}+\nu(\frac{\partial^2 v}{\partial x^2}+\frac{\partial^2 v}{\partial y^2})=0, \\ \frac{\partial u}{\partial x}+\frac{\partial v}{\partial y}=0. \end{cases} \tag{6}$$

Let us differentiate between the first and second equations of system (6) with respect to x and y by conducting the additional operation, getting rid of the pressure, replacing the first two equations of system (6) with one third-order differential equation

$$\frac{\partial^3 u}{\partial y^3}+\frac{\partial^3 u}{\partial x^2\partial y}-\frac{\partial^3 v}{\partial x^3}-\frac{\partial^3 v}{\partial x\partial y^2}=0. \tag{7}$$

Let us introduce a vector stream function $\vec{\psi}$, with its expression $\vec{u}=\operatorname{rot}\vec{\psi}$, that connects the distribution of the velocity field of an incompressible flow [14]. In the two-dimensional case, the vector function $\vec{\psi}$ has only one component $\psi_z=\psi(x,y)$, which connects the components of the velocity field in the following form:

$$u=\frac{\partial\psi}{\partial y},\ v=-\frac{\partial\psi}{\partial x}. \tag{8}$$

Substituting (8) into (7) yields a biharmonic equation with respect to the stream function

$$\frac{\partial^4\psi}{\partial x^4}+2\frac{\partial^4\psi}{\partial x^2\partial y^2}+\frac{\partial^4\psi}{\partial y^4}=0. \tag{9}$$

Taking into account (8), we conclude that the latter equation describes the distribution of the velocity field in the flow that is considered.

Let us supplement Equation (9) with boundary conditions on the top and bottom surfaces. For a viscous fluid, the no-slip conditions [14] on the moving boundary, denoted by S, are as follows:

$$\vec{u}|_S=U_S \tag{10}$$

and can be written in the form of derivatives along the normal and tangent, respectively

$$\left.\frac{\partial\psi}{\partial n}\right|_S=U_S,\ \left.\frac{\partial\psi}{\partial\tau}\right|_S=0 \text{ or } \psi|_S=const. \tag{11}$$

For further calculations, let us use the biharmonic Equation (9) and boundary conditions (11) to construct an analytical solution of the hydrodynamic problem of the flow of a viscous fluid in a rectangular cavity.

3.2. Stokes Flow in a Rectangular Cavity

The two-dimensional Stokes flow of an incompressible viscous fluid can be described as a biharmonic problem with the stream function satisfying the biharmonic equation

$$\Delta^2 \psi = 0. \tag{12}$$

where Δ is the Laplacian operator in two dimensions.

The flow in a rectangular cavity $|x| < a$, $|y| < b$ arises with the participation of tangential velocities U_+ and U_- on the top $(y = b)$ and bottom $(y = -b)$ walls, while the side walls remain stationary $x = \pm a$, and therefore, the boundary conditions for Equation (12) have the form:

$$\begin{aligned} &\psi = 0, \ \frac{\partial \psi}{\partial x} = 0, \text{ if } x = \pm a, \ |y| \le b, \\ &\psi = 0, \ \frac{\partial \psi}{\partial y} = U_{\pm}, \text{ if } y = \pm b, \ |x| \le a. \end{aligned} \tag{13}$$

The velocities U_+ and U_- can both depend on coordinate x and on time t simultaneously. Periodic functions with a definite period T and its dependence on time are of particular interest. So the stream function ψ, which is a solution to the quasi-stationary limiting problem, will also be periodic with a period T.

Using the linear boundary value problem (12), (13), the representation for the stream function in a rectangular cavity can be presented as a sum of two functions ψ_1 and ψ_2 describing a symmetric and antisymmetric velocity field. The tangential velocities $U_+^{(1)} = -U_-^{(1)} = U_1$ and $U_+^{(2)} = U_-^{(2)} = U_2$ applied on the upper and lower walls, respectively, of the cavity excite these fields. In this case, an arbitrary load velocity with even on X functions $U_+(x)$ and $U_-(x)$ can be represented in the form

$$U_1(x) = \frac{U_+^{(1)} - U_-^{(1)}}{2}, \quad U_2(x) = \frac{U_+^{(2)} + U_-^{(2)}}{2}. \tag{14}$$

3.2.1. Construction of a Solution to a Symmetric Problem with Constant Velocities

Using the superposition method, a solution for a symmetric problem with constant velocities can be constructed as a sum of two Fourier series in the complete orthogonal system of functions [15–17].

$$\begin{aligned} \psi_{EE} =& b \sum_{m=1}^{\infty} (-1)^m \frac{X_m^{(1)}}{\alpha_m} (b \tanh \alpha_m b \frac{\cosh \alpha_m y}{\cosh \alpha_m b} - y \frac{\sinh \alpha_m y}{\cosh \alpha_m b}) \cos \alpha_m x \\ & - a \sum_{l=1}^{\infty} (-1)^l \frac{Y_l^{(1)}}{\beta_l} (a \tanh \beta_l a \frac{\cosh \beta_l x}{\cosh \beta_l a} - x \frac{\sinh \beta_l x}{\cosh \beta_l a}) \cos \beta_l y, \end{aligned} \tag{15}$$

where ψ_{EE} is the stream function expressing the flow of the symmetric problem, $\alpha_m = \frac{(2m-1)\pi}{2a}$, $\beta_l = \frac{(2l-1)\pi}{2b}$.

The first part of the equation in (15) is the solution for the strip $|y| \le b$, $-\infty < x < \infty$, while the second part is the solution for the strip $|x| \le a$, $-\infty < y < \infty$. For the first and second series, there is the required number of degrees of functional freedom in order to satisfy the boundary conditions on two opposite boundaries of the rectangle and to satisfy the requirement of completeness of the system of functions on different sides.

The unknown coefficients of the Fourier series $X_m^{(1)}$, $Y_l^{(1)}$ can be calculated by solving the system

$$\begin{cases} X_m^{(1)} b\Delta_1(\alpha_m b) - \sum\limits_{l=1}^{\infty} Y_l^{(1)} \frac{4\alpha_m^2\beta_l}{(\beta_l^2+\alpha_m^2)^2} = (-1)^{m-1}\alpha_m U_m^{(1)},\ 1 \leq m \leq \infty, \\ Y_l^{(1)} a\Delta_1(\beta_l a) - \sum\limits_{m=1}^{\infty} X_m^{(1)} \frac{4\beta_l^2\alpha_m}{(\alpha_m^2+\beta_l^2)^2} = 0,\ 1 \leq l \leq \infty, \end{cases} \tag{16}$$

where

$$\Delta_1(\xi) = \tanh\xi + \frac{\xi}{\cosh^2\xi} \tag{17}$$

and $U_m^{(1)}$ — Fourier coefficients of the even function $U_1(x)$.

Using the boundary conditions: the first equation is satisfied by the boundary condition $\frac{\partial\psi_{EE}}{\partial y} = \pm U_1(x)$ at $y = \pm b$, multiplied by $\cos\alpha_m x$ and integrated over x from $-a$ to a, and the second—by fulfilling the boundary condition $\frac{\partial\psi_{EE}}{\partial x} = 0$ at $x = \pm a$ for the desired flow function $\psi_{EE}(x,y)$, multiplied by $\cos\beta_l y$ and integrated over y from $-b$ to b.

At infinity, the asymptotics of the coefficients $X_m^{(1)}$, $Y_l^{(1)}$ take the form

$$\begin{aligned} X_m^{(1)} &= \frac{2\pi^2 U_1(\alpha)}{ab(\pi^2-4)} - \frac{\pi U_1'(a)}{2ab\alpha_m} + \Re(E_\lambda^{(1)}\alpha_m^{-\lambda_1}) + o(m^{-3}),\ m \to \infty, \\ Y_l^{(1)} &= \frac{4\pi U_1(a)}{ab(\pi^2-4)} - \frac{\pi U_1'(a)}{2ab\beta_l} - \Re(E_\lambda^{(1)}\beta_l^{-\lambda_1}) + o(l^{-3}),\ l \to \infty, \end{aligned} \tag{18}$$

where $\lambda_1 = 1.7396 + i1.1190$ is the root with the lowest positive real part of the transcendental equation $\cos(\frac{\pi\lambda_1}{2}) = -\lambda_1 - 1$.

In the case when the function $U_1(x)$ is continuous together with the first and second derivatives on the interval $|x| \leq a$, we have

$$U_1(x) - U_1(a) = \sum_{m=1}^{\infty} (-1)^{m-1}\overline{U}_m \cos\alpha_m x,\ \overline{U}_m = O(\alpha_m^{-3}),\ m \to \infty, \tag{19}$$

$$U_m - \frac{2}{a\alpha_m} U_1(a) = \overline{U}_m. \tag{20}$$

Let us use the expression

$$U_1'(a) = \sum_{m=1}^{\infty} \alpha_m \overline{U}_m, \tag{21}$$

which follows from the differentiation of the uniformly convergent Fourier series (19) for the function $U_1(x) - U_1(a)$.

When $U_1(x) \neq 0$, then with the increase in m the value of $|\alpha_m U_m|$ does not fall. This condition affects the stability of the numerical solution of an infinite system.

Consider the case when $U_1(x) = U = const$ on the interval $|x| \leq a$. According to the formula

$$U_m^{(1)} = \frac{1}{a}\int_{-a}^{a} U_1(x)\cos\alpha_m x dx, \tag{22}$$

the Fourier coefficients for this case take the form $U_m^{(1)} = \frac{2U}{a\alpha_m}$. Therefore, the peculiarity of the system (16) will be that the right-hand-side terms will grow. Therefore, it is impossible to use existing data in the study of the asymptotics of unknown coefficients in systems of this type because the right-hand-side terms do not satisfy the necessary decreasing condition $O(\frac{1}{\alpha_m^2})$ [18].

To use the method of analysis of regular systems, let us apply new unknown coefficients $x_m^{(1)}$ and $y_l^{(1)}$ [19] according to formulas

$$X_m^{(1)} = X_1 + x_m^{(1)}, \ Y_l^{(1)} = Y_1 + y_l^{(1)}, \tag{23}$$

where X_1 and Y_1 are some constants. Substituting (23) into (16), we obtain one more system for determining the unknown coefficients.

$$\begin{aligned} x_m^{(1)} b\Delta_1(\alpha_m b) - \sum_{l=1}^{\infty} y_l^{(1)} \frac{4\beta_l \alpha_m^2}{(\alpha_m^2 + \beta_l^2)^2} &= F_m^{(1)}, \ m = 1, 2, \ldots, \\ y_l^{(1)} a\Delta_1(\beta_l a) - \sum_{m=1}^{\infty} x_m^{(1)} \frac{4\beta_l^2 \alpha_m}{(\alpha_m^2 + \beta_l^2)^2} &= G_l^{(1)}, \ l = 1, 2, \ldots, \end{aligned} \tag{24}$$

where

$$F_m^{(1)} = 4Y_1\alpha_m^2 \sum_{l=1}^{\infty} \frac{\beta_l}{(\alpha_m^2 + \beta_l^2)^2} - X_1 b\Delta_1(\alpha_m b) + \frac{2}{a}U,$$

$$G_l^{(1)} = 4X_1\beta_l^2 \sum_{m=1}^{\infty} \frac{\alpha_m}{(\alpha_m^2 + \beta_l^2)^2} - Y_1 a\Delta_1(\beta_l a).$$

Let us impose a decreasing condition $O(\frac{1}{\alpha_m^2})$ on $F_m^{(1)}$ and $G_l^{(1)}$. Set the coefficients

$$\begin{aligned} F_m^{(1)} &= \left(\frac{2b}{\pi}Y_1 - bX_1 + \frac{2}{a}U\right) + \frac{\pi}{6b\alpha_m^2}Y_1 + O(m^{-4}), \ m \to \infty, \\ G_l^{(1)} &= \left(\frac{2a}{\pi}X_1 - aY_1\right) + \frac{\pi}{6a\beta_l^2}X_1 + O(l^{-4}), \ l \to \infty. \end{aligned} \tag{25}$$

In the equations, the condition of decreasing the right-hand-side terms must be satisfied. As a result, we obtain the values of the constants X_1 and Y_1 as a result of equating the main terms to zero

$$X_1 = \frac{2\pi^2}{ab(\pi^2 - 4)}U, \ Y_1 = \frac{4\pi}{ab(\pi^2 - 4)}U. \tag{26}$$

Therefore, the infinite system of linear algebraic equations (24) with respect to unknown coefficients $x_m^{(1)}$ and $y_l^{(1)}$, in general, satisfies the regularity conditions [18], and for such a system the asymptotic law for the solutions is true

$$\lim_{m\to\infty} x_m^{(1)} = \lim_{l\to\infty} y_l^{(1)} = A. \tag{27}$$

It follows from this condition that there exists a main solution that is bounded, and it can be found using the reduction method. The numbers of unknown coefficients $x_m^{(1)}$ and $y_l^{(1)}$ are finite (M and L), and therefore, in order to find the unknown coefficients $x_m^{(1)}$ and $y_l^{(1)}$, it is necessary to solve a finite system of $M + L$ linear equations.

Next, let us calculate the unknown stream function $\psi_{EE}(x,y)$. Substitute (23) in (15) and obtain the relation

$$\psi_{EE}(x,y) = \psi_{EE}^{(a,b)}(x,y) + \psi_{EE}^{(x,y)}(x,y), \tag{28}$$

where

$$\psi_{EE}^{(a,b)}(x,y) = X_l b S_a^{(1)}(x,y) - Y_1 a S_b^{(1)}(x,y),$$

$$\psi_{EE}^{(x,y)}(x,y) = b\sum_{m=1}^{\infty} \frac{(-1)^m}{\alpha_m} x_m^{(1)} p_m^{(1)}(y)\cos\alpha_m x - \alpha \sum_{l=1}^{\infty} \frac{(-1)^l}{\beta_l} x_l^{(1)} q_l^{(1)}(x)\cos\beta_l y,$$

$$p_m^{(1)}(y) = b\tanh\alpha_m b\frac{\cosh\alpha_m y}{\cosh\alpha_m b} - y\frac{\sinh\alpha_m y}{\cosh\alpha_m b},$$
$$q_l^{(1)}(x) = a\tanh\beta_l a\frac{\cosh\beta_l x}{\cosh\beta_l a} - x\frac{\sinh\beta_l x}{\cosh\beta_l a},$$
$$S_a^{(1)}(x,y) = \sum_{m=1}^{\infty}\frac{(-1)^m}{\alpha_m}x_m^{(1)}p_m^{(1)}(y)\cos\alpha_m x,$$
$$S_b^{(1)}(x,y) = \sum_{l=1}^{\infty}\frac{(-1)^l}{\beta_l}x_l^{(1)}q_l^{(1)}(x)\cos\beta_l y.$$

In a rectangular cavity, the terms of the equation $\frac{\cosh\alpha_m y}{\cosh\alpha_m b}$ and $\frac{\sinh\alpha_m y}{\cosh\alpha_m b}$ are quantities of the order $e^{\alpha_m(|y|-1)}$ of that; the series in (24) inside the cavity and on the boundary of the region converge uniformly [15,16,18]. There is no need to improve convergence for these series. But on the border, there are diverging rows $S_a^{(1)}(x,y)$ and $S_b^{(1)}(x,y)$.

To transform the expressions $p_m^{(1)}(y)$ and $q_l^{(1)}(x)$, let us use the relations

$$\frac{1}{\cosh\xi} = 2\sum_{r=0}^{\infty}(-1)^r e^{-(2r+1)\xi}, \quad \frac{\sinh\xi}{\cosh^2\xi} = 2\sum_{r=0}^{\infty}(-1)^r(2r+1)e^{-(2r+1)\xi}. \tag{29}$$

Let us perform certain transformations to obtain expressions for $S_a^{(1)}(x,y)$ and $S_b^{(1)}(x,y)$, namely,

$$\begin{aligned} S_a^{(1)}(x,y) &= \sum_{r=0}^{\infty}(-1)^r[(2rb+b-y)S_1(x,2rb+b-y) + (2rb+b+y)S_1(x,2rb+b+y)], \\ S_a^{(1)}(x,y) &= \sum_{r=0}^{\infty}(-1)^r[(2ra+a-x)S_2(y,2ra+a-x) + (2ra+a+x)S_2(y,2ra+a+x)], \end{aligned} \tag{30}$$

where

$$S_1(\xi,\eta) = \sum_{m=1}^{\infty}\frac{(-1)^m}{\alpha_m}e^{-\alpha_m\eta}\cos\alpha_m\xi \quad = -\frac{a}{\pi}\arctan\left[\frac{\cos(\pi\xi/2a)}{\sinh(\pi\eta/2a)}\right],$$
$$S_2(\xi,\eta) = \sum_{l=1}^{\infty}\frac{(-1)^l}{\beta_l}e^{-\beta_l\eta}\cos\beta_l\xi \quad = -\frac{b}{\pi}\arctan\left[\frac{\cos(\pi\xi/2b)}{\sinh(\pi\eta/2b)}\right].$$

By finding that the terms slowly coincide and adding them, let us obtain the functions $S_1(\xi,\eta)$ and $S_2(\xi,\eta)$. Now, in expression (24), the series uniformly coincide both at all points of the region and on the boundary. For the functions $S_1(\xi,\eta)$ and $S_2(\xi,\eta)$ at the boundary of the region, we encountered a singularity, so the calculations were carried out on the basis of the passage to the limit.

Let us analyze the convergence of the series for the velocity field. Velocity components can be calculated using the formulas given above, as the corresponding derivatives with respect to and from the stream function

$$
\begin{aligned}
u_{EE}(x,y) =& b\sum_{m=1}^{\infty}\frac{(-1)^m}{\alpha_m}X_m^{(1)}\left(b\tanh\alpha_m b\frac{\alpha_m\sinh\alpha_m y}{\cosh\alpha_m b}-y\frac{\alpha_m\cosh\alpha_m y}{\cosh\alpha_m b}-\frac{\sinh\alpha_m y}{\cosh\alpha_m b}\right)\cos\alpha_m x\\
&+a\sum_{l=1}^{\infty}(-1)^l Y_l^{(1)}\left(a\tanh\beta_l a\frac{\cosh\beta_l x}{\cosh\beta_l a}-x\frac{\sinh\beta_l x}{\cosh\beta_l a}\right)\sin\beta_l y\\
=& b\sum_{m=1}^{\infty}(-1)^m X_m^{(1)}\left(b\tanh\alpha_m b\frac{\sinh\alpha_m y}{\cosh\alpha_m b}-y\frac{\cosh\alpha_m y}{\cosh\alpha_m b}\right)\cos\alpha_m x\\
&-b\sum_{m=1}^{\infty}\frac{(-1)^m}{\alpha_m}X_m^{(1)}\frac{\sinh\alpha_m y}{\cosh\alpha_m b}\cos\alpha_m x-a\sum_{l=1}^{\infty}(-1)^l Y_l^{(1)}\left(a\tanh\beta_l a\frac{\cosh\beta_l x}{\cosh\beta_l a}-x\frac{\sinh\beta_l x}{\cosh\beta_l a}\right)\sin\beta_l y,\\
v_{EE}(x,y) =& b\sum_{m=1}^{\infty}(-1)^m X_m^{(1)}\left(b\tanh\alpha_m b\frac{\cosh\alpha_m y}{\cosh\alpha_m b}-y\frac{\sinh\alpha_m y}{\cosh\alpha_m b}\right)\sin\alpha_m x\\
&+a\sum_{l=1}^{\infty}\frac{(-1)^l}{\beta_l}Y_l^{(1)}\left(a\tanh\beta_l a\frac{\beta_l\sinh\beta_l x}{\cosh\beta_l a}-x\frac{\beta_l\cosh\beta_l x}{\cosh\beta_l a}-\frac{\sinh\beta_l x}{\cosh\beta_l a}\right)\cos\beta_l y\\
=& b\sum_{m=1}^{\infty}(-1)^m X_m^{(1)}\left(b\tanh\alpha_m b\frac{\cosh\alpha_m y}{\cosh\alpha_m b}-y\frac{\sinh\alpha_m y}{\cosh\alpha_m b}\right)\sin\alpha_m x\\
&-a\sum_{l=1}^{\infty}\frac{(-1)^l}{\beta_l}Y_l^{(1)}\frac{\sinh\beta_l x}{\cosh\beta_l a}\cos\beta_l y+a\sum_{l=1}^{\infty}(-1)^l Y_l^{(1)}\left(a\tanh\beta_l a\frac{\sinh\beta_l x}{\cosh\beta_l a}-x\frac{\cosh\beta_l x}{\cosh\beta_l a}\right)\cos\beta_l y.
\end{aligned}
\tag{31}
$$

Based on Formula (28), there are expressions for the velocity component

$$
\begin{aligned}
u_{EE}(x,y) &= u_{EE}^{(a,b)}(x,y)+u_{EE}^{(x,y)}(x,y),\\
v_{EE}(x,y) &= v_{EE}^{(a,b)}(x,y)+v_{EE}^{(x,y)}(x,y),
\end{aligned}
\tag{32}
$$

where $u_{EE}^{(x,y)}(x,y)$ and $v_{EE}^{(x,y)}(x,y)$ are possible to express from Formula (31). The coefficients take the form $x_m^{(1)}$ and $y_l^{(1)}, u_{EE}^{(a,b)}(x,y)$, and $v_{EE}^{(a,b)}(x,y)$ and have the sums of terms with constant coefficients X_1 and Y_1. Expressions for $u_{EE}^{(a,b)}(x,y)$ and $v_{EE}^{(a,b)}(x,y)$ are as follows:

$$
\begin{aligned}
u_{EE}^{(a,b)}(x,y) =& X_1 b\sum_{r=0}^{\infty}(-1)^r[(2rb+b-y)S_3(x,2rb+b-y)-(2rb+b+y)S_3(x,2rb+b+y)]\\
&-X_1 b\sum_{r=0}^{\infty}(-1)^r[S_1(x,2rb+b-y)-S_1(x,2rb+b+y)]\\
&+Y_1 a\sum_{r=0}^{\infty}(-1)^r[(2ra+a-x)S_4(y,2ra+a-x)+(2ra+a+x)S_4(y,2ra+a+x)],\\
v_{EE}^{(a,b)}(x,y) =& X_1 b\sum_{r=0}^{\infty}(-1)^r[(2rb+b-y)S_5(x,2rb+b-y)+(2rb+b+y)S_5(x,2rb+b+y)]\\
&-Y_1 a\sum_{r=0}^{\infty}(-1)^r[S_2(y,2ra+a-x)+S_2(y,2ra+a+x)]\\
&+Y_1 a\sum_{r=0}^{\infty}(-1)^r[(2ra+a-x)S_6(y,2ra+a-x)-(2ra+a+x)S_6(y,2ra+a+x)],
\end{aligned}
\tag{33}
$$

where

$$
S_3(\xi,\eta)=\sum_{m=1}^{\infty}(-1)^m e^{-\alpha_m\eta}\cos\alpha_m\xi=-\frac{1}{2}\frac{\cos(\pi\xi/2a)\cosh(\pi\eta/2a)}{\cos^2(\pi\xi/2a)+\sinh^2(\pi\eta/2a)},
$$

$$
S_4(\xi,\eta)=\sum_{l=1}^{\infty}(-1)^l e^{-\beta_l\eta}\sin\beta_l\xi=-\frac{1}{2}\frac{\sin(\pi\xi/2b)\sinh(\pi\eta/2b)}{\cos^2(\pi\xi/2b)+\sinh^2(\pi\eta/2b)},
$$

$$S_5(\xi,\eta) = \sum_{m=1}^{\infty}(-1)^m e^{-\alpha_m\eta}\sin\alpha_m\xi = -\frac{1}{2}\frac{\sin(\pi\xi/2a)\sinh(\pi\eta/2a)}{\cos^2(\pi\xi/2a)+\sinh^2(\pi\eta/2a)},$$

$$S_6(\xi,\eta) = \sum_{l=1}^{\infty}(-1)^l e^{-\beta_l\eta}\cos\beta_l\xi = -\frac{1}{2}\frac{\cos(\pi\xi/2b)\cosh(\pi\eta/2b)}{\cos^2(\pi\xi/2b)+\sinh^2(\pi\eta/2b)},$$

components $S_1(\xi,\eta)$ and $S_2(\xi,\eta)$ are expressed by Formula (30), and $S_1(\xi,0) = -a/2$, $S_1(\pm a,\eta) = 0, S_2(\xi,0) = -b/2, S_2(\pm b,\eta) = 0$.

The series that are included in the solution coincide quickly, so it is possible to select a part to sum to the final values. The accuracy of the fulfillment of the boundary conditions is associated with an infinite number of members of the series; when using the reduced series, there is an error in solving the boundary value problem.

3.2.2. Construction of a Solution to an Antisymmetric Problem with Constant Velocities

Similarly to how the general solution $\psi_{EE}(x,y)$ was found using the superposition method, let us find the solution to the boundary value problem [15,16]

$$\begin{aligned}\psi_{EO} =& b\sum_{m=1}^{\infty}(-1)^m\frac{X_m^{(2)}}{\alpha_m}\left(b\coth\alpha_m b\frac{\sinh\alpha_m y}{\sinh\alpha_m b} - y\frac{\cosh\alpha_m y}{\sinh\alpha_m b}\right)\cos\alpha_m x\\ &- a\sum_{k=1}^{\infty}(-1)^k\frac{Y_k^{(2)}}{\gamma_k}\left(a\tanh\gamma_k a\frac{\cosh\gamma_k x}{\cosh\gamma_k a} - x\frac{\sinh\gamma_k x}{\sinh\gamma_k a}\right)\sin\gamma_k y,\end{aligned} \tag{34}$$

where ψ_{EO} is the stream function expressing the flow of the antisymmetric problem, $\gamma_k = \frac{k\pi}{b}$.

When the boundary conditions are satisfied, let us obtain a system of linear algebraic equations for the unknown Fourier coefficients $X_m^{(2)}$ and $Y_k^{(2)}$ and write it in the form

$$\begin{aligned}X_m^{(2)}b\Delta_2(\alpha_m b) - \sum_{k=1}^{\infty}Y_k^{(2)}\frac{4\delta_k\alpha_m^2}{(\alpha_m^2+\delta_k^2)^2} &= \alpha_m U_m^{(2)}, \quad m = 1,2,\ldots,\\ Y_k^{(2)}a\Delta_1(\delta_k a) - \sum_{m=1}^{\infty}X_m^{(2)}\frac{4\delta_k^2\alpha_m}{(\alpha_m^2+\delta_k^2)^2} &= 0, \quad l = 1,2,\ldots,\end{aligned} \tag{35}$$

where

$$\Delta_2(\xi) = \coth\xi - \frac{\xi}{\sinh^2\xi}, \tag{36}$$

and $\delta_k = \frac{k\pi}{b}$, $U_m^{(2)}$—Fourier coefficients of an even function $U_2(x)$.

Let us suppose that $U_2(x) = U = const$ for $|x| \le a$. The Fourier coefficients in this case will have the form

$$U_m^{(2)} = \frac{(-1)^{m-1}}{a}\int_{-a}^{a}U_2(x)\cos\alpha_m x dx = \frac{2U}{a\alpha_m}. \tag{37}$$

To neglect the influence of a non-decreasing free term, let us introduce new unknown coefficients $x_m^{(2)}$ and $y_k^{(2)}$

$$X_m^{(2)} = X_2 + x_m^{(2)}, \quad Y_k^{(2)} = Y_2 + y_k^{(2)}, \tag{38}$$

At infinity, the asymptotic of the coefficients $X_m^{(2)}$ and $Y_k^{(2)}$ takes the form

$$\begin{aligned} x_m^{(2)} b\Delta_2(\alpha_m b) - \sum_{k=1}^{\infty} y_k^{(2)} \frac{4\delta_k \alpha_m^2}{(\alpha_m^2 + \delta_k^2)^2} &= F_m^{(2)}, \quad m = 1, 2, \dots, \\ y_k^{(2)} a\Delta_1(\delta_k a) - \sum_{m=1}^{\infty} x_m^{(2)} \frac{4\delta_k^2 \alpha_m}{(\alpha_m^2 + \delta_k^2)^2} &= G_k^{(2)}, \quad l = 1, 2, \dots, \end{aligned} \tag{39}$$

On the right-hand-side, we obtain the values

$$\begin{aligned} F_m^{(2)} &= 4Y_2\alpha_m^2 \sum_{k=1}^{\infty} \frac{\delta_k}{(\alpha_m^2 + \delta_k^2)^2} - X_2 b\Delta_2(\alpha_m b) + \frac{2}{a}U, \\ G_k^{(2)} &= 4X_2\delta_k^2 \sum_{m=1}^{\infty} \frac{\alpha_m}{(\alpha_m^2 + \delta_k^2)^2} - Y_2 a\Delta_1(\delta_k a). \end{aligned} \tag{40}$$

For $F_m^{(2)}$ and $G_k^{(2)}$, the decrease condition $O\left(\frac{1}{\alpha_m^2}\right)$ is satisfied. For system (39), the law of asymptotic expressions can be applied since it satisfies the regularity conditions [18].

$$\lim_{m\to\infty} x_m^{(2)} = \lim_{k\to\infty} y_k^{(2)} = B. \tag{41}$$

The solution is sought by a simple reduction method. The numbers of unknown coefficients $x_m^{(2)}$ and $y_k^{(2)}$ are finite (M and K) and can be found by solving a finite system of linear equations.

Let us also take $x_m^{(2)}$ and $y_k^{(2)}$ for the known values. We calculate the stream function

$$\psi_{EO}(x,y) = \psi_{EO}^{(a,b)}(x,y) + \psi_{EO}^{(x,y)}(x,y), \tag{42}$$

where

$$\begin{aligned} \psi_{EO}^{(x,y)}(x,y) &= b\sum_{m=1}^{\infty} \frac{(-1)^n}{\alpha_m} x_m^{(2)} p_m^{(2)}(y) \cos\alpha_m x - a\sum_{k=1}^{\infty} \frac{(-1)^k}{\delta_k} y_k^{(2)} q_k^{(2)}(x) \sin\delta_k y, \\ \psi_{EO}^{(a,b)}(x,y) &= X_2 b\sum_{m=1}^{\infty} \frac{(-1)^m}{\alpha_m} p_m^{(2)}(y) \cos\alpha_m x - Y_2 a\sum_{k=1}^{\infty} \frac{(-1)^k}{\delta_k} q_k^{(2)}(x) \sin\delta_k y, \end{aligned}$$

$$\begin{aligned} p_m^{(2)}(y) &= b\coth\alpha_m b\frac{\sinh\alpha_m y}{\sinh\alpha_m b} - y\frac{\cosh\alpha_m y}{\sinh\alpha_m b}, \\ q_k^{(2)}(x) &= a\tanh\delta_k a\frac{\cosh\delta_k x}{\cosh\delta_k a} - x\frac{\sinh\delta_k x}{\cosh\delta_k a}. \end{aligned}$$

Let us use the ratios

$$\frac{1}{\sinh\xi} = 2\sum_{r=0}^{\infty} e^{-(2r+1)\xi}, \quad \frac{\cosh\xi}{\sinh^2\xi} = 2\sum_{r=0}^{\infty} (2r+1)e^{-(2r+1)\xi}, \tag{43}$$

to transform $p_m^{(2)}(y)$ and $q_k^{(2)}(x)$. Consequently, we find an expression for $\psi_{EO}^{(a,b)}(x,y)$

$$\begin{aligned} \psi_{EO}^{(a,b)}(x,y) =& X_2 b\sum_{r=0}^{\infty}[(2rb+b-y)S_1(x, 2rb+b-y) - (2rb+b+y)S_1(x, 2rb+b+y)] \\ &- Y_2 a\sum_{r=0}^{\infty}(-1)^r[(2ra+a-x)S_{14}(y, 2ra+a-x) + (2ra+a+x)S_{14}(y, 2ra+a+x)], \end{aligned} \tag{44}$$

where

$$S_{14}(\xi,\eta)=\sum_{k=1}^{\infty}\frac{(-1)^k}{\delta_k}e^{-\delta_k\eta}\sin\delta_k\xi=-\frac{b}{\pi}\arctan\left[\frac{\sin(\pi\xi/b)}{\exp(\pi\eta/b)+\cos(\pi\xi/b)}\right].$$

The velocity components, as derivatives with respect to x and y of the stream function, can be represented as

$$\begin{aligned}u_{EO}(x,y)&=u_{EO}^{(a,b)}(x,y)+u_{EO}^{(x,y)}(x,y),\\ v_{EO}(x,y)&=v_{EO}^{(a,b)}(x,y)+v_{EO}^{(x,y)}(x,y),\end{aligned}\tag{45}$$

where $u_{EO}^{(x,y)}(x,y)$ and $v_{EO}^{(x,y)}(x,y)$ are expressed from the following formulas with coefficients $x_m^{(2)}$ and $y_k^{(2)}$

$$\begin{aligned}u_{EO}^{(x,y)}(x,y)=&\,b\sum_{m=1}^{\infty}(-1)^m x_m^{(2)}\left(b\coth\alpha_m b\frac{\cosh\alpha_m y}{\sinh\alpha_m b}-y\frac{\sinh\alpha_m y}{\sinh\alpha_m b}\right)\cos\alpha_m x\\ &-b\sum_{m=1}^{\infty}\frac{(-1)^m}{\alpha_m}x_m^{(2)}\frac{\cosh\alpha_m y}{\sinh\alpha_m b}\cos\alpha_m x-a\sum_{k=1}^{\infty}(-1)^k y_k^{(2)}q_k^{(2)}(x)\cos\delta_k y,\\ v_{EO}^{(x,y)}(x,y)=&\,a\sum_{k=1}^{\infty}(-1)^k y_k^{(2)}\left(a\tanh\delta_k a\frac{\sinh\delta_k x}{\cosh\delta_k a}-x\frac{\cosh\delta_k x}{\cosh\delta_k a}\right)\sin\delta_k y\\ &-a\sum_{k=1}^{\infty}\frac{(-1)^k}{\delta_k}y_k^{(2)}\frac{\sinh\delta_k x}{\cosh\delta_k a}\sin\delta_k y+b\sum_{m=1}^{\infty}(-1)^m x_m^{(2)}p_m^{(2)}(y)\sin\alpha_m x,\end{aligned}\tag{46}$$

and $u_{EO}^{(a,b)(x,y)}$ and $v_{EO}^{(a,b)}(x,y)$ have the sums of all components with constant coefficients X_2 and Y_2; they can be calculated as derivatives with respect to x and y of the component of the stream function $\psi_{EO}^{(a,b)}(x,y)$,

$$\begin{aligned}u_{EO}^{(a,b)}(x,y)=&\,X_2 b\sum_{m=1}^{\infty}(-1)^m\left(b\coth\alpha_m b\frac{\cosh\alpha_m y}{\sinh\alpha_m b}-y\frac{\sinh\alpha_m y}{\sinh\alpha_m b}\right)\cos\alpha_m x\\ &-X_2 b\sum_{m=1}^{\infty}\frac{(-1)^m}{\alpha_m}\frac{\cosh\alpha_m y}{\sinh\alpha_m b}\cos\alpha_m x-Y_2 a\sum_{k=1}^{\infty}(-1)^k q_k^{(2)}(x)\cos\delta_k y\\ =&\,X_2 b\sum_{r=0}^{\infty}[(2rb+b-y)S_3(x,2rb+b-y)+(2rb+b+y)S_3(x,2rb+b+y)]\\ &-X_2 b\sum_{r=0}^{\infty}[S_1(x,2rb+b-y)+S_1(x,2rb+b+y)]\\ &-Y_2 a\sum_{r=0}^{\infty}(-1)^r[(2ra+a-x)S_{15}(y,2ra+a-x)+(2ra+a+x)S_{15}(y,2ra+a+x)],\end{aligned}\tag{47}$$

where

$$S_{15}(\xi,\eta)=\sum_{k=1}^{\infty}(-1)^k e^{-\delta_k\eta}\cos\delta_{k\xi}=\frac{1}{2}\left[\frac{\sinh(\pi\eta/b)}{\cosh(\pi\eta/b)+\cos(\pi\xi/b)}-1\right].$$

$$
\begin{aligned}
v_{EO}^{(a,b)}(x,y) &= Y_2 a \sum_{k=1}^{\infty} (-1)^k \left(a \tanh \delta_k a \frac{\sinh \delta_k x}{\cosh \delta_k a} - x \frac{\cosh \delta_k x}{\cosh \delta_k a} \right) \sin \delta_k y \\
&\quad - Y_2 a \sum_{k=1}^{\infty} \frac{(-1)^k}{\delta_k} \frac{\sinh \delta_k x}{\cosh \delta_k a} \sin \delta_k y + X_2 b \sum_{m=1}^{\infty} (-1)^m p_m^{(2)}(y) \sin \alpha_m x \\
&= X_2 b \sum_{r=0}^{\infty} [(2rb + b - y) S_5(x, 2rb + b - y) - (2rb + b + y) S_5(x, 2rb + b + y)] \\
&\quad - Y_2 a \sum_{r=0}^{\infty} [S_{14}(y, 2ra + a - x) - S_{14}(y, 2ra + a + x)] \\
&\quad + Y_2 a \sum_{r=0}^{\infty} (-1)^r [(2ra + a - x) S_{16}(y, 2ra + a - x) - (2ra + a + x) S_{16}(y, 2ra + a + x)],
\end{aligned}
\tag{48}
$$

where

$$
S_{16}(\xi, \eta) = \sum_{k=1}^{\infty} (-1)^k e^{-\delta_k \eta} \sin \delta_k \xi = -\frac{1}{2} \frac{\sin(\pi \xi / b)}{\cosh(\pi \eta / b) + \cos(\pi \xi / b)}.
$$

With a constant velocity distribution on the boundary, the stream function $\psi_{EO}(x, y)$ can be calculated by combining Formulas (42) and (44). Velocity components $u_{EO}(x, y)$ and $v_{EO}(x, y)$ are calculated by combining (45)–(48).

4. Advection of Fluid

4.1. Advection Equations of a Moving Fluid Particle

Any small, non-inert fluid particle moves with a velocity equal to the flow velocity at the point at which it is located. This means that

$$
\vec{V}_{particle} = \vec{V}_{flow} \tag{49}
$$

and this will be the formal expression of advection. This equation is defined in Lagrangian hydromechanics [14]: the kinematics of the fluid itself are such that each particle of the fluid undergoes passive advection.

The velocity of a particle in the two-dimensional case $V_{particle}$ is, of course, given by the rate of change in its position:

$$
\vec{V}_{particle} = \left(\frac{dx}{dt}, \frac{dy}{dt} \right), \tag{50}
$$

where (x, y)—the coordinates of the radius vector of the particle in the Cartesian coordinate system.

The fluid velocity is specified according to other considerations, including solving a system of partial differential equations, for example, the Euler equations, the Navier–Stokes equations, or the Stokes equations. In other words, the analysis of the motion of individual fluid particles provides that a hydrodynamic problem has been solved, which allows for an arbitrary point at an arbitrary time instant to determine the magnitude of the velocity vector of the flow under consideration

$$
\vec{V}_{fluid} = (u(x, y, t), v(x, y, t)). \tag{51}
$$

Then condition (49) leads to a system of ordinary differential equations, which are called advection equations [20,21]

$$
\frac{dx}{dt} = u(x, y, t), \quad \frac{dy}{dt} = v(x, y, t), \tag{52}
$$

In other words, Equation (52) describes the motion of a Lagrangian liquid particle in a Eulerian velocity field [14].

From the point of view of the theory of dynamical systems, two ordinary differential equations (52) are more than enough to obtain a non-integral or chaotic dynamical system. The right-hand sides of the equations do not even need to be very complicated.

In two-dimensional space, to obtain a chaotic motion of a particle, it is necessary that the flow depends on time. Stationary 2D advection is integrated.

The greatest point of interest from the point of view of the randomness of the motion of individual fluid particles in hydrodynamic systems is two-dimensional flows. In this case, the velocity components are the derivatives of the stream function ψ and are expressed by Formula (8).

If Equation (8) is combined with advection equations (52), then they turn into Hamiltonian canonical equations for a system with one degree of freedom

$$\frac{dx}{dt} = \frac{\partial \psi}{\partial y}, \quad \frac{dy}{dt} = -\frac{\partial \psi}{\partial x}, \tag{53}$$

with initial conditions $x = x_0, y = y_0$ at $t = 0$.

Kinematic equations (53) can be interpreted as a Hamiltonian dynamical system with one degree of freedom, where both play the role of canonical variables and are conjugate coordinates. Any of these coordinates can be taken as a generalized coordinate. Then, the second Cartesian coordinate will be the conjugate generalized impulse. The stream function ψ plays the role of the Hamiltonian. The phase space in this problem is configuration space.

The system of differential equations (53) describes the motion of passive non-inertial particles in the two-dimensional case in terms of the stream function, regardless of whether the fluid is viscous or not. There is no contradiction or paradox here because the Hamiltonian nature of kinematics arises precisely from incompressibility. This does not depend on whether the motion is dynamically dissipative or not. To determine the position of the particles, it is necessary to integrate the equations of motion (53) of each particle within a certain time interval.

4.2. Numerical Modeling of Closed Loop Advection Process

After finding the velocity field in a rectangular cavity, one can begin to study the problem of mixing a viscous fluid with slow motions of the Stokes flow. Below, there are examples of calculations obtained on the basis of understanding the analytical velocity field. The periodic motion of the rectangular cavity walls is given by

$$\begin{aligned} U_{top} &= \begin{cases} U_0, & nT \le t < \left(n + \frac{1}{2}\right)T \\ 0, & \left(n + \frac{1}{2}\right)T \le t < (n+1)T, \quad n = 1, 2, \ldots, \end{cases} \\ U_{bot} &= \begin{cases} 0, & nT \le t < \left(n + \frac{1}{2}\right)T \\ -U_0, & \left(n + \frac{1}{2}\right)T \le t < (n+1)T, \quad n = 1, 2, \ldots. \end{cases} \end{aligned} \tag{54}$$

Let the top wall move from left to right with velocity U_0 during the first half of the period, while the bottom wall is motionless, and during the second half of the period, the bottom wall moves from right to left with velocity $-U_0$, while the upper wall is motionless.

In the future, it is convenient to normalize the problem to the width of the cavity $2b$ and to the period T of motion of the boundaries of the rectangular cavity. Let us introduce a dimensionless parameter $D = \frac{U_0 T}{2a}$ characterizing the movement of each of the movable walls, where U_0—the modulus of the maximum wall velocity.

As an example, let us consider the mixing process in a rectangular cavity with parameters U_0 and D corresponding to the data of the Ottino experiment [12].

Let us consider the process of advection of a selected volume of liquid in the form of a circular region of radius $r = 0.1$ centered at the origin, the dimensions of which coincide with the dimensions of the spot from the Ottino experiment. The initial position of the circular spot is shown in Figure 2a.

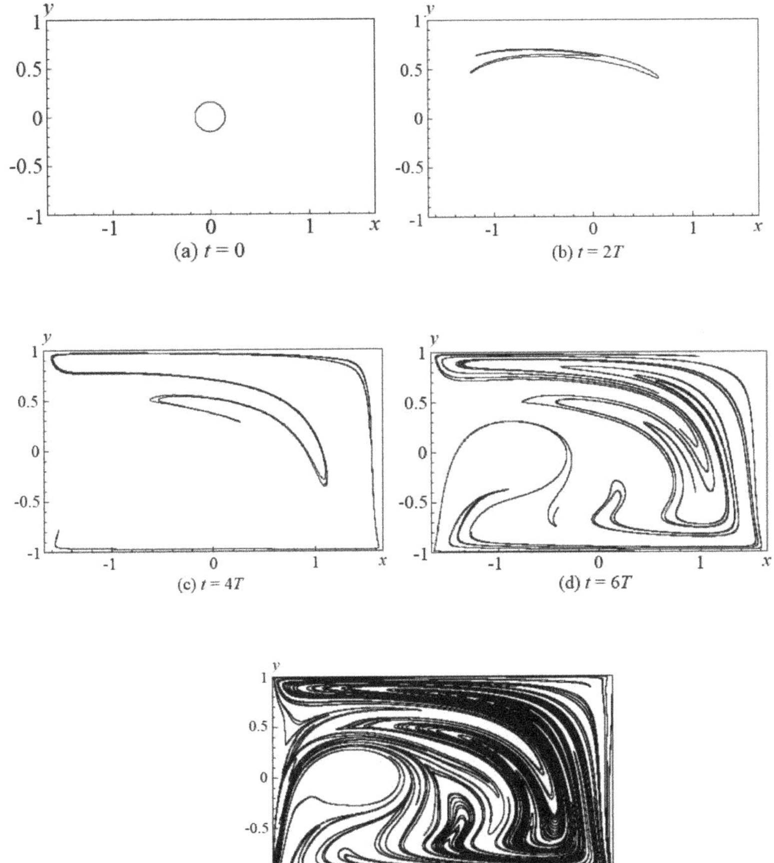

Figure 2. Deformation of the selected volume of fluid at a constant velocity U_0.

In order to numerically simulate the fluid advection process depicted in Figure 2e at $D = 6.24$, the following procedure was chosen. Let us fix the value $U_0 = 10.24$, increase T from 0 to $8T$ (corresponds to the value $D = 6.24$), and monitor the advection process of the selected spot. This approach minimizes the accumulation of error. Consideration of the advection process during only one period T with a sufficiently large value U_0 leads to an erroneous result.

It should be noted that the process of advection of the contour is based on the piecewise spline cubic interpolation method, developed by Prof. A. Gourjii [11].

The images obtained illustrate that numerical calculations in the process of solving the problem quite accurately illustrate the advection process. The results are in agreement with the experiment carried out by Ottino [12]. As in the experiment, we obtained the Period-1 island, where the mixing process does not take place (Ottino's article [12] demonstrates this phenomenon).

5. Conclusions

Using the superposition method, an analytical distribution of the velocity field of the flow of a viscous fluid moving in a rectangular cavity under the action of constant tangential velocities applied to the upper and lower walls is obtained. Solutions are obtained for the general case of given functions on the moving boundaries of a rectangular cavity. Despite the cumbersome calculations and mathematical transformations, the final solutions turned out to be quite simple and give the exact distribution of the velocity field in a rectangular region.

The singularity in the vicinity of a corner point of a rectangular cavity is investigated, and a good convergence of the series is obtained with a small number of terms in Fourier series.

The process of advection of the selected volume of fluid with periodic movement of the cavity walls was numerically modeled using the contour advection technique developed by Prof. A. Gourjii. The technique is based on the piecewise spline cubic interpolation that is applied to the points lying on the boundary of the selected volume of the fluid to be advected inside the rectangular cavity.

The results obtained are in good agreement with the experiment taken from Ottino's work. The performed simulations with the selected volume in a circular form correspond to the full mixing process, which is described in the Ottino's work.

Author Contributions: Conceptualization, V.S., O.K., O.B., O.P., I.L., I.U., and O.V.; methodology, V.S., O.K., O.B., O.P., I.L., I.U., and O.V.; formal analysis, V.S., O.K., O.B., O.P., I.L., I.U., and O.V.; investigation, V.S., O.K., O.B., O.P., I.L., I.U., and O.V.; writing—original draft preparation, V.S., O.K., O.B., O.P., I.L., I.U., and O.V.; and writing—review and editing, V.S., O.K., O.B., O.P., I.L., I.U., and O.V. All authors have read and agreed to the published version of the manuscript.

Funding: This research received no external funding.

Data Availability Statement: Data are contained within the article.

Acknowledgments: The authors express their sincere gratitude for the opportunity to publish the work in this journal on a free basis.

Conflicts of Interest: The authors declare no conflicts of interest.

References

1. Aref, H. Stirring by chaotic advection. *J. Fluid Mech.* **1984**, *143*, 1–21. [CrossRef]
2. Lefèvre, A.; Mota, J.P.B.; Rodrigo, A.J.S.; Saatdjian, E. Chaotic advection and heat transfer enhancement in Stokes flows. *Int. J. Heat Fluid Flow* **2003**, *24*, 310–321. [CrossRef]
3. Van der Woude, D.; Clercx, H.J.H.; Van Heijst, G.J.F.; Veleshko, V.V. Stokes flow in a rectangular cavity by rotlet forcing. *Phys. Fluids* **2007**, *19*, 083602. [CrossRef]
4. Zhang, D.; Zumbrunnen, D.A. Chaotic mixing of two similar fluids in the presence of a third dissimilar fluid. *AIChE J.* **1996**, *42*, 3301–3309. [CrossRef]
5. Boyl, P.L.; Aref, H.; Stremler, M.A. Topological fluid mechanics of stirring. *J. Fluid Mech.* **2000**, *403*, 277–304. [CrossRef]
6. Vikhansky, A. Chaotic advection of finite-size bodies in a cavity flow. *Physic Fluids* **2003**, *15*, 1830–1836. [CrossRef]
7. Karami, M.; Shirani, E.; Jarrahi, H.; Peerhossaini, H. Mixing by Time-Dependent Orbits in Spatiotemporal Chaotic Advection. *J. Fluids Eng.* **2015**, *137*, 011201. [CrossRef]
8. Beebe, D.J.; Adrian, R.J.; Olsen, M.G.; Stremler, M.A.; Aref, H.; Jo, B.H. Passive mixing in microchannels: Fabrication and flow experiments. *MéCanique Ind.* **2001**, *2*, 343–348. [CrossRef]
9. Gorban, N.V.; Kapustyan, A.V.; Kapustyan, E.A.; Khomenko, O.V. Strong Global Attractor for the Three-Dimensional Navier–Stokes System of Equations in Unbounded Domain of Channel Type. *J. Autom. Inf. Sci.* **2015**, *47*, 48–59. [CrossRef]

10. Lin, L.; Yang, Z.; Dong, S. Numerical approximation of incompressible Navier–Stokes equations based on an auxiliary energy variable. *J. Comput. Phys.* **2019**, *388*, 1–22. [CrossRef]
11. Gourjii, A.A.; Meleshko, V.V.; van Heijst, G.J.F. Method of the Piece-Spline Interpolation in the Advection Problem for an Arbitrary Velocity Field. *Dop. AN Ukrainy.* **1996**, *8*, 48–54.
12. Ottino, J.M.; Leong, C.W. Experiments on mixing due to chaotic advection in a cavity. *J. Fluid Mech.* **1989**, *209*, 463–499. [CrossRef]
13. Meyer, R.E. *Introduction to Mathematical Fluid Dynamics*; Dover Publications: New York, NY, USA, 2010; 190p.
14. Milne-Thomson, L.M. *Theoretical Hydrodynamics*, 5th ed.; Dover Publications: New York, NY, USA, 2013; 768p.
15. Meleshko, V.V. Steady Stokes flow in a rectangular cavity. *Proc. R. Soc. Lond.* **1996**, *452*, 1999–2022. [CrossRef]
16. Meleshko, V.V. Biharmonic problem in a rectangle. *Appl. Sci. Res.* **1997**, *58*, 217–249. [CrossRef]
17. Sobchuk, V.; Barabash, O.; Musienko, A.; Tsyganivska, I.; Kurylko, O. Mathematical Model of Cyber Risks Management Based on the Expansion of Piecewise Continuous Analytical Approximation Functions of Cyber Attacks in the Fourier Series. *Axioms* **2023**, *12*, 924. [CrossRef]
18. Gomilko, A.; Savytskiy, O.; Trofymchuk, O. Superposition, Eigenfunctions and Orthogonal Polynomials Methods in Elasticity and Acoustic Boundary Value Problems. *Kyiv Nauk. Dumka* **2016**, 436p.
19. Sobchuk, V.V.; Zelenska, I.O. Construction of asymptotics of the solution for a system of singularly perturbed equations by the method of essentially singular functions. *Bull. Taras Shevchenko Natl. Univ. Kyiv. Phys. Math.* **2023**, *2*, 184–192. [CrossRef]
20. Aref, H. The development of chaotic advection. *Phys. Fluids* **2002**, *14*, 1315–1325. [CrossRef]
21. Aref, H. Chaotic advection of fluid particles. *Philos. Trans. R. Soc. Lond.* **1990**, *333*, 273–288. [CrossRef]

axioms

MDPI

Article

A Study Using the Network Simulation Method and Nondimensionalization of the Fiber Fuse Effect

Juan Francisco Sanchez-Pérez [1,*], Joaquín Solano-Ramírez [2], Fulgencio Marín-García [3] and Enrique Castro [1]

[1] Department of Applied Physics and Naval Technology, Universidad Politécnica de Cartagena (UPCT), Campus Muralla del Mar, 30202 Cartagena, Spain; enrique.castro@upct.es
[2] Department of Mechanical Engineering, Materials and Manufacturing, Universidad Politécnica de Cartagena (UPCT), Campus Muralla del Mar, 30202 Cartagena, Spain; joaquin.solano@upct.es
[3] Department of Automation Engineering, Electrical Engineering and Electronic Technology, Universidad Politécnica de Cartagena (UPCT), Campus Muralla del Mar, 30202 Cartagena, Spain; pentxo.marin@upct.es
* Correspondence: juanf.sanchez@upct.es

Abstract: This paper presents an innovative approach to modelling the fiber optic fusion effect using the Network Simulation Method (NSM). An analogy between the heat conduction equations and electrical circuits is developed, allowing a complex physical problem to be transformed into an equivalent electrical system. Using NGSpice, thermal interactions in an anisotropic optical fiber under high optical power conditions are simulated. The methodology addresses the distribution of the temperature in the system, considering thermal variations and temperature-dependent material characteristics. In an NSM equivalent circuit, the effect of applying the spark is modelled by a switch that switches the spark-generating source on and off. It can be seen that temperature variation with time, or temperature rise rate (K/s), depends on the applied power. In addition, the mathematical method of nondimensionalization is used to study the real influence of each parameter of the problem on the solution and the relationship between the variables. Four optical fiber cases are analysed, each characterised by different areas and refractive indices, revealing how these variables affect the propagation of the melting phenomenon. The results highlight the effectiveness of the NSM in solving nonlinear and coupled problems in thermal engineering, providing a solid framework for future research in the optimisation of optical communication systems.

Keywords: network simulation method; mathematical modelling; non-linear material characteristics; coupled differential equations; nondimensionalization; heat transfer

MSC: 76M55; 80M10; 37N30

1. Introduction

The fiber fusion effect, also known as optical discharge, refers to a phenomenon that takes place in fiber optic cables when high-density radiation is transmitted. This process involves an initial stage of optical breakdown, which is succeeded by a plasma spark that moves along the fiber towards the source of radiation, causing significant damage to large portions of the fiber optic lines (see Figure 1). This effect was initially explained by Blow et al. during the years 1987–1988 [1–3]. A more detailed description of the problem, as well as the properties used to solve it, can be found in the article by Starikova et al. [4].

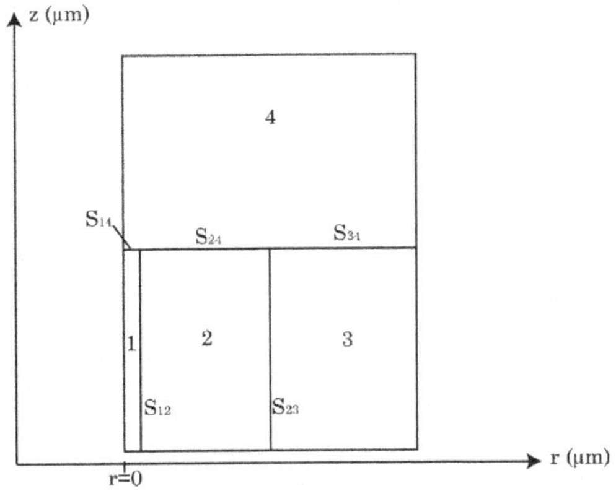

Figure 1. The computational space is integrated by four distinct regions with varying thermophysical characteristics: the core (1), the cladding (2), the guard envelope (3), and the metal plate (4). Thermal equilibrium is maintained at the interfaces between these regions.

In the book *Fiber Fuse*, Todoroki, S. [5] describes the phenomenon of fiber fusion, which causes a serious problem for current optical communication systems. High-power light often causes catastrophic damage to optical devices. When the fiber melts, a heated region of the fiber cable emits a few watts of light and travels towards the light source, destroying its core region. The book includes the classification of its propagation mode and the self-pulse effect.

Due to the drastic consequences of this phenomenon, it has been studied and analysed by several researchers. Ha, W et al. [6] examine the non-linear fiber fusion effect (FFE) in hollow optical fibers (HOF), which feature a central void encircled by a ring core with a high refractive index, along with a silica outer layer, in contrast to traditional solid-core fibers. They provide thorough comparisons regarding threshold power, the formation of holes, and penetration depth.

In the study conducted by Shuto, Y. [7], the focus is on understanding how core melting and fiber melting occurs in a single-mode fiber optic connector. The process of heat flow in the core, which leads to the melting of the fiber core, is evaluated using the explicit finite difference method. Meanwhile, Xiao et al. [8] explore the conditions that trigger fiber fusion (IFF), a severe type of damage that impacts all optical fibers, particularly those made of silica. An analysis of fibers with various chemical compositions is performed prior to IFF, revealing for the first time a consistent relationship between critical temperatures and the optical powers they transmit.

The work of Konin et al. [9] studies and analyses the internal structure of microcavities in single-mode and multimode acrylate and polyimide-coated optical fibers, which appear due to the melting that occurs when a plasma spark propagates through the core. The study is carried out on the structure of the microcavities on the outer and lateral surfaces of the fibers.

Shuto, Y. [10] examines the impact of fiber melting in multicore fibers (MCF) through the explicit finite difference method, utilising a thermochemical model for SiOx production. The analysis presumes that MCF varieties possess a uniform refractive index profile akin to that found in doubly coated single-mode fibers. This study is influenced by the presence of optical power restrictions caused by the fiber melting effect and the limited transmission bandwidth set by fiber optic amplifiers.

In order to complete the state of the art of the problem addressed in this article, we can highlight a series of references that may be useful when it comes to deepening the knowledge of the fiber fuse phenomenon [8,11–13], as well as being able to clearly see some of the industrial applications that have been made using this effect [14–16].

This article wants to contribute to the analysis of the fiber fusion effect by using a new approach to modelling it with the NSM. So, the numerical model of the optical breakdown starting process in the fiber and the thermophysical characteristics of optical fibers are shown. Subsequently, the equivalent formulation of the physical problem in the SNM will be presented. With the results obtained, the initial phenomenon, as well as the propagation of this defect, can be better understood.

To solve the model, the NSM has been used. This is a numerical simulation method, which is a widely tested method, by Peusner, L., Nagel, L. and Nagel, L. [17–19]. In this method, the equations defining the physical problem are transformed into electrical circuits, with a behaviour in their response equivalent to the physical equations.

The open-source program NGSpice has been used to solve the different circuits that make up the equivalent problem. NGSpice provides the numerical solutions to the problem, and by means of the inverse path to the one used to transform the original problem, the solutions to the physical problem can be obtained, and in this way, conclusions can be drawn about the results.

Furthermore, the nondimensionalisation numerical procedure makes it possible to determine the influence of each study variable of the problem by grouping them into monomials. This technique has been used in several engineering problems, Sánchez-Pérez et al. [20].

This paper presents a model based on the heat transfer equation in the initial stage of fiber fusion. With this model, the temperature distribution is obtained in the same, in the stationary phase, neglecting the transient. With this model, the temperature distribution in the same, in the transient phase and studying certain cases is obtained. The plasma spark process movement is neglectable. The calculations were performed using NGSpice V42 and Matlab R2020. In addition, the study of nondimensionalization is indicated for the study of the influence of the variables.

2. Materials and Methods

This research investigates an anisotropic optical fiber with cylindrical geometry. A cylindrical coordinate system is employed for modelling, with the z-axis aligned with the fiber's axis and the r-axis along its span. The computational space, depicted in Figure 1, is axisymmetric, allowing for 2D analysis in the z-r plane. Symmetry conditions are applied at the axis of symmetry (r = 0). The distribution of temperature does not depend on the polar angle. The computational domain illustrated in Figure 1 is made up of four elements, each exhibiting distinct thermophysical characteristics. The conditions for thermal equilibrium are satisfied at the boundaries between these elements.

A single-mode fiber (SMF-28e) with a stepped refractive index profile is examined. The fiber is pressed against a duraluminum plate, and the starting temperature of both is $T_0 = 293$ K.

The material properties of the fiber are obtained from SMF-28e specifications, while the duraluminum plate adheres to ISO standard 2024. Table 1 provides a summary of the materials and dimensions of each region.

Table 1. Values for the different simulation cases [4].

Case	λ, nm	n_1	n_2	V	A_{eff}, µm^2
1	1080	1.4483	1.4439	2.76	13.25
2	1310	1.4552	1.4508	2.17	15.29
3	1550	1.4617	1.4573	1.88	17.27
4	2050	1.4662	1.4618	1.39	23.49

The core of the fiber (1), its cladding (2), the protective reinforcement cladding (3), and the metal plate (4) in Figure 1 have contact contours with each other at S_{12}, S_{14}, S_{23}, S_{24}, and S_{34}.

The distribution of the temperature T(r,z,t) within the computational domain is ruled by the heat conduction expression as follows:

$$\rho_i C_{p_i} \frac{\partial T}{\partial t} = k_i \left(\frac{\partial^2 T}{\partial r^2} + \frac{1}{r} \frac{\partial T}{\partial r} + \frac{\partial^2 T}{\partial z^2} \right) + Q \tag{1}$$

where i = 1–4 is the section number (Figure 1), ρ_i are the densities $(\mathrm{kg/m^3})$, C_{p_i} are the specific heat capacities (J/(kg K)), k_i is the thermal conductivity of the materials (W/(mK)), and Q is the heat source, whose intensity is obtained by optical radiation (W/m^3). In the article [4], the authors show temperature-dependent functions.

Assuming that the temperature changes across the interface continuously, at edges S_{12}, S_{14}, S_{23}, S_{24}, and S_{34} of the calculation scheme, the heat flow equilibrium conditions apply:

$$\left(k_i \frac{\partial T}{\partial r} l_r + k_i \frac{\partial T}{\partial z} l_z \right)_{S_{ij}} = \left(k_j \frac{\partial T}{\partial r} l_r + k_j \frac{\partial T}{\partial z} l_z \right)_{S_{ij}} \tag{2}$$

where l_r and l_z are the unit vector projections onto the r and z axes. The outer contour is considered to be quite well conducting with T_0 = 293 K.

The heat source, Q, is determined by:

$$Q(r,z) = \alpha(r,\ z) \frac{P}{A_{eff}} \Gamma(r,z) \tag{3}$$

where $\alpha(r,\ z)$ is equal to the aggregation of the under normal conditions absorption coefficient α_0 and the electron gas absorption coefficient α_e. describes the non-linear absorption of radiation in chaotically localised defects in the fiber. Defects appear in the fiber core because of chemical reactions in fabrication, as shown by Carslow, H.S. et al. and Davis et al. [21,22]. P is the input power (W), Γ is the normalised Gaussian distribution $\Gamma(\mathrm{x}) = \frac{1}{\sqrt{2\pi}} e^{-\frac{x^2}{2}}$ and A_{eff} is the effective area of the mode point (m^2). Γ takes a two-dimensional form due to the solution is a two-dimensional layer:

$$\Gamma(r,z) = \Gamma(r) \cdot \Gamma(z) \tag{4}$$

In the article [23], the GeE′ concentration ions are obtained by:

$$n_{GeE'} = n_p e^{-\frac{E_f}{k_B T}} \tag{5}$$

where $E_f = 2.5$ eV is the GeE′ formation energy, $n_p = 1.72 \times 10^{15}$ m^{-3} is the GeE′ centre concentration at 293 K, and k_B is the Boltzmann constant. The quartz, due to free electrons conductivity, will be stated by:

$$\sigma = e\mu_e n_e = e\mu_e n_p e^{-\frac{E_f}{k_B T}} \tag{6}$$

where e is the modulus of charge of the electrons, μ_e is the electron drift velocity, with 5×10^{-3}m^2/(V·s) [24], and $n_e = n_{GeE\prime}$. Considering (5) the electron gas absorption coefficient in the fiber, Equation (3), will equal to this expression:

$$\alpha_e = \frac{k_B n_1}{\sqrt{2}} \left[\sqrt{1 + \left(\frac{\mu_0 c_0 \sigma}{k_0 n_1^2} \right)^2} - 1 \right]^{\frac{1}{2}} \approx \frac{\mu_0 c_0 \sigma}{2n_1} = \frac{\mu_0 c_0}{2n_1} e\mu_e n_p e^{-\frac{E_f}{k_B T}} \tag{7}$$

where n_1 is the refractive index at the core, μ_0 is the magnetic permeability, c_0 is the vacuum speed of light and k_0 is the vacuum wavenumber.

The effective area of the model in Equation (3) is solved employing the effective radius for each of the wavelengths, Marcuse et al. [25]

$$A_{eff} = \pi a^2 \left(0.65 + \frac{1.619}{V^{\frac{3}{2}}} + \frac{2.879}{V^6} \right)^2 \tag{8}$$

where a is the fiber core radius (see Table 1). The parameter V is the normalised frequency [4]:

$$V = \frac{2\pi a}{\lambda} \sqrt{n_1^2 - n_2^2} \tag{9}$$

where λ is the transported radiation wavelength, n_2 is the fiber cladding refractive index.

Finally, in Table 1, Starikova, V. A. et al. [4] presents different values of wavelength, core refractive index, cladding refractive index and area to simulate different cases with the NSM and in Table 2, Starikova, V. A. et al. [4] gives some values of the different parameters that appear in the equations that make up the mathematical model.

Table 2. Values of the constants for the calculation model [4].

Description	Value	Units
Boltzmann's constant	$1.38{\cdot}10^{-23}$	J/K
Core refractive index	1.4617	
Charge of electron	$1.6{\cdot}10^{-19}$	C
Concentration	$1.72{\cdot}10^{15}$	m^{-3}
Input power	1.10	W
Formation energy GeE0	$4.0054{\cdot}10^{-19}$	J
Light velocity	$3{\cdot}10^{8}$	m/s
Core radius	$4.1{\cdot}10^{-6}$	m
Core layer thickness	$4.1{\cdot}10^{-6}$	m
Magnetic constant	$1.2566{\cdot}10^{-6}$	H/m
Drift mobility of electrons	$5{\cdot}10^{-3}$	m^2/(V·s)

2.1. Mathematical Model of the Heat Transfer Mechanism

The mathematical model we will discuss pertains to a cylindrical structure composed of potentially diverse materials whose properties are subject to temperature variations, as outlined by Fernández-García, M. et al. [26].

As previously mentioned, the model incorporates heat transfer mechanisms.

For conduction processes, Fourier's law is employed to quantify heat transfer:

$$\alpha\left(\frac{\partial^2 T}{\partial x^2}+\frac{\partial^2 T}{\partial y^2}+\frac{\partial^2 T}{\partial z^2}\right)+\frac{Q}{\rho c_e}=\frac{\partial T}{\partial t}\,;\alpha=\frac{k}{\rho c_e} \tag{10}$$

In the equation above, T represents temperature (K), α is thermal diffusivity (m^2/s), k is thermal conductivity (W/mK), c_e is specific heat capacity (J/kg K), ρ is density (kg/m^3), t is time (s), and x, y, and z are spatial coordinates. As stated earlier, thermal conductivity, density, specific heat, and, consequently, thermal diffusivity will be declared as temperature functions.

Given the cylindrical geometry of the problem, it is advantageous to formulate it in cylindrical coordinates. The angle, φ; the radius, r; and the height, z, define the equation illustrated in Figure 2:

$$\frac{1}{r}\frac{\partial}{\partial r}\left(k\,r\frac{\partial T}{\partial r}\right)+\frac{1}{r^2}\frac{\partial}{\partial \varphi}\left(k\frac{\partial T}{\partial \varphi}\right)+\frac{\partial}{\partial z}\left(k\frac{\partial T}{\partial z}\right)+Q=\rho c_e\frac{\partial T}{\partial t} \tag{11}$$

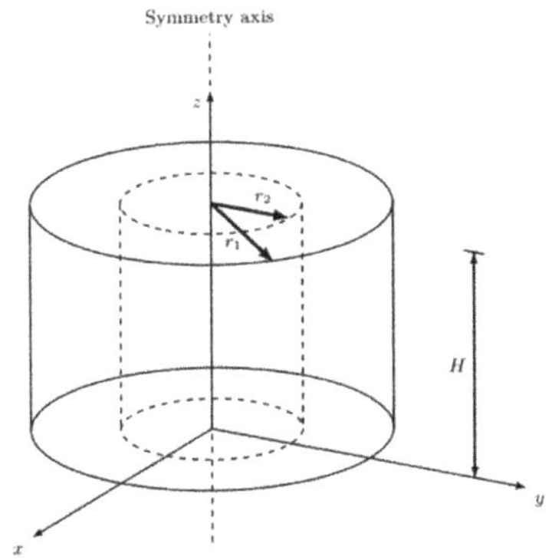

Figure 2. Cylindrical geometry.

It can be simplified, because of the symmetry of the problem, to two dimensions, axial and radial, leaving Equation (11) as follows:

$$\frac{1}{r}\frac{\partial}{\partial r}\left(k\,r\frac{\partial T}{\partial r}\right)+\frac{\partial}{\partial z}\left(k\frac{\partial T}{\partial z}\right)+Q=\rho c_e\frac{\partial T}{\partial t} \tag{12}$$

It is obtained the following, if it is developed the above expression:

$$\frac{1}{r}\frac{k}{\rho c_e}\frac{\partial T}{\partial r}+\frac{k}{\rho c_e}\frac{\partial^2 T}{\partial r^2}+\frac{k}{\rho c_e}\frac{\partial^2 T}{\partial z^2}+\frac{Q}{\rho c_e}=\frac{\partial T}{\partial t} \tag{13}$$

Grouping the properties together streamlines their integration into the network model. This is particularly beneficial considering their temperature-dependent nature.

To account for convective heat transfer, Newton's law is applied:

$$\frac{dQ_b}{dt}=Ah(T_s-T_e) \tag{14}$$

where Q_b represents the heat transfer (J), h is the heat transfer coefficient (W/m^2 K), A is the heat transfer surface area (m^2), T_s is the surface temperature of the solid (K), and T_e is the ambient temperature (K).

The final phenomenon to be considered is thermal radiation, which is modelled using the Stefan–Boltzmann law:

$$\frac{dQ_r}{dt} = \varepsilon\sigma\left(T_s^4 - T_e^4\right)dS \tag{15}$$

where ε is the emissivity and σ is the Stefan–Boltzmann constant (W/m^2 K^4).

2.2. Network Model

A physical phenomenon that is modelled mathematically can be solved using the NSM. Each member of the mathematical model equation can be assigned an equivalent electrical element. In this case, we are dealing with a heat transfer problem which will have a corresponding electrical equivalent.

The equivalence between thermal and electrical variables has been extensively employed in heat transfer problems by Hao, L. et al. and Kreith, F. et al. [27,28]; however, the resolution methodology is different. Numerous engineering problems have been successfully solved through this method, as shown by Alhama, F. et al., Del Cerro Velázquez, F et al., Alhama, F. et al., Sánchez-Pérez, J.F. et al., and Solano, J. et al., [29–33].

To adapt Equation (14) for use with the NSM, we will express the term resulting from multiplying all summands on the left-hand side as thermal diffusivity, given its temperature-dependent variables. Additionally, through mathematical manipulation, the second derivative terms will be accomplished as two in-series resistors.

$$\frac{1}{r}\alpha\frac{\partial T}{\partial r} + \alpha\frac{\partial^2 T}{\partial r^2} + \alpha\frac{\partial^2 T}{\partial z^2} + \frac{Q}{\rho c_e} = \frac{\partial T}{\partial t} \tag{16}$$

To represent the second derivatives as resistors, it is compulsory to isolate them from variable terms. To achieve this, they are split into two components (Equation (18)). One component will be electrically analogous to a voltage-controlled current source, while the other will be represented by in-series-connected two resistors, as described by Fernández-García, M. et al. [26].

$$\alpha\frac{\partial^2 T}{\partial r^2} = (\alpha - 1)\frac{\partial^2 T}{\partial r^2} + \frac{\partial^2 T}{\partial r^2} \tag{17}$$

For the $\frac{\partial^2 T}{\partial z^2}$ term, the same procedure is followed as for the $\frac{\partial^2 T}{\partial r^2}$ term, leaving Equation (16) as follows:

$$\frac{1}{r}\alpha\frac{\partial T}{\partial r} + (\alpha - 1)\frac{\partial^2 T}{\partial r^2} + \frac{\partial^2 T}{\partial r^2} + (\alpha - 1)\frac{\partial^2 T}{\partial z^2} + \frac{\partial^2 T}{\partial z^2} + \frac{Q}{\rho c_e} = \frac{\partial T}{\partial t} \tag{18}$$

Any second-order partial derivative without variable terms is represented in the circuit as in-series-connected two resistors. Similarly, any second-order or first-order partial derivative involving multiplicative dependent terms is represented as a voltage-controlled current source. Finally, the time derivative is represented as a capacitor. Consequently, our circuit will be configured as follows:

$\frac{1}{r}\alpha\frac{\partial T}{\partial r}$, $(\alpha - 1)\frac{\partial^2 T}{\partial r^2}$, $(\alpha - 1)\frac{\partial^2 T}{\partial z^2} + \frac{Q}{\rho c_e}$: some voltage-controlled current sources

$\frac{\partial^2 T}{\partial r^2}$, $\frac{\partial^2 T}{\partial z^2}$: two in-series-connected resistors; and $\frac{\partial T}{\partial t}$: one capacitor.

Given the temperature-dependent nature of the involved terms, voltage-controlled sources will be employed. Before applying the NSM, the differential equations are spatially discretised by splitting the space into n-volume elements, as depicted in Figure 3. This discretisation allows for the representation of the equations in finite difference form. Ultimately, the balance of currents at the centre of each cell is ensured by the electrical elements constituting the electrical circuit.

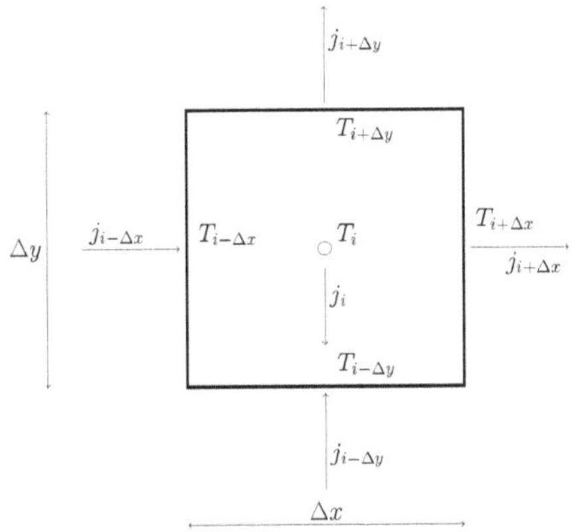

Figure 3. Volume element terminology.

Employing the terminology presented in Figure 3, the spatial discretisation of first and second derivatives is achieved through equilibrium considerations between central nodes and cell edges, as described by Kreith, F. and Zheng, W. et al. [28,34]. For instance, the finite difference approximation of the first derivative is given by:

$$\frac{\partial T}{\partial r} = \frac{T_{i+1,\,j} - T_{i-1,\,j}}{\Delta r} \tag{19}$$

where $\Delta r = r_{i+1,\,j} - r_{i-1,\,j}$, and the second derivative is:

$$\frac{\partial^2 T}{\partial r^2} = \frac{T_{i+1,\,j} + T_{i-1,\,j} - 2T_{i-1,\,j}}{\frac{\Delta^2 r}{2}} \tag{20}$$

In Equation (20) the value of the equivalent resistance for each node, R_z, when implementing the electrical element is:

$$R_{z,l} = \frac{1}{\frac{\Delta^2 r}{2}} \quad R_{z,r} = \frac{1}{\frac{\Delta^2 r}{2}} \quad R_{z,d} = \frac{1}{\frac{\Delta^2 z}{2}} \quad R_{z,u} = \frac{1}{\frac{\Delta^2 z}{2}} \tag{21}$$

Consequently, the circuit representing our problem, incorporating all the previously discussed elements, is illustrated in Figure 4. Each of the circuits in Figure 4a represents the unit cell defined in the geometry section. The boundary conditions, radiation, convection and spark gap effects are implemented by voltage-controlled current sources. The remaining voltage-controlled current sources represent the variation of the density variation, Figure 4b, the variation in the thermal conductivity, Figure 4c, the variation of the specific heat capacity, Figure 4d, and the variation in the thermal diffusivity, Figure 4e.

The network model is then solved by employing the circuit simulation program NGSpice, Holger, V. [35].

NGSpice (version ngspice-42), Holger, V. [35], employs computational algorithms to solve circuits understood from coupled and non-linear mathematical models, such as the one proposed in this article. These algorithms, rooted in the work of Nagel, L.W. [18,19], include Gear's time-stepping methods, Gear, C. W. [36], and trapezoidal integration, Nagel, L. [19]. Efficiency and accuracy are achieved by minimising local truncation errors and promoting stability in the numerical solution convergence [37].

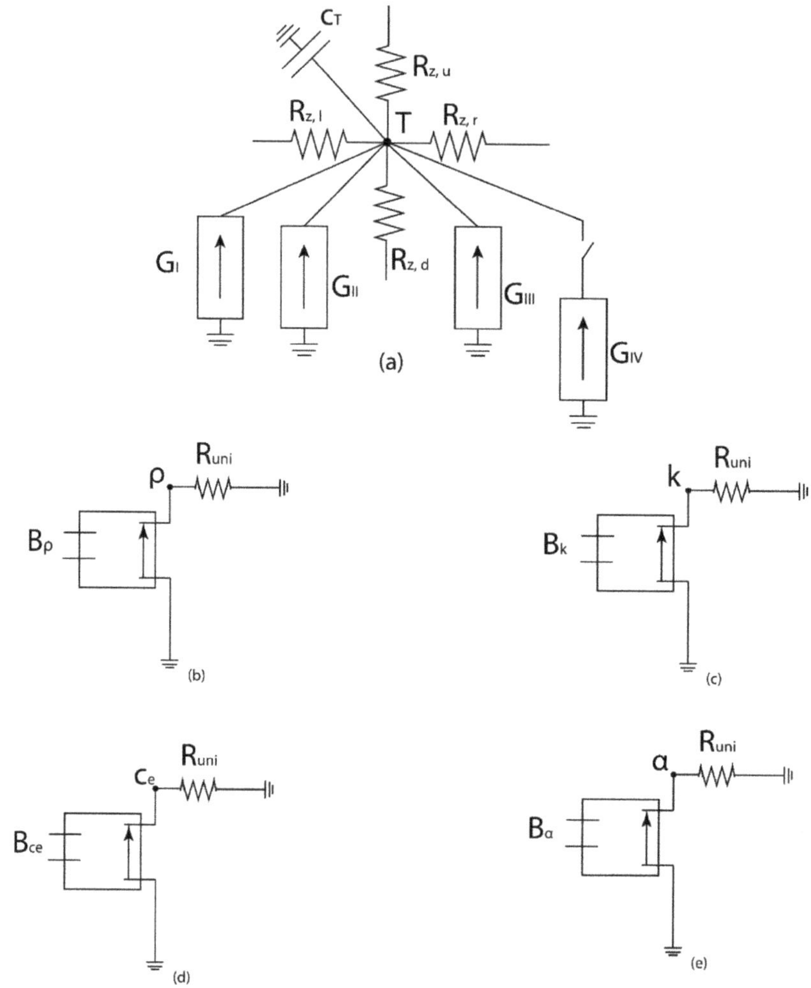

Figure 4. Volume element network model. (**a**) Temperature, (**b**) density, (**c**) thermal conductivity, (**d**) specific heat capacity, and (**e**) thermal diffusivity.

The novelty in the present work lies in the modelling of the spark application by implementing the discharge of a current source controlled by a switch; in Figure 4a, it can be seen that the G_{IV} source corresponds to the spark generator. This switch, when closed, discharges the source at the set time. Table 3 shows the different spark application times, which correspond to the time the switch remains closed. After the set time has elapsed, the switch opens, simulating the completion of the spark.

The section that makes up the optical fiber has also been simplified to include the core, the sheath, the protective layer and the metal where the spark is initiated. This reduction of the domain allows for reduced computational time, as the mesh is smaller.

Table 3. Temperature rise rate values for each simulation in r_T (K/s).

t (s)	P (W)	r_{T1} (K/s)	r_{T2} (K/s)	r_{T3} (K/s)	r_{T4} (K/s)
1	1	3816	3307	2928	2152
0.1	1	3816	3307	2928	2152
0.001	1	3816	3307	2928	2152
1	0.01	38.16	33.07	29.28	21.52
1	0.001	3.816	3.307	2.928	2.152
0.001	0.001	3.816	3.307	2.928	2.152

2.3. Nondimensionalization

Nondimensionalisation is a technique that requires a deep knowledge of the problem and a well-defined set of equations that represent the problem under study. The difference between this work and some previous ones lies in the importance of Q, which, in this problem, initiates the temperature change in the system. Thus, its importance with respect to the rest of the variables is studied. The difference is that this article has to be customised and take into account the Q energy source.

The following is a brief explanation of the procedure to be followed in order to apply this technique. Firstly, the dimensionless variables are established, which are as follows:

$$Q' = \frac{Q}{Q_{max}};\ t' = \frac{t}{\tau};\ T' = \frac{T - T_i}{T_e - T_i};\ r' = \frac{r}{R};\ z' = \frac{z}{H} \tag{22}$$

where Q_{max} is the maximum power obtained, T_i is the initial temperature, T_e is the ambient temperature, H is the height, and τ is the steady state time and R is the radius.

Applying the $\pi - theorem$, we obtain the following dimensionless numbers:

$$\pi_1 = \frac{\alpha\tau}{R^2};\ \pi_2 = \frac{R^2}{H^2};\ \pi_3 = \frac{\alpha h\tau}{Rk};\ \pi_4 = \frac{hR}{k} \tag{23}$$

Here, π_1 represents the temperature change associated with diffusion phenomena, while π_2 represents the cylinder's dimensions geometric relationship. π_3 predominates in convection phenomena. π_4 = hD/k, where D is the cylinder diameter. This is the Nusselt number, Nu, which describes the heat transfer coefficient, h, and the thermal conductivity of the material, k [27].

$$\pi_5 = \frac{Q_{max}R^2}{k} \tag{24}$$

π_5 relates the maximum rate of temperature rise to the driving effects. As can be seen, the effect of Q on heat transfer in the system depends, logically, on geometrical factors, R, which in turn is related to H through π_1, π_2 and on the thermal conductivity, k, which in turn is related to density and c_p through π_1, since all of them are included in α. Finally, the time to reach steady state, is obtained with τ :

$$\tau = \frac{R^2}{\alpha} f\left(\frac{R^2}{H^2}, \frac{Q_{max}R^2}{k}, \frac{hR}{k}\right) \tag{25}$$

where f is an unknown function. From Equation (25) it follows that the steady state depends on the heat generated by the fiber melting effect, the geometry of the optical fiber and the conductivity of the material.

3. Results

In Figures 5–10, the same process is represented, with equal spark application time and equal power, but for the four different cases that can be seen in Table 1. Thus, section (a) corresponds to case 1 and is the one with the smallest area and index n_1. Section

(b) corresponds to case 2, section (c) to case 3 and section (d) is for the last case, 4, which has the largest area and the highest index n_1.

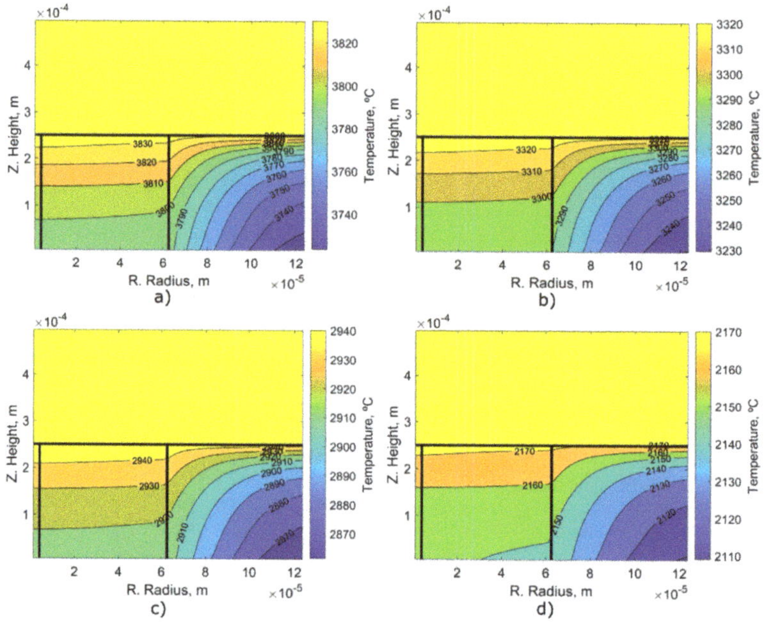

Figure 5. Results for the 4 cases with a spark application time of 1 s. Case 1 (**a**), Case2 (**b**), Case 3 (**c**) and Case 4 (**d**).

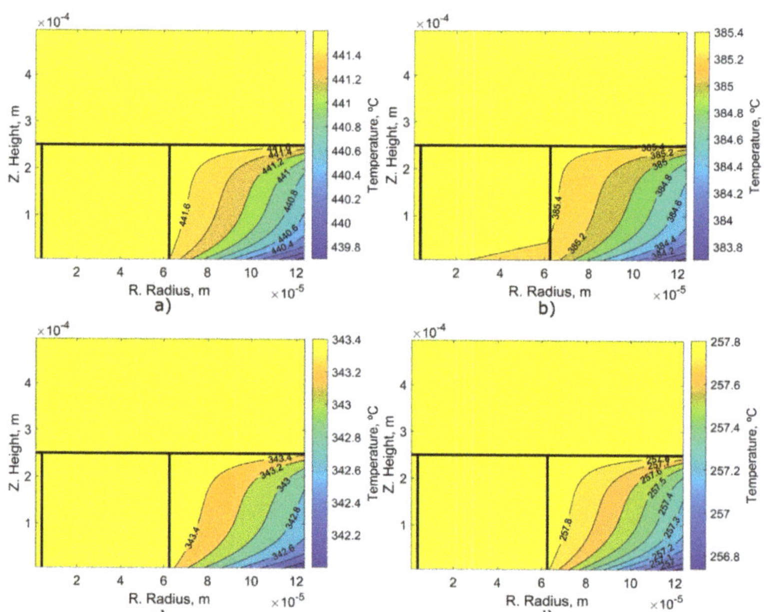

Figure 6. Results for the 4 cases with a spark application time of 0.1 s. Case 1 (**a**), Case2 (**b**), Case 3 (**c**) and Case 4 (**d**).

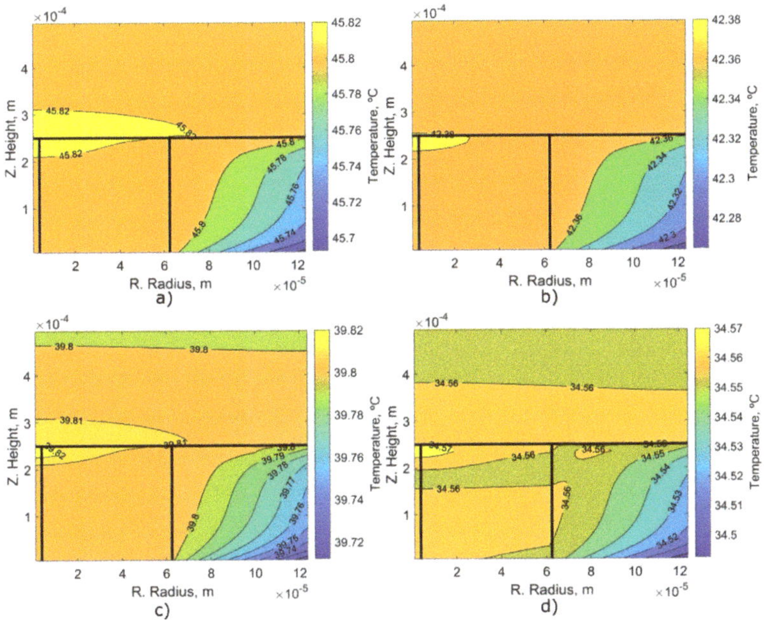

Figure 7. Results for the 4 cases with a spark application time of 1 ms. Case 1 (**a**), Case2 (**b**), Case 3 (**c**) and Case 4 (**d**).

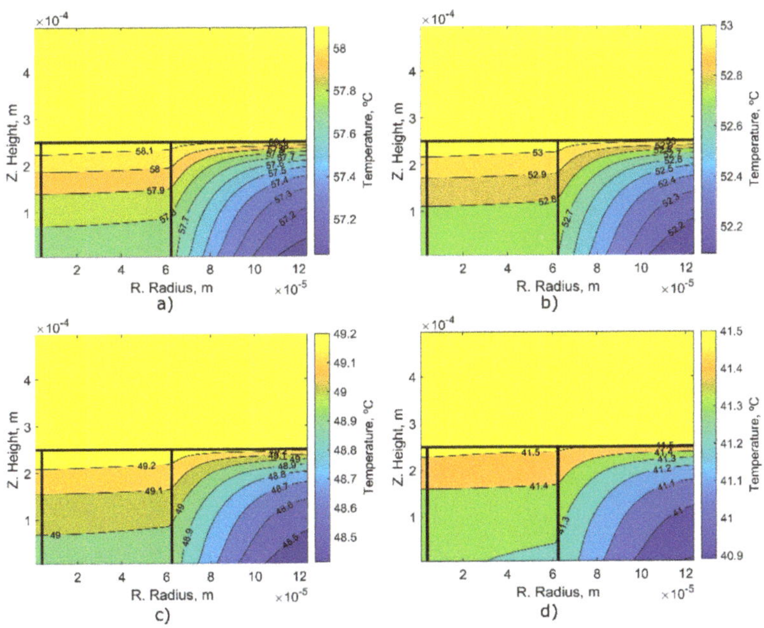

Figure 8. Results for the 4 cases with a spark application time of 1 s and power of 10 mW. Case 1 (**a**), Case2 (**b**), Case 3 (**c**) and Case 4 (**d**).

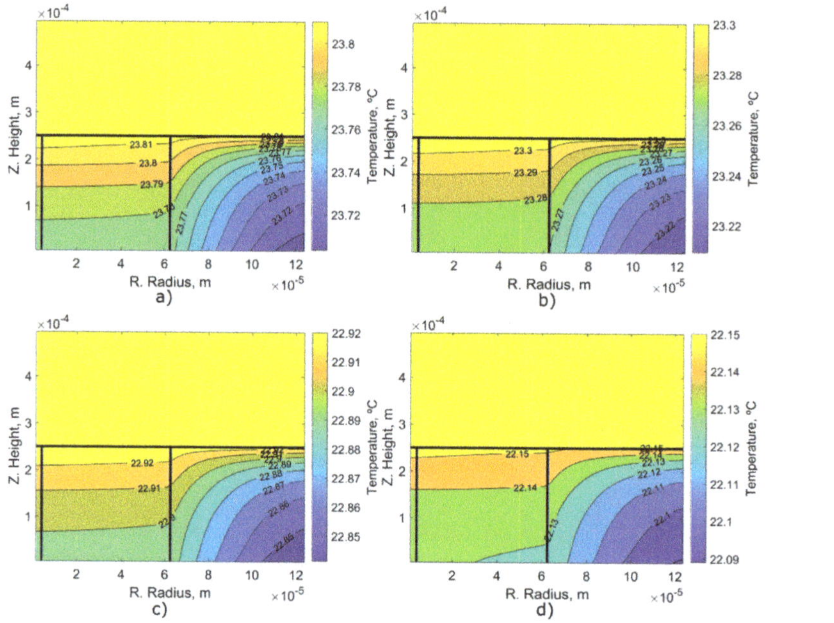

Figure 9. Results for the 4 cases with a spark application time of 1 s and power of 1 mW. Case 1 (**a**), Case2 (**b**), Case 3 (**c**) and Case 4 (**d**).

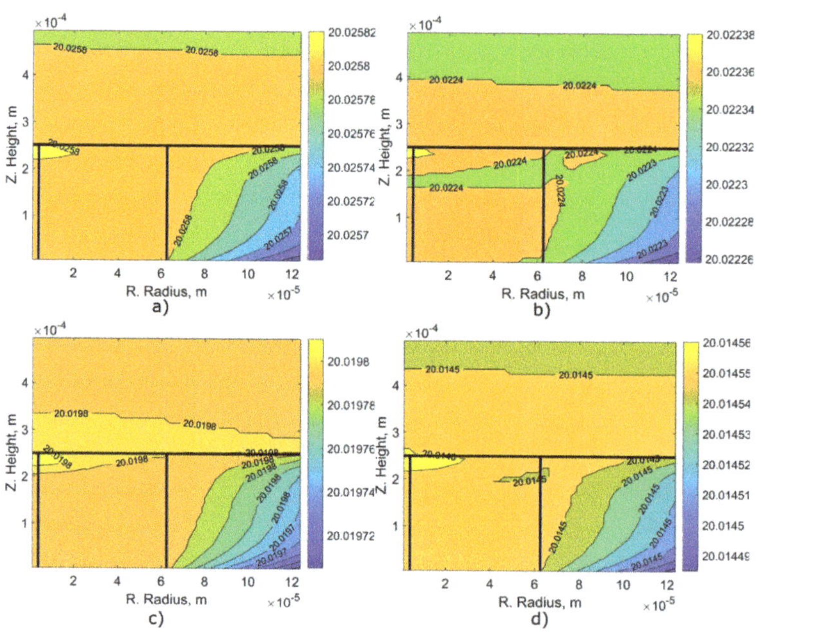

Figure 10. Results for the 4 cases with a spark application time of 1 ms and power of 1 mW. Case 1 (**a**), Case2 (**b**), Case 3 (**c**) and Case 4 (**d**).

This section can be organised into subheadings. It should provide a clear and concise summary of the experimental findings, their interpretation, and the resulting experimental conclusions.

In Figure 5, the temperature rise speed corresponding to r_T to the $\frac{Q}{\rho c_e}$ term in Equation (10) is higher in section (a) and the lowest in section (d). Due to the cross-section of the optical fiber, which is smaller in section (a), the generation of energy is greater in less surface area, so the temperature rise speed is higher than in the rest of the cases. On the other hand, in case 4, which has the largest cross-section, the rate of rise is the lowest since the larger cross-section means that the energy dissipation is greater.

Table 3 shows the different values obtained by NSM of r_T (K/s) for different spark application times, t (s), and applied power, P (W). The simulation time is always 1 s, and t is the application time of Q.

The behaviour of the problem in Figures 6–10 is similar to that described in Figure 5. It is clear that the temperature reached is conditioned by the time of application of the spark and the power of the spark. Figure 6 shows that with the reduction of the time from 1 s (Figure 5) to 0.1 s (Figure 6), the temperature reached is lower than that reached by applying the spark for 1s.

Next, a study of the variables of the problem will be carried out using the expression obtained by means of nondimensionalization. Substituting the value of α into expression (25) gives Equation (26). As can be seen, the variables that only appear in a monomial are the specific heat capacity, c_e, density, ρ, heat transfer coefficient, h, and maximum heat transfer.

$$\tau = \frac{\rho c_e R^2}{k} f\left(\frac{R^2}{H^2}, \frac{Q_{max} R^2}{k}, \frac{hR}{k}\right) \quad (26)$$

In this work, the effect of material density on heat transfer with a spark application time of 1 s and power of 1 W will be studied. Table 4 and Figure 11 show the results obtained from the study, where it can be seen how the effect of this variable on temperature is studied at two points with different materials, cladding and the guard envelope. The position for T_1, cladding, is ($6.25 \cdot 10^{-5}$, $1.25 \cdot 10^{-4}$) m, and for T_2, guard envelope, is ($12.37 \cdot 10^{-5}$, $1.25 \cdot 10^{-4}$) m. Thus, the effect of variations with respect to a base case is studied. For case 1, the value of the fibre density is halved so that, as shown in expression (26), the simulation time must be halved to obtain the same temperature value in 1. However, since the value of the density of the envelope guard is not also halved, the value in 2 must be different. For case 2, only the value of the guard envelope density is halved, and the simulation time of the base case is maintained, so as expected the value of T_1 is the same and T_2 is not, as it is influenced by the heat transmission from the fibre. Finally, in case 3, both densities are halved, so according to expression (26), the simulation time must also be halved. In this case, by halving both densities, in contrast to case 1, the same temperature values are obtained as in the base case.

Table 4. Study of the density of materials.

Case	ρ_{Fiber} (kg/m^3)	ρ_{guard} (kg/m^3)	t (s)	T_1 (°C)	T_2 (°C)
Base	2220	1190	1	3804	3743
1	1110	1190	0.5	3804	3690
2	2220	595	1	3804	3770
3	1110	595	0.5	3804	3743

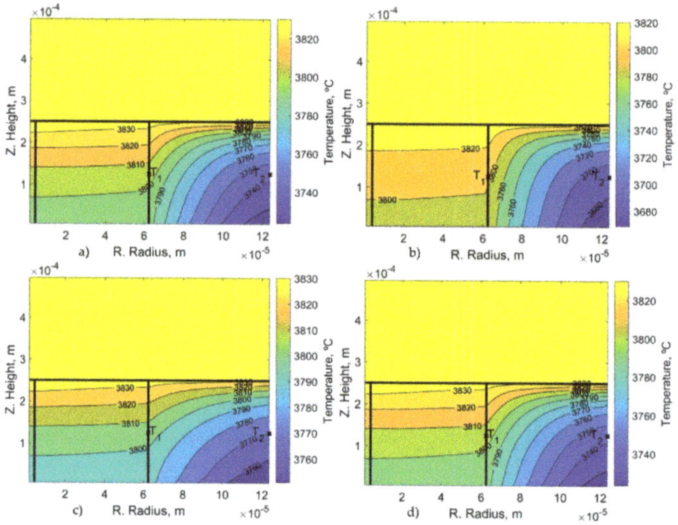

Figure 11. Results for the 4 cases with a spark application time of 1 s and power of 1 W. Base (**a**), Case 1 (**b**), Case 2 (**c**) and Case 3 (**d**). See Table 4.

4. Discussion

Table 3 shows that the r_{Ti} remain constant as long as the applied power does not vary. As the power decreases, the rate of rise does vary, and this variation is of the same factor as the power decrease factor.

A strong dependence can be established between the rate of rise, the characteristics of the section and the applied power.

These results obtained in the simulation agree with the analysis of the behaviour of the equations and parameters governing the fiber optic fusion process.

Through nondimensionalization, it has been possible to establish which variables are relevant and which variables are superfluous, as seen in the Results section. It has been possible to reduce the number of variables that intervene or have a significant weight in the problem.

Thus, the factor α_e has a value of $\alpha_e \approx 8.888 \cdot 10^{-11}\ \text{m}^{-1}$ which makes its influence practically negligible and the factor $\alpha(r,\ z) = \alpha_0 + \alpha_e \approx \alpha_0 = 1\ \text{m}^{-1}$. The gamma function, $\Gamma(\text{x}) = \frac{1}{\sqrt{2\pi}} e^{-\frac{x^2}{2}} = 0.159$, is a constant value. With this it can be seen how the heat generated and the rate of rise only relies on the applied power and the effective area of the optical fiber, $Q(r,z) = \alpha(r,\ z) \frac{P}{A_{eff}} \Gamma(r,z) = 0.159\ \frac{P}{A_{eff}}$. With this result, it can be assured that the simulations present results in agreement with the analysis of the equations.

5. Conclusions

In this work, we have studied the phenomenon of optical fiber fusion by plasma spark. A methodology has been developed in NSM that has allowed us to design a circuit with the same behaviour as the physical process. One aspect to highlight is the control that we have been able to carry out on the time and application of the spark, as well as the applied power; this has allowed us to check the effect that each of these terms has, reaching the conclusion that the parameter that most influences the rate of temperature rise is the power, as can be seen in Table 3.

In the analysis of the equations that govern the process (see Section 4 Discussion), it was found that most of the terms are either constant or their influence is negligible, leaving as main variables those that define the section, the material and the power of the spark.

The results obtained are used to study the behaviour of different materials with respect to the damage caused by the fusion of the optical fiber caused by a high-energy spark and to establish a power limit for each type of material that allows different protection devices to be designed according to the material selected.

It is interesting how the temperature varies depending on the material selected. This result leads to the selection of the most suitable materials for this defect, which has an impact on the design of better-quality fiber optic cables.

Author Contributions: Conceptualization, J.F.S.-P. and E.C.; methodology, J.F.S.-P., J.S.-R. and F.M.-G.; software, J.F.S.-P. and J.S.-R.; validation, J.F.S.-P., J.S.-R., E.C. and F.M.-G.; formal analysis, J.F.S.-P., J.S.-R., E.C. and F.M.-G.; writing—original draft preparation, J.F.S.-P., J.S.-R., E.C. and F.M.-G.; writing—review and editing, J.F.S.-P., J.S.-R., E.C. and F.M.-G. All authors have read and agreed to the published version of the manuscript.

Funding: This research received no external funding.

Data Availability Statement: The original contributions presented in this study are included in the article. Further inquiries can be directed to the corresponding author. The data presented in this study are available on request from the corresponding author.

Conflicts of Interest: The authors declare no conflicts of interest.

References

1. Kashyap, R. Self-propelled self-focusing damage in the optical fibres. In *Lasers 1987, Proceedings of the Tenth International Conference on Lasers and Applications, Lake Tahoe, NV, USA, 7–11 December 1987*; Duarte, F.J., Ed.; STS Press: McLean, VA, USA, 1988; pp. 859–866.
2. Kashyap, R.; Blow, K.J. Observation of catastrophic self-propelled self-focusing in optical fibres. *Electron. Lett.* **1988**, *24*, 47–49. [CrossRef]
3. Kashyap, R.; Sayles, A.H.; Cornwell, G.F. Heat-flow modeling and visualization of catastrophic self-propagating damage in single-mode optical fibers at low powers. In *Laser-Induced Damage in Optical Materials: 1996*; SPIE: Bellingham, WA, USA, 1997; pp. 586–591.
4. Starikova, V.A.; Konin, Y.A.; Petukhova, A.Y.; Aleshkina, S.S.; Petrov, A.A.; Perminov, A.V. Mathematical Model of Fuse Effect Initiation in Fiber Core. *Algorithms* **2023**, *16*, 331. [CrossRef]
5. Todoroki, S. *Fiber Fuse*; NIMS Series; Springer: Berlin/Heidelberg, Germany, 2014. [CrossRef]
6. Ha, W.; Jeong, Y.; Oh, K. Fiber fuse effect in hollow optical fibers. *Opt. Lett.* **2011**, *36*, 1536–1538. [CrossRef] [PubMed]
7. Shuto, Y. End Face Damage and Fiber Fuse Phenomena in Single-Mode Fiber-Optic Connectors. *J. Photonics* **2016**, *2016*, 2781392. [CrossRef]
8. Xiao, Q.; Tian, J.; Yan, P.; Li, D.; Gong, M. Exploring the initiation of fiber fuse. *Sci. Rep.* **2019**, *9*, 11655. [CrossRef]
9. Konin, Y.A.; Scherbakova, V.A.; Bulatov, M.I.; Malkov, N.A.; Lucenko, A.S.; Starikov, S.S.; Grachev, N.A.; Perminov, A.V.; Petrov, A.A. Structural characteristics of internal microcavities produced in optical fiber via the fuse effect. *J. Opt. Technol.* **2021**, *88*, 672–677. [CrossRef]
10. Shuto, Y. Fiber Fuse Simulation in Multi-Core Fibers for Space Division Multiplexed Transmission. *J. Electr. Electron. Eng.* **2022**, *10*, 162–169.
11. Lin, G.-R.; Baiad, M.D.; Gagne, M.; Liu, W.-F.; Kashyap, R. Harnessing the fiber fuse for sensing applications. *Opt. Express* **2014**, *22*, 8962. [CrossRef]
12. Mizuno, Y.; Lee, H.; Hayashi, N.; Nakamura, K.; Todoroki, S.-I. Plastic Optical Fiber Fuse and Its Impact on Sensing Applications. Available online: http://www.youtube.com/ (accessed on 20 November 2024).
13. Leal-Junior, A.G.; Marques, C.; Lee, H.; Nakamura, K.; Mizuno, Y. Sensing Applications of Polymer Optical Fiber Fuse. *Adv. Photonics Res.* **2022**, *3*, 2100210. [CrossRef]
14. Xiao, Q.; Tian, J.; Li, D.; Huang, Y.; Wang, Z.; Yan, P.; Gong, M. An Efficient Non-Invasive Method to Fabricate In-Fiber Microcavities Using a Continuous-Wave Laser. *IEEE Photonics Technol. Lett.* **2020**, *32*, 573–576. [CrossRef]

15. Tian, J.D.; Wang, Z.H.; Xiao, Q.R.; Li, D.; Yan, P.; Gong, M.L. On the initiation of fiber fuse damage in high-power ytterbium-doped fiber lasers. *Photonics Res.* **2022**, *10*, 2513–2525. [CrossRef]
16. Tian, J.D.; Xiao, Q.R.; Li, D.; Zhang, Z.; Yin, H.Y.; Yan, P.; Gong, M.L. Fiber Fuse Damage Effect in Fiber Lasers: A Review. *Chin. J. Lasers-Zhongguo Jiguang* **2021**, *48*, 81–105.
17. Peusner, L. *The Principles of Network Thermodynamics: Theory and Biophysical Applications*; Entropy Limited: Amador, CA, USA, 1987.
18. Nagel, L. SPICE (Simulation Program with Integrated Circuit Emphasis). In Proceedings of the 16th Midwest Symposium on Circuit Theory, Waterloo, ON, Canada, 12 April 1973.
19. Nagel, L.W. *SPICE2: A Computer Program to Simulate Semiconductor Circuits*; College of Engineering, University of California: Berkeley, CA, USA, 1975.
20. Sánchez-Pérez, J.F.; Alhama, I. Universal curves for the solution of chlorides penetration in reinforced concrete, water-saturated structures with bound chloride. *Commun. Nonlinear Sci. Numer. Simul.* **2020**, *84*, 105201. [CrossRef]
21. Carslow, H.S.; Jaeger, J.C.; Morral, J.E. Conduction of heat in solids. *J. Eng. Mater. Technol.* **1986**, *108*, 378. [CrossRef]
22. Davis, D.D., Jr.; Mettler, S.C.; DiGiovanni, D.J. Experimental data on the fiber fuse. In Proceedings of the 27th Annual Boulder Damage Symposium: Laser-Induced Damage in Optical Materials, Boulder, CO, USA, 30 October–1 November 1995; SPIE: Bellingham, WA, USA, 1996; pp. 202–210.
23. Hanafusa, H.; Hibino, Y.; Yamamoto, F. Formation mechanism of drawing-induced E′ centers in silica optical fibers. *J. Appl. Phys.* **1985**, *58*, 1356–1361. [CrossRef]
24. Shuto, Y.; Yanagi, S.; Asakawa, S.; Kobayashi, M.; Nagase, R. Fiber fuse phenomenon in step-index single-mode optical fibers. *IEEE J. Quantum Electron.* **2004**, *40*, 1113–1121. [CrossRef]
25. Marcuse, D. Loss analysis of single-mode fiber splices. *Bell Syst. Tech. J.* **1977**, *56*, 703–718. [CrossRef]
26. Hao, L.; Xu, F.; Chen, Q.; Wei, M.; Chen, L.; Min, Y. A thermal-electrical analogy transient model of district heating pipelines for integrated analysis of thermal and power systems. *Appl. Therm. Eng.* **2018**, *139*, 213–221. [CrossRef]
27. Kreith, F.; Bohn, M.S. *Principles of Heat Transfer*; Harper and Row Publishers Inc.: New York, NY, USA, 1986.
28. Alhama, F.; Campo, A. Electric Network Representation of the Unsteady Cooling of a Lumped Body by Nonlinear Heat Transfer Modes. *J. Heat Transf.* **2002**, *124*, 988–992. [CrossRef]
29. Del Cerro Velázquez, F.; Gómez-Lopera, S.A.; Alhama, F. A powerful and versatile educational software to simulate transient heat transfer processes in simple fins. *Comput. Appl. Eng. Educ.* **2008**, *16*, 72–82. [CrossRef]
30. Alhama, F.; González-Fernández, C.F. Network simulation method for solving phase-change heat transfer problems with variable thermal properties. *Heat Mass Transf.* **2002**, *38*, 327–335. [CrossRef]
31. Sánchez-Pérez, J.F.; Marín, F.; Morales, J.L.; Cánovas, M.; Alhama, F. Modeling and simulation of different and representative engineering problems using Network Simulation Method. *PLoS ONE* **2018**, *13*, e0193828. [CrossRef]
32. Solano, J.; Balibrea, F.; Moreno, J.A.; Marín, F. Dry Friction Analysis in Doped Surface by Network Simulation Method. *Mathematics* **2023**, *11*, 1341. [CrossRef]
33. Fernández-Gracía, M.; Sánchez-Pérez, J.F.; del Cerro, F.; Conesa, M. Mathematical Model to Calculate Heat Transfer in Cylindrical Vessels with Temperature-Dependent Materials. *Axioms* **2023**, *12*, 335. [CrossRef]
34. Zheng, W.; Zhu, J.; Luo, Q. Distributed Dispatch of Integrated Electricity-Heat Systems with Variable Mass Flow. *IEEE Trans. Smart Grid* **2023**, *14*, 1907–1919. [CrossRef]
35. Holger, V.; Atkinson, G.; Nenzi, P.; Warning, D. Software "NgSpice". Available online: https://ngspice.sourceforge.io/index.html (accessed on 20 November 2024).
36. Gear, C.W. The automatic integration of ordinary differential equations. *Commun. ACM* **1971**, *14*, 176–179. [CrossRef]
37. Solano, J.; Mulas-Pérez, J.; Balibrea, F.; Moreno-Nicolás, J.A. Truncation Error of the Network Simulation Method: Chaotic Dynamical Systems in Mechanical Engineering. *Mathematics* **2024**, *12*, 3441. [CrossRef]

axioms

MDPI

Article

A Confidence-Interval Circular Intuitionistic Fuzzy Method for Optimal Master and Sub-Franchise Selection: A Case Study of Pizza Hut in Europe

Velichka Nikolova Traneva [1,*], Venelin Todorov [2,3,*], Stoyan Tranev Tranev [4] and Ivan Dimov [2]

1 Department of Natural Sciences, Prof. Assen Zlatarov University, Prof. Yakimov Blvd. 1, 8010 Bourgas, Bulgaria
2 Institute of Information and Communication Technologies, Bulgarian Academy of Sciences, Acad. G. Bonchev Str. Bl. 25A, 1113 Sofia, Bulgaria; ivdimov@bas.bg
3 Institute of Mathematics and Informatics, Bulgarian Academy of Sciences, Acad. G. Bonchev Str. Bl. 8, 1113 Sofia, Bulgaria
4 Department of Social Sciences, Prof. Assen Zlatarov University, Prof. Yakimov Blvd. 1, 8010 Bourgas, Bulgaria; tranev@abv.bg
* Correspondence: veleka13@gmail.com (V.N.T.); venelinltodorov@gmail.com (V.T.)

Abstract: Effective franchise selection is crucial for global brands like Pizza Hut to maintain consistent quality and operational excellence amidst a competitive landscape. This paper introduces a novel confidence-interval circular intuitionistic fuzzy set (CIC-IFS) framework, designed to address the intricate challenges of master and sub-franchise selection in the European market. By integrating competence coefficients of decision-makers into the final evaluations, the model allows for a more accurate representation of expert judgments. Decision-makers can choose from various scenarios, ranging from super pessimistic to super optimistic, using ten forms of aggregation operations over index matrices. The proposed approach leverages confidence intervals within the circular intuitionistic fuzzy set paradigm to capture the uncertainty, vagueness, and hesitancy inherent in the decision-making process. A case study involving Pizza Hut's European operations demonstrates the model's efficacy in differentiating potential franchisees and identifying those best aligned with the brand's values. The results indicate a significant improvement in selection accuracy compared to traditional methods and other fuzzy approaches, thereby enabling Pizza Hut to make more informed decisions and solidify its market position.

Keywords: aggregation operations; confidence-interval circular intuitionistic fuzzy sets; decision-making; master franchise; sub-franchise

MSC: 60J22; 62P12; 65C05; 68W20

1. Introduction

In the highly competitive global fast-food industry, selecting the right franchise partners is essential for maintaining brand reputation, operational consistency, and market success. For a brand like Pizza Hut, which operates across various cultural and economic landscapes, the complexity of franchise selection is amplified. Traditional selection methods often fall short in addressing the uncertainties and subjective judgments inherent in this process. The term "master international franchising" describes the legal arrangement whereby a franchisor grants an independently owned sub-franchisor the exclusive right to use the business format for a predetermined period of time in exchange for the development of a certain number of franchises in a given nation [1]. The master franchisee is in charge of vetting potential local franchisees, marketing franchises, educating potential franchisees, and handling franchise and royalty payments.The two main categories of master franchising are area development and sub-franchising.

Under the former, the area developer takes on responsibility for a specific region, in which he agrees to create and operate a predetermined number of outlets within a predetermined time frame [1]; under the latter, the master franchisee functions as a franchisor, selling sub-franchises within a given territory. Using worldwide master franchising has numerous benefits for the company [1], such as quick time to market, accelerated system growth rate, low capital expenditure, and the master franchisee is familiarity with foreign markets. Conventional franchise selection techniques frequently depend on deterministic criteria and subjective assessment, which might not fully account for the inherent ambiguities and uncertainties seen in real-world situations.

A circular intuitionistic fuzzy set (C-IFS) [2] is an extension of classical fuzzy sets [3] that allows for the representation of data with dual levels of uncertainty, defining both membership and non-membership boundaries. The confidence interval, on the other hand, provides a statistical framework for assessing the reliability of the obtained results, enabling decision-makers to evaluate the likelihood of successfully choosing franchise partners. The C-IFS offers an effective way to represent the uncertainty under the form of circle around the point, which present the degree of truth and falsity of the element of the set, associated with evaluating potential franchise partners. By integrating parameters that reflect both confidence and ambiguity, the confidence-interval circular intuitionistic approach for franchise selection (CIC-IFFr) allows for a more accurate and reliable assessment of candidates.

The preferred decision-making processes of several DMs in selecting, rating, and evaluating based on multiple unrelated criteria are referred to MCGDM. However, because of the complexity of the decision-making environment and the ambiguity and uncertainty of DMs' preference information, tradition fuzzy sets (FSs) [3,4] and their extensions, including spherical fuzzy sets [5], complemental fuzzy sets [6], Z-numbers [7], intuitionistic fuzzy sets (IFSs) [8–12], hesitant fuzzy sets (HFSs) [13–16], Pythagorean fuzzy sets [17,18], Fermatean fuzzy sets [19–21], interval-valued fuzzy sets [22], picture fuzzy sets [23–27], q-rung orthopair fuzzy sets [28,29], circular IFSs [11,30,31], and elliptic IFS [32] have been applied to solve MCGDM problems. The "Extensions" of the IFSs are thoroughly compared in the study [33]. The authors of [33] have shown that a Hesitant fuzzy set [16] can be fully characterized by IFS. The authors also demonstrate in [33] that interval-valued IFSs (IVIFSs) [22] can represent the Picture fuzzy sets [23], the Cubic sets [34], the Neutrosophic fuzzy sets [35], and the Support-intuitionistic fuzzy sets [36]. The last two generalizations of interval-valued intuitionistic fuzzy sets have emerged in the last few years under the form of elliptic (E-IFSs) [37] and circular (C-IFSs) [2]. A circle with radius r that centers the IFSs [8] membership and nonmembership degrees is called a C-IFS [2]. A semi-major and semi-minor axis surrounds the place where the membership and non-membership degrees of IFSs [8] are shown by an ellipse called an E-IFS [37].

Our aim is to enhance MCGDM algorithms on circular IF data, as they are extensions of interval-valued IFSs, as supported by the evidence presented in [33]. Standard IFSs are enhanced by C-IFSs, which introduce an uncertainty region with an adaptable and adjustable radius [2]. This instability is efficiently captured by the circular area defined in C-IF sets, which symbolizes the various degrees of belief and skepticism associated with a choice [11,38]. For intelligent systems functioning in a variety of domains where judgments must be made, C-IF theory offers a promising direction forward.

These apps, which mostly rely on AI techniques [39], have the potential to support intelligent decision-making in a range of uncertain situations. Though C-IF theory and its application in decision scenarios have advanced, Chen [11] highlights the lack of enough attention in the existing literature on the necessity for a systematic and thorough methodology for C-IF assignment modeling. Using C-IF sets in assignment-based decision scenarios presents a structured approach to manage preferences and uncertainty, which is one of the specific shortcomings of current techniques. Furthermore, the C-IF scoring functions that are currently in use have drawbacks such instability, dependence on particular datasets, and incompleteness in reflecting the intrinsic uncertainty of C-IF data. In the practical world of circular intuitionistic fuzziness decision-making, score functions are essential for comparing and arranging C-IF data in order to create a hierarchy. Several studies have presented scoring functions tailored for C-IF contexts, including works by Çakır et al. [40,41], Çakır and Tas [30], Chen [38], Kahraman et al. [42], and Otay and Kahraman [43]. There are still restrictions and application-specific practical issues with the scoring functions as they stand today, even with these improvements.

To account for the optimistic and pessimistic dispositions of decision-makers, Çakır et al. [40,41] and Xu and Wen [44] employed a parameter during the circular function radius normalization process. However, the very crude formula used by Xu and Wen [44] and Çakır et al. [40,41] does not fully account for the wide range of uncertainty present in C-IF data. Çakır and Tas [30] included parameters that represented the inclinations of decision-makers when transforming C-IF values into optimistic and pessimistic point estimations. Their suggested C-IF scoring method, however, does not fully utilize all of the information properties of the C-IF set; rather, it merely extends the conventional IF score function. Furthermore, using the reciprocal of the radius, Kahraman et al. [42] and Otay and Kahraman [43] created a vector normalization approach to provide relative fuzzy scores in the C-IF configuration. However, when the radius approaches 0 in relation to the C-IF data, a noteworthy point becomes apparent. Since the denominator drops to 0 in certain circumstances, the relative scoring technique no longer makes sense. Chen [38] boosted C-IF scoring with improved parameters; however, the approach has instability problems. When there are numerous decision-makers, Chen [45] recommends using a (nine-point) linguistic rating scale to facilitate the collecting of corresponding IF values for the construction of C-IF data. To overcome the shortcomings of the current C-IF scoring techniques, ref. [11] presents a parameterized C-IF scoring framework. It provides guidance on creating a specific C-IF assignment model, which is essential for handling preferences and uncertainty in decision-making situations.

In order to improve the decision-making process for master and sub-franchise selection, this study suggests a unique method that makes use of confidence-interval circular intuitionistic fuzzy sets (CIC-IFSs) and confidence-interval circular intuitionistic fuzzy IMs (CIC-IFIMs), which we define here for the first time. By embedding confidence intervals and C-IFSs [2], the proposed model captures not only the uncertainty and vagueness, but also the hesitancy associated with expert evaluations. The integration of competence coefficients further refines the decision-making process by weighting expert opinions according to their perceived reliability. The confidence-interval circular intuitionistic fuzzy franchising method (CIC-IFFr) combines the robustness of confidence intervals with the advantages of CIC-IFSs, which manages imprecise and uncertain information, to produce a more thorough and trustworthy evaluation framework. By definition, each element is surrounded by a circle with a radius, which size varies on the probability level of β.

In this model, the criteria values are expressed as CIC-IF numbers, and are established by experts with dynamic ranks. Each condition's significance is assessed by the investor. The input data are transformed into circular intuitionistic fuzzy data based on a confidence probability coefficient β determined by the decision maker. Decision-makers can choose from various scenarios, ranging from super pessimistic to super optimistic, using ten forms of aggregation operations over index matrices (IMs) [46]. The suggested CIC-IFFr technique integrates probabilistic information into the CIC-IFS, which may be useful in ensuring the quality and integrity of the CIC-IFS data. This study focuses on the European market for Pizza Hut [47], examining the efficacy of the CIC-IFFr approach in selecting franchisees that meet the brand's strategic and operational criteria. By leveraging this advanced fuzzy logic methodology, the paper aims to demonstrate how CIC-IFS can facilitate better-informed and more resilient franchise selection decisions, ultimately contributing to Pizza Hut's sustainable growth and competitive advantage in Europe. This model's benefit is that it may be used with confidence interval circular IF data, as well as regular data.

The rest of the paper is as follows: A survey of the literature on franchise selection in the face of uncertainty is given in Section 2. The confidence interval circular intuitionistic index matrices (CIC-IFIM), sets (CIC-IFSs), triples (CIC-IFTs), and certain operations and relations with them are defined in Section 3. A confidence interval circular IF method for the most benevolent franchisor is proposed in Section 4. A case study of Pizza Hut in Europe is presented in Section 5 to illustrate the usefulness and feasibility of our methodology. Section 6 discusses the recently developed CIC-IFFr methodology. Ultimately, a review of the results, recommendations for further research, and implications for franchise management round up Section 7.

2. Review of Literature on Franchise Selection under Uncertainty

Fuzzy logic, as created by [3], is a helpful tool when handling unclear or partial data. Fuzzy logic has been effectively applied to multi-criteria decision-making situations because of the fact that human judgments are typically imprecise when selecting an option based on numerous factors that vary in importance. A linguistic criteria values-based approach is described in [48], which can be applied to fuzzy criteria-based multi-criteria decision-making problems. Fuzzy franchisee selection models are created by the studies [49,50] using neural networks and an Analytic Hierarchical Process (AHP). One of the first generalizations of fuzzy sets, intuitionistic fuzzy sets (IFSs, [8]), exhibit some hesitancy. They work better at illustrating the uncertainty of the environment. To choose the best franchise candidates, we have also developed software for performing IF selection of the franchisor using IFIMFr approach [51], based on the concept of index matrices (IMs, [52]). In [31], the creation of Circular Intuitionistic Fuzzy Multicriteria Analysis (C-IFFr) for Petrol Station Franchisor Selection is discussed. We have presented elliptic intuitionistic fuzzy algorithm (E-IFFr) [32] for the optimal franchise organization selection, which is based on the toolset of index matrices (IMs) theories and elliptic intuitionistic fuzzy sets (E-IFSs). In [53], we use confidence interval elliptic-IF data to expand the optimal method (E-IFFr) for choosing a franchise organization for the courier franchisor.

3. Preliminaries

The definitions of the confidence interval circular intuitionistic index matrices (CIC-IFIM), sets (CIC-IFSs), triples (CIC-IFTs), and some operations and relationships between them are among the concepts that are introduced in this part.

In 1963, Zadeh [3] introduced fuzzy sets. A class of items with a continuum of membership grades is called a fuzzy set. A membership function belonging between zero and one characterizes such a set. As an expansion of Lotfi Zadeh is fuzzy set concept, Atanassov [8] proposed intuitionistic fuzzy sets (IFSs) in 1983. Sets with varying degrees of membership and non-membership are known as IFSs. Let us review the fundamental definitions of intuitionistic fuzzy pairs (IFPs), relations and operations with them [54].

3.1. Intuitionistic Fuzzy Pairs

An object of the type $\langle a, b\rangle = \langle \mu(p), \nu(p)\rangle$, where $a, b \in [0,1]$ and $a + b \leq 1$, is used to assess a proposition p [54]. $\mu(p)$ and $\nu(p)$, respectively, define the degrees of membership and non-membership. Given two IFPs, let $x = \langle a, b\rangle$ and $y = \langle c, d\rangle$. A few operations are recalled according to [54–57],

$$\neg x = \langle b, a\rangle; x \wedge_1 y = \langle \min(a,c), \max(b,d)\rangle;$$

$$x \vee_1 y = \langle \max(a,c), \min(b,d)\rangle; x \wedge_2 y = x + y = \langle a + c - a.c, b.d\rangle;$$

$$x@y = \langle \tfrac{a+c}{2}, \tfrac{b+d}{2}\rangle; x \vee_2 y = x.y = \langle a.c, b + d - b.d\rangle;$$

$$\alpha.x = \langle 1 - (1-a)^{\alpha}, b^{\alpha}\rangle (\text{for } \alpha > 0); \tag{1}$$

$$x - y = \langle \max(0, a-c), \min(1, b+d, 1-a+c)\rangle;$$

$$x : y = \begin{cases} \langle \min(1, a/c), \min(\max(0, 1 - a/c), \max(0, (b-d)/(1-d)))\rangle \text{if } c \neq 0 \ \&d \neq 1 \\ \langle 0, 1\rangle \text{ otherwise} \end{cases}$$

and some relations [54],

$$\begin{array}{lll} x \geq y & \text{iff} & a \geq c \text{ and } b \leq d; \quad x \geq_{\square} y \quad \text{iff} \quad a \geq c; \\ x \geq_{\diamond} y & \text{iff} & b \leq d. \end{array} \tag{2}$$

One of the most recent IFS expansions is the circular IFSs, which Atanasov presented in 2020 [2]. They work well as a method of showing the fuzziness of data. Let us review the definitions of Circular Intuitionistic Fuzzy Sets (C-IFSs) and Circular Intuitionistic Fuzzy Triples (C-IFTs) before extending them.

3.2. Circular Intuitionistic Fuzzy Sets (C-IFSs) [2,58]

The C-IFS is a mathematical construct that represents uncertainty under the form of a circle to depict degrees of truth and falsity associated with the elements of a set. Assume that A is a subset of E, which is fixed. The set $A_u^* = \{\langle x, \mu_A(x), \nu_A(x); u\rangle | x \in E\}$, where $\mu_A(p) + \nu_A(p) \leq 1$ and $u \in [0, \sqrt{2}]$ is the radius of the circle surrounding each element $x \in E$, is called Circular IFS (C-IFS). The $\mu_A : E \to [0;1]$ and $\nu_A : E \to [0,1]$ denote the degree to which element $x \in E$ belongs to a fixed set $A \subseteq E$ in terms of membership (validity, etc.) and non-membership (non-validity, etc.). The function $\pi_A = 1 - \mu_A(x) - \nu_A(x)$ ($\pi_A : E \to [0;1]$) relates to the level of uncertainty. The set A_u^* can be rewritten in the form

$$A_u^* = \{\langle x, E_u(\mu_A(x), \nu_A(x))\rangle | x \in E\}, \tag{3}$$

where E_u is a part of a circle (section, [2]) with the center in point $\mu_A(x), \nu_A(x)$ and a radius u that lies in intuitionistic fuzzy triangle. The graphical representation of the C-IFS is made in [2].

3.3. Circular Intuitionistic Fuzzy Triples (C-IFTs)

A circular intuitionistic fuzzy triple (C-IFT) is defined as an object with the following form [31]: $\langle a(p), b(p); u\rangle = \langle \mu(p), \nu(p); u\rangle$. The assertion p has two degrees of truth and falsity, which are $a(p)(\mu(p)) \in [0,1]$ and $b(p)(\nu(p)) \in [0,1]$, and $a(p) + b(p) \leq 1$. $r \in [0, \sqrt{2}]$ is the radius of the circle around $\langle a(p), b(p)\rangle$.

Let two C-IFTs be given: $x_{u_1} = \langle a, b; u_1\rangle$ and $y_{u_2} = \langle c, d; u_2\rangle$. Let us denote the set of radii $R = \{R_1, R_2, \ldots, R_n\}$. The domain for the operation $*$ is R. When $*$ represents the minimum operation, the result from $*(R_1, R_2, \ldots, R_n) = min(R_1, R_2, \ldots, R_n)\}$ yields the smallest value among the selected radii. Conversely, when $*$ represents the maximum operation, the result $*(R_1, R_2, \ldots, R_n) = max(R_1, R_2, \ldots, R_n)\}$ yields the the largest value among the selected radii.

In [31], the operations defined below are defined over C-IFTs:

$$\begin{aligned}
x_{u_1} \wedge_* y_{u_2} &= \langle \min(a,c), \max(b,d); *(u_1,u_2)\rangle; \\
x_{u_1} \vee_* y_{u_2} &= \langle \max(a,c), \min(b,d); *(u_1,u_2)\rangle; \\
x_{u_1} +_* y_{u_2} &= \langle a+c-a.c, b.d; *(u_1,u_2)\rangle; \\
x_{u_1} \bullet_* y_{u_2} &= \langle a.c, b+d-b.d; *(u_1,u_2)\rangle;
\end{aligned} \tag{4}$$

3.4. Confidence Interval Circular Intuitionistic Fuzzy Sets (CIC-IFSs)

We first extend the C-IFSs to Confidence Interval Circular Intuitionistic Fuzzy Sets (CIC-IFSs) in this section.

The definition of CIC-IFSs is based on building a confidence interval for the unknown mean Mu by adding and subtracting a margin of error from $\overline{x}$, the mean of our random sample [59], and the definition of C-IFSs [2]. The confidence level α for this interval is represented by a number, such 10, 5, or 1 percent. A higher confidence level corresponds to a larger confidence interval. There are two scenarios for computing the confidence interval for a mean, depending on whether it is applied to exact numbers [59], fuzzy numbers [60], or intuitionistic fuzzy numbers [60]:

- Confidence interval for a mean Mu with known standard deviation σ is

$$\left[\overline{x} - z_{\alpha/2}\frac{\sigma}{\sqrt{n}}; \overline{x} + z_{\alpha/2}\frac{\sigma}{\sqrt{n}}\right] \tag{5}$$

In case the data are fuzzy or intuitionistic fuzzy, we use the operations of (1) in (5). A probability for the process used to compute the confidence interval is the confidence level $1-\alpha$. If the population is normal, and we know σ, we may safely apply the following process to generate the confidence interval for Mu. Under the assumption that $\overline{x}$ has a normal distribution, $n \geq 30$ suffices if σ is known, but the normality of the population is unknown, as long as the population is relatively symmetric and free of outliers.

- Confidence interval for a mean Mu with uncertain σ.

When the population is normally distributed, but the standard deviation σ is unknown [59,60], Student's t distribution should be utilized instead of the normal z distribution. This is particularly important when the sample size is small. With the exception of substituting z for t and σ for s, the confidence interval formula for an unknown σ is similar to the expression for a known σ:

$$\left[\overline{x} - t_{\{\alpha/2;df\}}\frac{s}{\sqrt{n}}; \overline{x} + t_{\{\alpha/2;df\}}\frac{s}{\sqrt{n}}\right], \tag{6}$$

where the df is the degree of freedom of the sample. When the data are fuzzy or intuitionistic fuzzy, we use the operations of (1) for calculating of the interval from (6).

Confidence-interval C-IFS (CIC-IFS) is defined here. Let A be a subset of a fixed universe E. The set

$$A_u^\beta = \{\langle x, \mu_A(x), \nu_A(x); u^\beta\rangle | x \in E\}, \tag{7}$$

where $\mu_A(p) \in [0,1], \nu_A(p) \in [0,1], \mu_A(p) + \nu_A(p) \leq 1$ and $\{u^\beta\} \in [0, \sqrt{2}]$ is the circle's radius around every element $x \in E$, is referred to as Confidence interval circular IFS (CIC-IFS) at a probability level of confidence *beta*. The functions $\mu_A : E \to [0,1]$ and $\nu_A : E \to [0,1]$ express the extent to which element $x \in E$ belongs to a fixed set $A \subseteq E$, and to which it does not. The degree of indeterminacy is correlated with the function $\pi_A = 1 - \mu_A(x) - \nu_A(x)$ ($\pi_A : E \to [0,1]$). Rewriting the set A_u^β in the form can be achieved by utilizing the concept from [2].

$$A_u^\beta = \{\langle x, E_{u^\beta}(\mu_A(x), \nu_A(x))\rangle | x \in E\}, \tag{8}$$

where E_{u^β} is a part of a circle with center in point $\mu_A(x), \nu_A(x)$ and a radius u^β that depend on the chosen confidence level α. Inspired by Atanassov's C-IFSs [2], the idea for constructing CIC-IFSs incorporated ideas from Torra [16] and intuitionistic hesitant fuzzy sets [61] by Chen et al.

$$H = \{\langle x, \{\langle \mu(x_i), \nu(x_i)\rangle | i = 1, \ldots, k_x\}\rangle | x \in E\}, \tag{9}$$

is the form of the hesitant IFS. The number of distinct values for element x is denoted by k_x.

For a fixed element $x \in E$, the numbers $a(x)$ and $c(x)$, respectively, indicate the left and right limits of the confidence interval for a given confidence probability β for the different values for the membership degree of $x - \mu_{k_1}, \ldots, \mu_{k_x}$. $b(x)$ and $d(x)$, respectively, represent the left and right boundaries of the confidence interval at a probability β for the different values of the non-membership degree of $x - \nu_{k_1}, \ldots, \nu_{k_x}$. The center and radius of the circle are then calculated using the following formulas, which are similar to those proposed in [2].

- A point having coordinates serves as the circle's center.

$$\langle \mu(x)^\beta, \nu(x)^\beta \rangle = \left\langle \frac{a(x) + c(x)}{2}, \frac{b(x) + d(x)}{2} \right\rangle. \tag{10}$$

The coordinates $\mu(x), \nu(x)$ of the circle's center are found by taking the arithmetic means of the different values for the membership degree of x ($\mu_{k_1}, \ldots, \mu_{k_x}$) and non-membership degree of x ($\nu_{k_1}, \ldots, \nu_{k_x}$). In contrast, the coordinates of the circle center for C-IFSs [2] are determined by taking the arithmetic mean of the largest and lowest values of the different membership and non-membership degrees of x, respectively.

- At a α confidence level, the circle's radius is

$$u^\beta(x) = \max_{1 \le i \le k_x} \left| \sqrt{(\mu(x)^\beta - \mu_{k_i}^\beta)^2 + (\nu(x)^\beta - \nu_{k_i}^\beta)^2} \right| \tag{11}$$

A new circle with the following radius is made:

$$u^\beta = \max_{x \in E} u^\beta(x) \tag{12}$$

Two CIC-IFSs, A_u^β and $B_w^{\beta_1}$, have comparable relations and operations to those described in [2].

3.5. Confidence Interval Circular Intuitionistic Fuzzy Triples (CIC-IFTs)

By expanding on the concept of C-IFT from [31], we define confidence interval circular triple (CIC-IFT) as follows:

$$\langle \mu(p), \nu(p); u^\beta \rangle = \langle a(p), b(p); u^\beta \rangle, \tag{13}$$

where $a(p) + b(p) \le 1$ and $a(p)(\mu(p)), b(p)(\nu(p))$.

Under the form of intuitionistic fuzzy pairs (IFPs), let us the experts $i = 1, \ldots, k_r$ evaluate the "truth degree" and "falsity degree" of the assertion p under the form of $\{\langle \mu(p_i), \nu(p_i)\rangle | i = 1, \ldots, k_r\}\rangle\}$.

Then, at a given probability level β, we compute the following values for the left and right limits of the confidence interval: $a(p)$ and $c(p)$, respectively, given the various membership degree values of p - $\mu_{k_1}, \ldots, \mu_{k_r}$. For a set of non-membership degree values of p - $\nu_{k_1}, \ldots, \nu_{k_r}$, the left and right boundaries of the confidence interval are $b(p)$ and $d(p)$, respectively.

Next, the circle's center and radius are computed in the same way as in Section 3.4.

- At a confidence level of α, the coordinates of the circle's center are as follows:

$$\langle \mu(p), \nu(p) \rangle = \left\langle \frac{a(p) + c(p)}{2}, \frac{b(p) + d(p)}{2} \right\rangle. \tag{14}$$

The coordinates $\mu(p), \nu(p)$ of the circle's center are obtained by taking the means of the different values for the membership $(\mu_{k_1}, \ldots, \mu_{k_r})$ and non-membership degrees $(\nu_{k_1}, \ldots, \nu_{k_r})$ of p.

- The radius of the circle is

$$u^{\beta}(p) = \max_{1 \le i \le k_r} |\sqrt{(\mu(p)^{\beta} - \mu^{\beta}_{k_i})^2 + (\nu(p)^{\beta} - \nu^{\beta}_{k_i})^2}|. \quad (15)$$

Let us consider the following two CIE-IFTs: $y^{\beta_1}_{u_2} = \langle c, d; u^{\beta_1}_2 \rangle$ and $x^{\beta}_{u_1} = \langle a, b; u^{\beta}_1 \rangle$. We are going to define an operation $* \in \{\min, \max\}$. In this section, we will expand the operations performed on C-IFTs [31,53,62] to CIC-IFTs:

$$\begin{array}{c} \neg x = \langle b, a; v^{\beta}_1 \rangle; x^{\beta}_{u_1} \wedge_* y^{\beta_1}_{u_2} = \langle \min(a, c), \max(b, d); *(u^{\beta}_1, u^{\beta_1}_2) \rangle; \\ x^{\beta}_{u_1} \vee_* y^{\beta_1}_{u_2} = \langle \max(a, c), \min(b, d); *(u^{\beta}_1, u^{\beta}_2) \rangle; \\ x^{\beta}_{u^{\beta}_1} +_* y^{\beta_1}_{u^{\beta_1}_2} = \langle a + c - a.c, b.d; *(u^{\beta}_1, u^{\beta_1}_2) \rangle; \\ x^{\beta}_{u_1} \bullet_* y^{\beta_1}_{u_2} = \langle a.c, b + d - b.d; *(u^{\beta}_1, u^{\beta_1}_2) \rangle; \\ x@y = \langle \frac{a+c}{2}, \frac{b+d}{2}; *(u^{\beta}_1, u^{\beta_1}_2) \rangle; \\ \alpha.x = \langle 1 - (1 - a)^{\alpha}, b^{\alpha}; *(u^{\beta}_1, u^{\beta_1}_2) \rangle (\text{for } \alpha > 0); \\ x - y = \langle \max(0, a - c), \min(1, b + d, 1 - a + c); *(u^{\beta}_1, u^{\beta_1}_2) \rangle; \\ x : y = \begin{cases} \langle \min(1, a/c), \min(\max(0, 1 - a/c), \max(0, (b - d)/(1 - d))); *(u^{\beta}_1, u^{\beta_1}_2) \\ \quad \text{if } c \neq 0 \ \& d \neq 1 \\ \langle 0, 1; \sqrt{2} \rangle \text{ otherwise} \end{cases} \end{array} \quad (16)$$

Here, we establish the relation that compares two CIC-IFTs in an analogous manner to those found in (2):

$$x \ge y \text{ iff } \quad a \ge c, b \le d, u^{\beta}_1 \ge u^{\beta}_2 \quad (17)$$

We extend the method from [62] to utilizing the distance between the ideal positive option $\langle 1, 0; \sqrt{2} \rangle$ and the alternatives x and y to rank them. x^{β} has higher rank than y^{β} iff

$$R^{circ}_{x^{\beta}} \le R^{circ}_{y^{\beta_1}}, where\ R^{circ}_{x^{\beta}} = \frac{1}{6}(2 - a - b)(|\sqrt{2} - u^{\beta}_1| + |\sqrt{2} - v^{\beta}_1| + |1 - a|). \quad (18)$$

3.6. Three-Dimensional Confidence Interval Circular Intuitionistic Fuzzy Index Matrices (3-D CIC-IFIM)

The theory of index matrices, or IMs, first appeared in 1987 [46]. Over IMs [52,63], a multitude of relations, operators, and operations are defined. Assume that $\mathcal{I}$ is a fixed set of indices. In this instance, we extend 3-D circular intuitionistic fuzzy IM (C-IFIM) [31] to include 3-D confidence interval C-IFIM (CIC-IFIM) $A^{\beta} = [K, L, H, \{\langle \mu_{k_i,l_j,h_g}, \nu_{k_i,l_j,h_g}; rf^{\beta}_{k_i,l_j,h_g} \rangle\}]$ for the first time in this manner:

$$\begin{array}{c|ccc} h_g \in H & l_1 & \ldots & l_n \\ \hline k_1 & \langle \mu_{k_1,l_1,h_g}, \nu_{k_1,l_1,h_g}; rf^{\beta}_{k_1,l_1,h_g} \rangle & \ldots & \langle \mu_{k_1,l_n,h_g}, \nu_{k_1,l_n,h_g}; rf^{\beta}_{k_1,l_n,h_g} \rangle \\ \vdots & \vdots & \ldots & \vdots \\ k_m & \langle \mu_{k_m,l_1,h_g}, \nu_{k_m,l_1,h_g}; rf^{\beta}_{k_m,l_1,h_g} \rangle & \ldots & \langle \mu_{k_m,l_n,h_g}, \nu_{k_m,l_n,h_g}; rf^{\beta}_{k_m,l_n,h_g} \rangle \end{array}, \quad (19)$$

where α is the confidence level, $(K, L, H \subset \mathcal{I}), K = \{k_1, \ldots, k_i, \ldots, k_m\}, L = \{l_1, \ldots, l_j, \ldots, l_n\}, H = \{h_1, \ldots, h_g, \ldots, h_f\}$, and the elements are CIC-IFTs.

Let $A^{\beta} = [K, L, H, \{\langle \mu_{k_i,l_j,h_g}, \nu_{k_i,l_j,h_g}; rf^{\beta}_{k_i,l_j,h_g} \rangle\}]$ and $B^{\beta_1} = [P, Q, R\{\langle \rho_{p_r,q_s,t_e}, \sigma_{p_r,q_s,t_e}; \delta f^{\beta_1}_{p_r,q_s,t_e}\}]$ are the CIC-IFIMs. Let $\beta^{new} = min(\beta, \beta_1)$.

We describe here a few fundamental operations on CIC-IFIMs that expand the ones found in [31,52]:

Addition-$(\circ_1, \circ_2, *)$:

$$A^{\beta} \oplus_{(\circ_1,\circ_2,*)} B^{\beta_1} = [K \cup P, L \cup Q, H \cup R, \{\langle \phi_{t_u,v_w,x_y}, \psi_{t_u,v_w,x_y}; \eta f^{\beta^{new}}_{t_u,v_w,x_y} \rangle\}], \tag{20}$$

where $\langle \circ_1, \circ_2 \rangle \in \{\langle \max, \min \rangle, \langle \min, \max \rangle, \langle average, average \rangle\}$ and $* \in \{\max, \min\}$,

$$\langle \phi_{t_u,v_w,x_y}, \psi_{t_u,v_w,x_y}; \eta f^{\beta^{new}}_{t_u,v_w,x_y} \rangle = \langle \circ_1(\mu_{k_i,l_j,x_y}, \rho_{p_r,q_s,x_y}), \circ_2(\nu_{k_i,l_j,x_y}, \sigma_{p_r,q_s,x_y}); *(rf^{\beta}_{t_u,v_w,x_y}, \delta f^{\beta_1}_{t_u,v_w,x_y}) \rangle).$$

Multiplication:

$$A^{\beta} \odot_{(\circ_1,\circ_2,*)} B^{\beta_1} = [K \cup (P - L), Q \cup (L - P), H \cup R, \{\langle \phi_{t_u,v_w,x_y}, \psi_{t_u,v_w,x_y}; \eta f^{\beta^{new}}_{t_u,v_w,x_y} \rangle\}], \tag{21}$$

where $\langle \phi_{t_u,v_w,x_y}, \psi_{t_u,v_w,x_y} \rangle$ is defined in [52], and $\eta f^{\beta^{new}}_{t_u,v_w,x_y} = *(rf^{\beta}_{t_u,v_w,x_y}, \delta f^{\beta_1}_{t_u,v_w,x_y})$.

Term-wise subtraction-(max,min):

$$A^{\beta} -_{(\max,\min)} B^{\beta_1} = A^{\beta} \oplus_{(\max,\min)} \neg B^{\beta_1}. \tag{22}$$

Term-wise multiplication:

$$A^{\beta} \otimes_{(\min,\max)} B^{\beta_1} = [K \cap P, L \cap Q, \{H \cup R, \{\langle \phi_{t_u,v_w,x_y}, \psi_{t_u,v_w,x_y}; \eta f^{\beta^{new}}_{t_u,v_w,x_y} \rangle\}], \tag{23}$$

where $\langle \phi_{t_u,v_w,x_y}, \psi_{t_u,v_w,x_y} \rangle$

$$= \langle \min(\mu_{k_i,l_j,x_y}, \rho_{p_r,q_s,x_y}), \max(\nu_{k_i,l_j,x_y}, \sigma_{p_r,q_s,x_y}) \rangle, \eta f^{\beta^{new}}_{t_u,v_w,x_y} = *(rf^{\beta}_{t_u,v_w,x_y}, \delta f^{\beta_1}_{t_u,v_w,x_y}). \tag{24}$$

Aggregation operation (AO) over CIC-IFIM A^{β} by one dimension: Let $* \in \{\min, \max\}$. Using the definition for the 10 operations from [64], denoted by $\#_i$, $(1 \le i \le 10)$, let us extend the aggregation operations over C-IFIT [31] so they can be used over two CIC-IFTs $x = \langle a, b; rf^{\beta}_1 \rangle$, and $y = \langle c, d; rf^{\beta_1}_2 \rangle$:

$$\begin{aligned}
x\#_1 y &= \langle ac, 1 - ac, *(rf^{\beta}_1, rf^{\beta}_2) \rangle, \\
x\#_2 y &= \langle ac, b + d - bd, *(rf^{\beta}_1, rf^{\beta}_2) \rangle, \\
x\#_3 y &= \langle \min(a, c), \max(b, d), *(rf^{\beta}_1, rf^{\beta}_2) \rangle, \\
x\#_4 y &= \langle \min(a, 1 - d), \max(b, d), *(rf^{\beta}_1, rf^{\beta}_2) \rangle, \\
x\#_5 y &= \langle 1 - \max(b, d), \max(b, d), *(rf^{\beta}_1, rf^{\beta}_2) \rangle, \\
x\#_6 y &= \langle \max(1 - b, c), 1 - \max(1 - b, c), *(rf^{\beta}_1, rf^{\beta}_2) \rangle, \\
x\#_7 y &= \langle \max(1 - b, c), \min(b, d), rf^{\beta}_1), *(rf^{\beta}_1, rf^{\beta}_2) \rangle, \\
x\#_8 y &= \langle 1 - \min(b, d), \min(b, d), *(rf^{\beta}_1, rf^{\beta}_2) \rangle, \\
x\#_9 y &= \langle 1 - bd, bd \rangle, *(rf^{\beta}_1, rf^{\beta}_2) \rangle, \\
x\#_{10} y &= \langle \min(1, 2 - b - d), \max(0, b + d - 1), *(rf^{\beta}_1, rf^{\beta}_2) \rangle.
\end{aligned} \tag{25}$$

Using the theorem from [64], we can prove the following:

$$x\#_1 y \le x\#_2 y \le x\#_3 y \le x\#_4 y \le x\#_5 y \le x\#_6 y$$

$$\le x\#_7 y \le x\#_8 y \le x\#_9 y \le x\#_{10} y.$$

Consider $k_0 \notin K$ as the fixed index. We recommend composing the aggregation operation $\alpha_{K,\#_q,*}(A^\beta, k_0)$ by K over 3-D CIC-IFIM A^β, extending those over IFIMs [64]:

$$\begin{array}{c|ccc} h_g \in H & l_1 & \dots & l_n \\ \hline k_0 & \underset{i=1}{\overset{m}{\#_q, *}} \langle \mu_{k_i,l_1,h_g}, \nu_{k_i,l_1,h_g}; rf^\beta_{k_i,l_1,h_g} \rangle & \dots & \underset{i=1}{\overset{m}{\#_q, *}} \langle \mu_{k_i,l_n,h_g}, \nu_{k_i,l_n,h_g}; rf^\beta_{k_i,l_1,h_g} \rangle \end{array} \quad (26)$$

In particular, we could use $\#_1^*$ to execute a super pessimistic aggregation operation (AO) in an environment with high inflation, $\#_5^*$ or $\#_6^*$, to execute an average AO in anticipation of minor changes in the market environment, and $\#_{10}^*$ to execute a super optimistic AO in an environment with stable market conditions.

Projection: Let $W \subseteq K$, $V \subseteq L$ and $U \subseteq H$. Then,

$$pr_{W,V,U} A^\beta = [W, V, U, \{\langle R_{p_r,q_s,e_d}, S_{p_r,q_s,e_d} \rangle\}], \quad (27)$$

where, for each $k_i \in W, l_j \in V$ and $e_d \in U$,

$$\langle R_{p_r,q_s,e_d}, S_{p_r,q_s,e_d} \rangle = \langle \mu_{k_i,l_j,h_g}, \nu_{k_i,l_j,h_g}; rf^\beta_{k_i,l_j,h_g}, rs^\beta_{k_i,l_j,h_g} \rangle. \quad (28)$$

Reduction: An IM A's operations-reduction $(k, \perp, \perp)$ is defined as follows:

$$A^\beta_{(k,\perp,\perp)} = [K - \{k\}, L, H, \{c^\beta_{t_u,v_w,e_d}\}],$$

where

$$c^\beta_{t_u,v_w,e_d} = a^\beta_{k_i,l_j,h_g} (t_u = k_i \in K - \{k\}, v_w = l_j \in L, e_d = h_g \in H). \quad (29)$$

Substitution:

$$\left[\frac{p}{k_i}; \perp, \perp\right] A^\beta = \left[(K - \{k_i\}) \cup \{p\}, L, H, \{a^\beta_{k_i,l_j,h_g}\}\right] \quad (30)$$

Composition: Let index set I and set $\mathcal{X}$ be fixed. The IMs $A_1^\beta, A_2^\beta, \dots,$ A_n^β are CIC-IFIMs over both sets be given. For $s (1 \le s \le n)$, let

$$(\forall p, q)(1 \le p < q \le n)(K^p \cap K^q = L^p \cap L^q = H^p \cap H^q = \oslash) \text{ and}$$

$$A_s^\beta = [K^s, L^s, H^s \{a^{\beta,s}_{k_i,l_j,h_g}\}]$$

$$= \begin{array}{c|ccccc} h_{s,g} \in H^s & l_{s,1} & \dots & l_{s,j} & \dots & l_{s,n_s} \\ \hline k_{s,1} & \mu_{k_{s,1},l_{s,1},h_{s,g}}, \nu_{k_{s,1},l_{s,1},h_{s,g}} & \dots & \mu_{k_{s,1},l_{s,j},h_{s,g}}, \nu_{k_{s,1},l_{s,j},h_{s,g}} & \dots & \mu_{k_{s,1},l_{s,n},h_{s,g}}, \nu_{k_{s,1},l_{s,n},h_{s,g}} \\ \vdots & \vdots & \dots & \vdots & \dots & \vdots \\ k_{s,i} & \mu_{k_{s,i},l_{s,1},h_{s,g}}, \nu_{k_{s,i},l_{s,1},h_{s,g}} & \dots & \mu_{k_{s,i},l_{s,j},h_{s,g}}, \nu_{k_{s,i},l_{s,j},h_{s,g}} & \dots & \mu_{k_{s,i},l_{s,n},h_{s,g}}, \nu_{k_{s,i},l_{s,n},h_{s,g}} \\ \vdots & \vdots & \dots & \vdots & \dots & \vdots \\ k_{s,m} & \mu_{k_{s,m},l_{s,m},h_{s,g}}, \nu_{k_{s,m},l_{s,m},h_{s,g}} & \dots & \mu_{k_{s,m},l_{s,j},h_{s,g}}, \nu_{k_{s,m},l_{s,j},h_{s,g}} & \dots & \mu_{k_{s,m},l_{s,n},h_{s,g}}, \nu_{k_{s,m},l_{s,n},h_{s,g}} \end{array}. \quad (31)$$

The following is the definition of the "composition" operation:

$$\flat\{A_s^\beta | 1 \le s \le n\} = [\bigcup_{s=1}^{n} K^s, \bigcup_{s=1}^{n} L^s, \bigcup_{s=1}^{n} H^s, \{\langle c_{1,t_{1,u},v_{1,w},d_{1,e}}, c_{2,t_{2,u},v_{2,w},d_{2,e}}, \dots, c_{n,t_{n,u},v_{n,w},d_{n,e}} \rangle\}], \quad (32)$$

where, for r $(1 \le r \le n)$,

$$c_{r,t_u,v_w,d_e} = \begin{cases} a^{\beta}_{r,k_i,l_j,h_g}, & \text{if } t_u = k_i \in K^r, v_w = l_j \in L^r \text{ and } d_e = h_g \in H^r \\ \perp, & \text{otherwise} \end{cases} \quad (33)$$

Decomposition: Given a set of n-dimensional vectors $\mathcal{X}$, an IM with elements from $\mathcal{X}$ is denoted by A^{β}. Then,

$$Pr_s(A^{\beta}) = \begin{cases} I_{\emptyset}, & \text{if } s \le 0 \text{ or } s > n \\ \\ A^{\beta}_s, & \text{otherwise} \end{cases}, \quad (34)$$

where $A^{\beta}_s = [K^s, L^s, H^s, \{a^{\beta,s}_{k_i,l_j,h_g}\}]$ and $a^s_{k_i,l_j,h_g}$ is the s-th component of vector $\langle a^1_{k_i,l_j,h_g}, a^2_{k_i,l_j,h_g}, \ldots, a^n_{k_i,l_j,h_g}\rangle$, which is an element of A^{β}. The operation "decomposition" ($\sharp$), which is the opposite of the operation "composition" ($\flat$), is defined as follows: $\sharp(A^{\beta}) = \{@Pr_s(A^{\beta})|1 \le s \le n\}$.

Internal subtraction of IMs' components:

Let A and B be 2-D CIC-IFIMs. Then,

$$IO_{-_{(\max,\min,*)}}(\langle k_i, l_j; rf^{\beta}_{k_i,l_j,h_g} A^{\beta}\rangle, \langle p_r, q_s; rfn^{\beta_1}_{k_i,l_j,h_g} B^{\beta_1}\rangle) \quad (35)$$

$$= [K, L, \{\langle \gamma_{t_u,v_w}, \delta_{t_u,v_w}; *(rf^{\beta}_{k_i,l_j,h_g}, rfn^{\beta_1}_{k_i,l_j,h_g})\rangle\}],$$

where $k_i \in K,\ l_j \in L;\ p_r \in P,\ q_s \in Q$ and

$$\langle \gamma_{t_u,v_w}, \delta_{t_u,v_w}\rangle = \begin{cases} \langle \mu_{t_u,v_w}, \nu_{t_u,v_w}; *(rf^{\beta}_{k_i,l_j,h_g}, rfn^{\beta_1}_{k_i,l_j,h_g})\rangle, & \text{if } t_u \ne k_i \in K, v_w \ne l_j \in L \\ \langle \max(0, \mu_{k_i,l_j} - \rho_{p_r,q_s}); *(rf^{\beta}_{k_i,l_j,h_g}, rfn^{\beta_1}_{k_i,l_j,h_g}) & \text{if } t_u = k_i \in K, \\ \min(1, \nu_{k_i,l_j} + \sigma_{p_r,q_s}, 1 - \mu_{k_i,l_j} + \rho_{p_r,q_s})\rangle & v_w = l_j \in L \end{cases} \quad (36)$$

4. A Confidence Interval Circular Intuitionistic Fuzzy Algorithm (CIC-IFFr) to Identify the Most Benefiting Franchisor

This section defines a new method known as CIC-IFFr for master and sub-franchise selection that uses confidence-interval circular intuitionistic fuzzy sets (CIC-IFSs) and confidence-interval intuitionistic fuzzy IMs (CIC-IFIMs), extending the circular IF algorithm for franchise selection [31]. The criteria values in this model are determined by experts with dynamic ranks and are expressed as CIC-IF numbers. The investor determines the significance of each condition. Circular intuitionistic fuzzy data are created from the input data based on a confidence probability coefficient β that the decision maker determines. Ten distinct scenarios—ranging from extremely pessimistic to extremely optimistic—are available for decision-makers to select from.

To find the best master and sub-franchise, let us expand the circular IF algorithm for franchise selection from [31].

In an undefined market, a franchising corporation in Europe is seeking applicants to be master (sub-)franchisees. The decision maker determines the confidence probability coefficient β. Candidates will be assessed using a system of criteria $\{c_1, \ldots, c_j, \ldots, c_n\}$ (for $j = 1, \ldots, n$). Experts $E = \{d_1, \ldots, d_s, \ldots, d_D\}$ are involved in the evaluation process of potential franchisees. Their competence coefficients are denoted as $r_s(1 \le s \le D)$. For $1 \le i \le m, 1 \le j \le n$, and $1 \le s \le D$, professional evaluations of possible franchisees are conducted. The assessments are provided as IF data ev_{k_i,c_j,d_s}. At time h_f, the final franchisee evaluations are computed as CIC-IFTs $fi^{\beta}{}_{k_i,v_e,h_f}$ (for $1 \le i \le m$). From the standpoint of the franchise brand v_e at a given moment h_f at a probability β, these CIC-IF priorities are weighed as $pk^{\beta}{}_{c_j,v_e,h_f}$ of the criteria c_j (for $j = 1, \ldots, n$). Finding the master (sub-)franchisee for Europe who best suits the franchise organization at a probability β is the optimal outcome.

To find the optimal solution of this problem, we need to expand the algorithm from [31] to convert the input data into CIC-IFTs at β confidence level. Ten scenarios are provided by the algorithm to help choose the best candidate. It makes use of the $*$-operation, which offers two choices: max and min, based on the level of environmental uncertainty.

The CIC-IFFr algorithm consists of the subsequent operations.

Step 1. The experts evaluate the candidates using the initial algorithmic criteria. IM $EVR[K, C, E, \{ev_{k_i,c_j,d_s}\}]$, $K=\{k_1, k_2, \ldots, k_m\}$, $C=\{c_1, c_2, \ldots, c_n\}$ and $E=\{d_1, d_2, \ldots, d_D\}$ is constructed. A C-IFT $r_s = \langle \delta_s, \epsilon_s; rad_s \rangle, (1 \leq s \leq D)$, where components can be interpreted as expressing the competence (δ_s) or ineptitude (ϵ_s) with a radius around center rad_s, should specify each expert's score coefficient. The IM $EVR^*[K, C, E, \{ev^*{}_{k_i,c_j,d_s}\}]$ was developed by:

$$EVR^* = r_1 pr_{K,C,d_1} EV \oplus_{(\circ_1,\circ_2)} r_2 pr_{K,C,d_2} EV \ldots \oplus_{(\circ_1,\circ_2)} r_D pr_{K,C,d_D} EV. \tag{37}$$

$$EVR := EVR^*(evr_{k_i,c_j,d_s} = evr^*_{k_i,c_j,d_s}, \forall k_i \in K, \forall c_j \in C, \forall d_s \in E).$$

The volatility in the market has left the specialists unsure about their assessments. Using the following methods, the assessments are converted into IFPs. The intervals of the expert assessments for each candidate at a given time h_f by all criteria are provided: $[p^{1,f}_{k_i,c_j,d_s}; p^{2,f}_{k_i,c_j,d_s}]$ and let

$$A_{min,i,j,s,f} = \min_{1 \leq i \leq m, 1 \leq j \leq n, 1 \leq s \leq D} p^{1,f}_{k_i,c_j,d_s} < \max_{1 \leq i \leq m, 1 \leq j \leq n, 1 \leq s \leq D} p^{2,f}_{k_i,c_j,d_s} = A_{max,i,j,s,f}. \tag{38}$$

For the interval between $[p^{1,f}_{k_i,c_j,d_s}; p^{2,f}_{k_i,c_j,d_s}]$, at a time point h_f, we employ the IFP [54] format to construct the c_j-th criterion and the d_s-th expert evaluation for the k_i-th candidate as follows:

$$\mu_{k_i,c_j,d_s,h_f} = \frac{p^{1,f}_{k_i,c_j,d_s} - A_{min,i,j,s,f}}{A_{max,i,j,s,f} - A_{min,i,j,s,f}}, \nu_{k_i,c_j,d_s,h_f} = \frac{A_{max,i,j,s,f} - p^{2,f}_{k_i,c_j,d_s}}{A_{max,i,j,s,f} - A_{min,i,j,s,f}}. \tag{39}$$

Some of the experts' conclusions might not be accurate. In [54], several techniques for altering the evaluations of flawed experts are investigated. Next, $EV[K, C, E, \{ev_{k_i,c_j,d_s}\}]$, $K=\{k_1, k_2, \ldots, k_m\}$, $C=\{c_1, c_2, \ldots, c_n\}$ and $E=\{d_1, d_2, \ldots, d_D\}$ are created by converting the IM EVR into intuitionistic fuzzy IM. The elements $\{ev_{k_i,c_j,d_s}\} = \langle \mu_{k_i,c_j,d_s}, \nu_{k_i,c_j,d_s} \rangle$ (for $1 \leq i \leq m, 1 \leq j \leq n, 1 \leq s \leq D$) of the matrix EV are unpredictable because of the state of the economy and they are IF valuations of the d_s-th expert for the k_i-th franchisor by the c_j-th criterion. $EV := EV^*(ev_{k_i,c_j,d_s} = ev^*_{k_i,c_j,d_s}, \forall k_i \in K, \forall c_j \in C, \forall d_s \in E)$. Next, we continue to *Step 2*.

Step 2. The resulting candidate scores ($ev_{k_i,c_j,d_s} \forall k_i \in K, \forall c_j \in L, \forall d_s \in E$) will be translated into CIC-IFTs at a certain β probability in order to represent the uncertainty in the data. Let us calculate the centers of the CIC-IFTs: $pi_{ave} = \overline{ev^*}_{k_i,c_j,d_s} (\forall k_i \in K, \forall c_j \in C, \forall d_s \in E)$ of the candidates' marks through the aggregation operation $\alpha_{E,\#_q}$ over EV^*.

We acquire the IM $PI^{ave}[K, C, h_f, \{pi^{ave}{}_{k_i,c_j,h_f}\}]$.

$$PI^{ave} = \alpha_{E,\#_2}(EV^*, h_f) = \left\{ \begin{array}{c|ccc} h_f & c_1 & \cdots & c_n \\ \hline k_1 & \overset{D}{\underset{s=1}{\#_2}} \langle \mu_{k_1,c_1,d_s}, \nu_{k_1,c_1,d_s} \rangle & \cdots & \overset{D}{\underset{s=1}{\#_2}} \langle \mu_{k_1,c_n,d_s}, \nu_{k_1,c_n,d_s} \rangle \\ \vdots & \vdots & \cdots & \vdots \\ k_m & \overset{D}{\underset{s=1}{\#_2}} \langle \mu_{k_m,c_1,d_s}, \nu_{k_m,c_1,d_s} \rangle & \cdots & \overset{D}{\underset{s=1}{\#_2}} \langle \mu_{k_m,c_n,d_s}, \nu_{k_m,c_n,d_s} \rangle \end{array} \right\}. \tag{40}$$

Let us use the operation "decomposition" to divide the degrees of belonging and non-belonging of the elements of PI^{ave} into index matrices PI^{ave}_{μ} and PI^{ave}_{ν}.

$$@Pr_1(PI^{ave}) = PI^{ave}_{\mu} = \left\{ \begin{array}{c|ccc} h_f & c_1 & \cdots & c_n \\ \hline k_1 & \overset{D}{\underset{s=1}{\#_2}} \mu_{k_1,c_1,d_s} & \cdots & \overset{D}{\underset{s=1}{\#_2}} \mu_{k_1,c_n,d_s} \\ \vdots & \vdots & \cdots & \vdots \\ k_m & \overset{D}{\underset{s=1}{\#_2}} \mu_{k_m,c_1,d_s} & \cdots & \overset{D}{\underset{s=1}{\#_2}} \mu_{k_m,c_n,d_s} \end{array} \right\}; \tag{41}$$

$$@Pr_2(PI^{ave}) = PI^{ave}_{\nu} = \left\{ \begin{array}{c|ccc} h_f & c_1 & \cdots & c_n \\ \hline k_1 & \overset{D}{\underset{s=1}{\#_2}} \nu_{k_1,c_1,d_s} & \cdots & \overset{D}{\underset{s=1}{\#_2}} \nu_{k_1,c_n,d_s} \\ \vdots & \vdots & \cdots & \vdots \\ k_m & \overset{D}{\underset{s=1}{\#_2}} \nu_{k_m,c_1,d_s} & \cdots & \overset{D}{\underset{s=1}{\#_2}} \nu_{k_m,c_n,d_s} \end{array} \right\}. \tag{42}$$

Let us use the "decomposition" operation to partition the degrees of belonging and non-belonging of the elements of EV^* into index matrices. We will investigate $EV^*_{\nu} = @Pr_2(EV^*)$, as well as $EV^*_{\mu} = @Pr_1(EV^*)$. Here, are definitions for the aggregation operations $\alpha_{E,\#_\sigma}(EV^*_{\mu}, h_f)$ and $\alpha_{E,\#_\sigma}(EV^*_{\nu}, h_f)$. These procedures calculate the standard deviation [59,60] of the expert judgments of the candidates according to the criteria, corresponding to their degrees of belonging and non-belonging.

$$\alpha_{E,\#_\sigma}(EV^*_{\mu}, h_f) \left\{ \begin{array}{c|ccc} h_f & c_1 & \cdots & c_n \\ \hline k_1 & \overset{D}{\underset{s=1}{\#_\sigma}} \mu_{k_1,c_1,d_s} & \cdots & \overset{D}{\underset{s=1}{\#_\sigma}} \mu_{k_1,c_n,d_s} \\ \vdots & \vdots & \cdots & \vdots \\ k_m & \overset{D}{\underset{s=1}{\#_\sigma}} \mu_{k_m,c_1,d_s} & \cdots & \overset{D}{\underset{s=1}{\#_\sigma}} \mu_{k_m,c_n,d_s} \end{array} \right\}; \tag{43}$$

$$\alpha_{E,\#_\sigma}(EV^*_{\nu}, h_f) \left\{ \begin{array}{c|ccc} h_f & c_1 & \cdots & c_n \\ \hline k_1 & \overset{D}{\underset{s=1}{\#_\sigma}} \nu_{k_1,c_1,d_s} & \cdots & \overset{D}{\underset{s=1}{\#_\sigma}} \nu_{k_1,c_n,d_s} \\ \vdots & \vdots & \cdots & \vdots \\ k_m & \overset{D}{\underset{s=1}{\#_\sigma}} \nu_{k_m,c_1,d_s} & \cdots & \overset{D}{\underset{s=1}{\#_\sigma}} \nu_{k_m,c_n,d_s} \end{array} \right\}. \tag{44}$$

Then, we calculate the value of ME at a level α, respectively, by

$$ME_z = z_{\alpha/2}\frac{\sigma_{average}}{\sqrt{D}} \text{ or } ME_{average,t} = t_{\alpha/2}\frac{s_{average}}{\sqrt{D}},$$

depending on whether there are more or fewer than thirty participating experts D in the evaluation, which is the value of ME at a level of confidence α.

We perform this by employing the averaged standard deviation $s_{average}$ of the expert evaluations for the k_i-th candidate for the c_j-th criterion [59] and the normal distribution, or t-distribution, respectively. Both when the evaluated IM EV has an intuitionistic fuzzy shape, and when it contains crisp number elements, the following computations can be used. The following calculations are performed during the process:

$$ME.\alpha_{E,\#_\sigma}(EV_\mu^*, h_f); ME.\alpha_{E,\#_\sigma}(EV_\nu^*, h_f);$$

$$PI_\mu^{leftCB}[K, C, h_f] = PI_\mu^{ave} \ominus_{(\circ_1,\circ_2,*)} ME.\alpha_{E,\#_\sigma}(EV_\mu^*, h_f);$$

$$PI_\mu^{rightCB}[K, C, h_f] = PI_\mu^{ave} \oplus_{(\circ_1,\circ_2,*)} ME.\alpha_{E,\#_\sigma}(EV_\mu^*, h_f);$$

$$PI_\nu^{leftCB}[K, C, h_f] = PI_\nu^{ave} \ominus_{(\circ_1,\circ_2,*)} ME.\alpha_{E,\#_\sigma}(EV_\nu^*, h_f)$$

$$\text{and } PI_\nu^{rightCB}[K, C, h_f] = PI_\nu^{ave} \oplus_{(\circ_1,\circ_2,*)} ME.\alpha_{E,\#_\sigma}(EV_\nu^*, h_f).$$

These IMs, produced by the "composition" procedure, show the left and right bounds of the confidence intervals for the expert opinions for each candidate based on the given criteria:

$$PI^{leftCB}[K, C, h_f] = \flat\{PI_\mu^{ave} \ominus_{(\circ_1,\circ_2,*)} ME.\alpha_{E,\#_\sigma}(EV_\mu^*, h_f), PI_\nu^{ave} \ominus_{(\circ_1,\circ_2,*)} ME.\alpha_{E,\#_\sigma}(EV_\nu^*, h_f);\}$$
$$PI^{rightCB}[K, C, h_f] = \flat\{PI_\mu^{ave} \oplus_{(\circ_1,\circ_2,*)} ME.\alpha_{E,\#_\sigma}(EV_\mu^*, h_f), PI_\nu^{ave} \oplus_{(\circ_1,\circ_2,*)} ME.\alpha_{E,\#_\sigma}(EV_\nu^*, h_f).\}$$

We next proceed to *Step 3*.

Step 3. The system for evaluating master (sub-)franchisees will now be optimized. We suggest using inter-criteria analysis to eliminate slower or more expensive criteria from the franchisee assessment system because research indicates that they closely correlate with other criteria in intuitionistic fuzzy settings (ICrA, [65]). Let an IFP be $\langle\gamma, \delta\rangle$.

If $\mu_{C_k,C_l} > \gamma$ and $\nu_{C_k,C_l} < \delta$, then the criteria C_k and C_l are in (γ, δ)-positive consonance. If $\mu_{C_k,C_l} < \gamma$ and $\nu_{C_k,C_l} > \delta$, then the criteria C_k and C_l are in (γ, δ)-negative consonance. In other cases, C_k and C_l are in (γ, δ)-dissonance.

For the IM $PI^{ave} = [K, C, h_f, \{pi^{ave}{}_{k_i,c_g,h_f}\}]$, consonant criteria are sought using the ICrA method. By applying the IM reduction operation on matrix PI^{ave}, the evaluation franchise system gets rid of more expensive, time-consuming, or sophisticated criteria. We proceed to *Step 4*.

Step 4. CIC-IFIM $A^\beta[K, C, h_f, \{a^\beta_{k_i,c_g,h_f}\}]$ can now be computed, which denotes the master (sub-)franchisees' existing evaluations utilizing the methodology from [31]:

$$\begin{array}{c|ccc} h_f & c_1 & \cdots & c_n \\ \hline k_1 & \langle\mu^\beta_{k_1,c_1}, \nu^\beta_{k_1,c_1}; rf^\beta_{k_1,c_1}\rangle & \cdots & \langle\mu^\beta_{k_1,c_n}, \nu^\beta_{k_1,c_n}; rf^\beta_{k_1,c_n}\rangle \\ \vdots & \vdots & \cdots & \vdots \\ k_m & \langle\mu^\beta_{k_m,c_1}, \nu^\beta_{k_m,c_1}; rf^\beta_{k_m,c_1}\rangle & \cdots & \langle\mu^\beta_{k_m,c_n}, \nu^\beta_{k_m,c_n}; rf^\beta_{k_m,c_n}\rangle \end{array}, \quad (45)$$

where $K = \{k_1, \ldots, k_i, \ldots, k_m\}, i = 1, \ldots, m; C = \{c_1, \ldots, c_j, \ldots, c_n\}, j = 1, \ldots, n.$

Its elements $a^\beta_{k_i,c_j,h_f}$ (for $i = 1, \ldots, m; j = 1, \ldots, n$) are generated as CIC-IFTs from the IFPs $pi^{ave}{}_{k_i,c_j,h_f}$ using the following operations.

for $j = 1$ to n
for $i = 1$ to m

$$\Big\{ \mu^{\beta}_{k_i,c_j,h_f} = \mu^{pi^T}_{k_i,c_j,h_f}; \nu^{\beta}_{k_i,c_j,h_f} = \nu^{pi^T}_{k_i,c_j,h_f} \tag{46}$$

$$r^{\beta}_{k_i,c_j,h_f} = \max_{1\le s\le D} |\sqrt{(\mu^{ev}_{k_i,c_j,d_s} - \mu^{pi^T}_{k_i,c_j,h_f})^2 + (\nu^{ev}_{k_i,c_j,d_s} - \nu^{pi^T}_{k_i,c_j,h_f})^2|} \Big\}.$$

We proceed to *Step 5*.

Step 5. Thus, a 3-D CIE-IFIM PK is produced. From the standpoint of the chain v_e, the coefficients utilized in the following operation determine how each assessment criterion is weighted for the master (sub-)franchisees:

$$PK^{\beta_1}[C, v_e, h_f, \{pk_{c_j,v_e,h_f}\}] = \begin{array}{c|c} h_f & v_e \\ \hline c_1 & pk_{c_1,v_e,h_f} \\ \vdots & \vdots \\ c_j & pk_{c_j,v_e,h_f} \\ \vdots & \vdots \\ c_n & pk_{c_n,v_e,h_f} \end{array}, \tag{47}$$

where $C = \{c_1, c_2, \ldots, c_n\}$ and the elements pk_{c_j,v_e,h_f} are CIC-IFTs.

The assessment CIC-IFIM

$$FI^{\beta^{new}}[K, v_e, h_f, \{fi^{\beta}_{k_i,v_e,h_f}\}] = A^{\beta} \odot_{(\circ_1,\circ_2,*)} PK^{\beta_1} \tag{48}$$

(for $1 \le i \le m$) for master (sub-)franchisees for the brand v_e includes all of the CIC-IF estimates for the k_i-th franchisee at a particular confidence probability β. $\beta^{new} = min(\beta, \beta_1)$. We go on to *Step 6*.

Step 6. The franchise chain v_e now uses the aggregation operation $\alpha_{K,\#_q,*}(FI^{\beta}, k_0)$ to select the most beneficial master (sub-)franchisee using scenarios ranging from extremely pessimistic to extremely optimistic, based on the value of $q, 1 \le q \le 10$:

$$\alpha_{K,\#_q,*}(FI^{\beta}, k_0) = \begin{array}{c|c} h_f & v_e \\ \hline k_0 & \underset{i=1}{\overset{m}{\#_q,*}} \langle \mu_{k_i,v_e,h_f}, \nu_{k_i,v_e,h_f}, rf^{\beta}_{k_i,v_e,h_f} \rangle \end{array}. \tag{49}$$

We go on to *Step 7*.

Step 7. At this point, the updated rating coefficients for the experts taking part in the assessment are acquired. Assume for the moment that the expert d_s ($s = 1, \ldots, D$) has used γ_s evaluation methods to choose a franchisee. The following processes were used to determine his score, at a specific confidence level β: $r^{\beta}_s = \langle \delta_s, \epsilon_s, \phi^1_s, \phi^2_s \rangle$. Following that, concepts from [54] will modify his updated score.

$$r^{\beta'}_s \langle \delta'_s, \epsilon'_s; \phi^{1'}_s \rangle = \begin{cases} \langle \frac{\delta\gamma+1}{\gamma+1}, \frac{\epsilon\gamma}{\gamma+1}; *(\phi^{1'}_s, \phi^1_s) \rangle, \text{ if the expert's assessment was accurate} \\ \langle \frac{\delta\gamma}{\gamma+1}, \frac{\epsilon\gamma}{\gamma+1}; *(\phi^{1'}_s, \phi^1_s) \rangle, \text{ if the expert has not provided any estimates} \\ \langle \frac{\delta\gamma}{\gamma+1}, \frac{\epsilon\gamma+1}{\gamma+1}; *(\phi^{1'}_s, \phi^1_s) \rangle, \text{if the expert has made an inaccurate assessment} \end{cases} \tag{50}$$

The procedure is finished.

The suggested CIE-IFFr approach has a complexity of $O(Dm^2n^2)$, based on the complexity of ICrA [66]. In the case of more ambiguity, the operation $* = \max$ is used; otherwise, $* = \min$.

The proposed CIE-IFFr technique can be applied to both crisp and CIC-IF data. It can be used without limitations for other kinds of MCGDM problems, and adjusts effectively to the different kinds of data that are present in a fuzzy environment. Ten options, ranging from extremely pessimistic to extremely optimistic, are provided by the suggested method. The procedure can be modified to work with multidimensional data by utilizing the CIC-IFIMs apparatus.

Because of this, the suggested CIC-IF optimal franchisor selection challenge maintains a societal viewpoint while accounting for the preferences of experts and decision-makers.

The CIC-IF data utilized in the optimum franchising problem study represent the uncertain fuzzy environment more than the C-IFTs ones and describe the data's uncertainty with a varied probability β, depending on the chosen confidence level from the decision-maker.

5. A Confidence-Interval Elliptic Intuitionistic Fuzzy Case Study for Selecting Master and Sub-Franchises for Pizza Hut in Europe

In this section, we develop the role of AmRest Holdings SE as the main franchisee, explaining its strategic responsibilities and the sub-franchising process. This introduces the application of the CIC-IFFr technique of Section 4, allowing readers to better understand the practical implications of selecting franchisees in Europe.

The optimal CIC-IF franchisee problem is: Pizza Hut, a global leader in the pizza industry, effectively utilizes this model through its master and sub-franchise arrangements [47]. In Europe, AmRest Holdings SE is a prominent master franchisee for Pizza Hut. The company manages the brand's presence across several European countries, including the Czech Republic, France, Hungary, Poland, and Slovakia. As a master franchisee, AmRest is responsible for the overall strategy, marketing, and operational standards for Pizza Hut in these regions. Additionally, the holding holds the authority to sub-franchise, selling the rights to operate individual Pizza Hut units to local entrepreneurs. AmRest Holdings SE (v_e) searches for sub-franchisees of Pizza Hut in European countries, including the Czech Republic, France, Hungary, Poland, and Slovakia.

Utilizing the knowledge of specialists d_1, d_2, and d_3, they develop a set of standards for assessing possible franchisees k_i (for $1 \leq i \leq 4$) in European nations. The Pizza Hut [47] franchise company's requirements form the basis of the procedure for selecting franchisees, which is composed of four groups of criteria:

- C_1—Financial stability and investment capability: Candidates for sub-franchisee must meet the following minimal standards in order to be considered: EUR 650,000 in net worth; EUR 350,000 in liquid assets; and a strong credit history and report. The prospective master franchisee needs to show that they have the financial wherewithal to contribute to the growth and development of the franchise system.
- C_2—Experience and market understanding: a competent applicant would possess extensive understanding of the local market conditions in addition to successful ownership or management experience in the retail or restaurant industries.
- C_3—Growth mindset: a well-defined and workable strategy for growing the franchise network inside the assigned region.
- C_4—An enthusiasm for operations is required of a Pizza Hut franchisee. They should be completely "hands-on" in the business, customer-focused, meticulous, and able to develop a team of people.

For each criterion (financial stability, experience, growth mindset, and operational enthusiasm), we have provided deeper insights into why these criteria are critical for sub-franchisee success. For instance, financial stability ensures the sub-franchisee can handle long-term commitments, while operational enthusiasm guarantees that they are hands-on in maintaining Pizza Hut's service standards.

The ranking coefficients for the experts $\{r_1, r_2, r_3\}(1 \leq s \leq 3)$ are given. Expert evaluations of the four courier franchise chains were determined by using the criteria; the results were then displayed as IF data ev_{k_i, c_j, d_s} (for $1 \leq i \leq 4, 1 \leq j \leq 4, 1 \leq s \leq 3$).

The sub-franchisees' final CIC-IF evaluations $fi^{beta}{}_{k_i,v_e,h_f}$ (for $1 \leq i \leq 4$) are based on the priorities $pk^{\beta}{}_{c_j,v_e}$ of criteria c_j (for $j = 1, \ldots, 4$), from the standpoint of the master franchise v_e at time h_f at a certain probability level 95%.

We utilize the CIC-IFFr method from Section 4 to determine the best solution to the problem in order to determine the ideal franchisee.

Step 1. 3-D $EV[K, C, E, \{es_{k_i,c_j,d_s}\}]$ are the professional judgments at this step. For the k_i-th franchisee (for $1 \leq i \leq 4, 1 \leq j \leq 4, 1 \leq s \leq 3$), is constructed the expert's estimations by the c_j-th criterion. The experts' rank coefficients are given as $\{r_1, r_2, r_3\} = \{\langle 0.4, 0.1\rangle, \langle 0.5, 0.1\rangle, \langle 0.6, 0.1\rangle\}$.

The matrix of assessments is calculated by the operations

$$EV^*[K, C, E, \{ev^*\}] = r_1 pr_{K,C,d_1} EV \oplus_{(\circ_1,\circ_2)} r_2 pr_{K,C,d_2} EV \oplus_{(\circ_1,\circ_2)} r_3 pr_{K,C,d_3} EV; EV := EV^*$$

and its IF form is

d_1	c_1	c_2	c_3	c_4
k_1	$\langle 0.12, 0.73\rangle$	$\langle 0.20, 0.69\rangle$	$\langle 0.21, 0.70\rangle$	$\langle 0.36, 0.52\rangle$
k_2	$\langle 0.36, 0.24\rangle$	$\langle 0.12, 0.69\rangle$	$\langle 0.20, 0.42\rangle$	$\langle 0.52, 0.24\rangle$
k_3	$\langle 0.12, 0.6\rangle$	$\langle 0.36, 0.43\rangle$	$\langle 0.36, 0.51\rangle$	$\langle 0.36, 0.42\rangle$
k_4	$\langle 0.28, 0.33\rangle$	$\langle 0.20, 0.51\rangle$	$\langle 0.52, 0.24\rangle$	$\langle 0.20, 0.51\rangle$

d_2	c_1	c_2	c_3	c_4
k_1	$\langle 0.14, 0.6\rangle$	$0.22, 0.33\rangle$	$\langle 0.18, 0.61\rangle$	$\langle 0.25, 0.34\rangle$
k_2	$\langle 0.25, 0.43\rangle$	$\langle 0.25, 0.61\rangle$	$\langle 0.11, 0.69\rangle$	$\langle 0.32, 0.42\rangle$
k_3	$\langle 0.18, 0.78\rangle$	$\langle 0.25, 0.51\rangle$	$\langle 0.46, 0.24\rangle$	$\langle 0.46, 0.15\rangle$
k_4	$\langle 0.32, 0.42\rangle$	$\langle 0.11, 0.69\rangle$	$\langle 0.53, 0.15\rangle$	$\langle 0.25, 0.52\rangle$

d_3	c_1	c_2	c_3	c_4
k_1	$\langle 0.13, 0.78\rangle$	$\langle 0.31, 0.51\rangle$	$\langle 0.13, 0.33\rangle$	$\langle 0.31, 0.60\rangle$
k_2	$\langle 0.31, 0.69\rangle$	$\langle 0.22, 0.78\rangle$	$\langle 0.31, 0.51\rangle$	$\langle 0.41, 0.51\rangle$
k_3	$\langle 0.13, 0.78\rangle$	$\langle 0.31, 0.60\rangle$	$\langle 0.22, 0.60\rangle$	$\langle 0.49, 0.24\rangle$
k_4	$\langle 0.13, 0.03\rangle$	$\langle 0.22, 0.69\rangle$	$\langle 0.40, 0.42\rangle$	$\langle 0.40, 0.50\rangle$

Step 2. It is assumed that we have stability in the economic situation in which franchisee candidates are evaluated. In this case, the realistic form of the aggregation operator $\alpha_{E,\#_6}$ is used. If the economic situation improves, then the optimistic form of the aggregation operation will be used $\alpha_{E,\#_10}$, while in the case of significant environmental instability and inflation, the pessimistic form $\alpha_{E,\#_1}$ of the aggregation operation will be applied. Now, let us use the realistic aggregation procedure to obtain the centers of the CIC-IFTs (or mathematical expectations). $\alpha_{E,\#_6}$ over EV^*. $pi_{ave} = \overline{ev^*}_{k_i,c_j,d_s} \forall k_i \in K, \forall c_j \in C, \forall d_s \in E)$ are the applicants' grades. We acquire the IM $PI^{ave}[K, C, h_f, \{pi^{ave}{}_{k_i,c_j,h_f}\}]$:

$PI^{ave} = \alpha_{E,\#_6}(EV^*, h_f) =$

h_f	c_1	c_2	c_3	c_4
k_1	$\langle 0.13, 0.71\rangle$	$\langle 0.24, 0.51\rangle$	$\langle 0.17, 0.66\rangle$	$\langle 0.31, 0.48\rangle$
k_2	$\langle 0.31, 0.39\rangle$	$\langle 0.2, 0.74\rangle$	$\langle 0.21, 0.57\rangle$	$\langle 0.41, 0.39\rangle$
k_3	$\langle 0.14, 0.72\rangle$	$\langle 0.31, 0.51\rangle$	$\langle 0.35, 0.45\rangle$	$\langle 0.44, 0.27\rangle$
k_4	$\langle 0.24, 0.49\rangle$	$\langle 0.17, 0.63\rangle$	$\langle 0.48, 0.27\rangle$	$\langle 0.28, 0.48\rangle$

We calculate the results in accordance with the three experts involved in the evaluation.

$$ME = ME_{average,t} = \frac{t_{\alpha/2} . s_{average}}{\sqrt{D}} = 0.19$$

at a given confidence level 95%.

Next, we compute the following IMs in order:

$$ME.\alpha_{E,\#_\sigma}(EV^*_\mu, h_f); ME.\alpha_{E,\#_\sigma}(EV^*_\nu, h_f);$$

$$PI_{\mu}^{leftCB}[K,C,h_f] = PI_{\mu}^{ave} \ominus_{(\circ_1,\circ_2,*)} ME.\alpha_{E,\#_\sigma}(EV_{\mu}^{*},h_f);$$

$$PI_{\mu}^{rightCB}[K,C,h_f] = PI_{\mu}^{ave} \oplus_{(\circ_1,\circ_2,*)} ME.\alpha_{E,\#_\sigma}(EV_{\mu}^{*},h_f);$$

$$PI_{\nu}^{leftCB}[K,C,h_f] = PI_{\nu}^{ave} \ominus_{(\circ_1,\circ_2,*)} ME.\alpha_{E,\#_\sigma}(EV_{\nu}^{*},h_f)$$

$$\text{and } PI_{\nu}^{rightCB}[K,C,h_f] = PI_{\nu}^{ave} \oplus_{(\circ_1,\circ_2,*)} ME.\alpha_{E,\#_\sigma}(EV_{\nu}^{*},h_f).$$

Step 3. At this stage, we applied $\gamma = 0.80$ and $\delta = 0.10$ to the matrix PI^{ave} using the ICrA. It is determined that there are no criteria that rely on consonants based on ICrA. In the $\mu - \nu$ view result matrix (cf. Table 1), the outcomes are displayed as an IM.

Table 1. The InterCriteria correlations are provided by the IFPs.

	C_1	C_2	C_3	C_4
C_1	—	$\langle 0.67, 0.28\rangle$	$\langle 0.77, 0.14\rangle$	$\langle 0.72, 0.22\rangle$
C_2	$\langle 0.67, 0.86\rangle$	—	$\langle 0.72, 0.24\rangle$	$\langle 0.78, 0.16\rangle$
C_3	$\langle 0.77, 0.14\rangle$	$\langle 0.72, 0.24\rangle$	—	$\langle 0.75, 0.22\rangle$
C_4	$\langle 0.72, 0.22\rangle$	$\langle 0.78, 0.16\rangle$	$\langle 0.75, 0.22\rangle$	—

Step 4. It is now possible to compute CIC-IFIM $A^{\beta}[K, C, h_f\{a^{\beta}_{k_i,c_g,h_f}\}]$, which indicates the sub-franchisees' present assessments with a confidence level of $\alpha = 5\%$ according to the following criteria:

h_f	c_1	c_2	c_3	c_4
k_1	$\langle 0.13, 0.70; 0.75\rangle$	$\langle 0.24, 0.52; 0.77\rangle$	$\langle 0.17, 0.66; 0.78\rangle$	$\langle 0.31, 0.48; 0.76\rangle$
k_2	$\langle 0.31, 0.39; 0.76\rangle$	$\langle 0.20, 0.66; 0.86\rangle$	$\langle 0.21, 0.57; 1.03\rangle$	$\langle 0.41, 0.39; 0.76\rangle$
k_3	$\langle 0.14, 0.72; 0.79\rangle$	$\langle 0.30, 0.51; 0.76\rangle$	$\langle 0.35, 0.45; 0.82\rangle$	$\langle 0.44, 0.27; 0.94\rangle$
k_4	$\langle 0.24, 0.48; 0.94\rangle$	$\langle 0.18, 0.63; 0.85\rangle$	$\langle 0.48, 0.28; 1.03\rangle$	$\langle 0.28, 0.49; 0.87\rangle$

Step 5. These coefficients are used in the next phase on a 3-D CIC-IFIM PK^{β} to determine the weights assigned to each evaluation criterion from the AmRest Holdings SE.

$PK^{\beta}[C, v_e, h_f, \{pk_{c_j,v_e,h_f}\}] =$

h_f	v_e
c_1	$\langle 0.80, 0.10; 0.02\rangle$
c_2	$\langle 0.60, 0.20; 0.02\rangle$
c_3	$\langle 0.80, 0.10; 0.02\rangle$
c_4	$\langle 0.90, 0.10; 0.02\rangle$

The CIC-IFIM $FI^{\beta}[K, v_e, h_f, \{fi_{k_i,v_e,h_f}\}] = A \odot_{(\circ_1,\circ_2,min)} PK^{\beta}$ (for $1 \le i \le m$) is created. We assume that the market environment is stable and the fuzziness of the parameters is lower, in which case we will apply the aggregation operation $\alpha_{K,\#_1 0,min}$, and operation $*$ on the radii of the C-IFTs will be the minimum. Based on the optimistic situation, (for $1 \le i \le m$) contains the complete estimates of the k_i-th franchisee:

$FI =$

h_f	v_e
k_1	$\langle 0.48, 0.16; 0.02\rangle$
k_2	$\langle 0.58, 0.10; 0.02\rangle$
k_3	$\langle 0.64, 0.06; 0.02\rangle$
k_4	$\langle 0.61, 0.06; 0.02\rangle$

Step 6. With a maximum acceptance degree of 0.64 and a minimum rejection degree of 0.06, the super optimistic aggregation process $\alpha_{K,\#_1 0,min}(FI^{\beta}, k_0)$, produces k_3 as the optimal Pizza Hut franchisee. If the future is unknown, and the environment in which decisions are made is unpredictable, the decision-makers in a gloomy condition (ultra pessimistic) will choose the candidate k_1 with the lowest degree of membership (0.48) and the largest degree of non-membership (0.16).

Step 7. Finally, we take into consideration that senior experts evaluated the experts' assessments for accuracy and concluded that they are correct from the standpoint of IF logic [54]. These are their updated rating coefficients, with a confidence level of $\alpha = 5\%$:

$$\{\langle 0.64, 0.09; 0.02\rangle, \langle 0.55, 0.09; 0.02\rangle, \langle 0.45, 0.09; 0.02\rangle\}.$$

The decision-maker will favor the extreme pessimistic scenario in situations where there is a great deal of uncertainty; the realistic scenario in situations where there are only minor deviations in the market parameters; and the super optimistic scenario in situations where the market parameters are stable uncertainty situations, as defined by CIE-IF logic; hence, we were unable to compare the recommended CIE-IFKP method for franchisor optimization with other methods.

The question of whether little differences in the input parameter values used had an effect on the model's conclusions arises after the CIC-IFFr results. Evaluating the created model's results' sensitivity and resistance to changes in the input variables is crucial to solving the CIC-IFFr problem. The CIC-IFFr outcomes are significantly influenced by the criterion weights.

A sensitivity study [67] with eight alternative scenarios has been carried out to examine the effects of varying the weight of each criterion on the ranking results by $\pm 10\%$, $\pm 25\%$, $\pm 50\%$, and $\pm 75\%$, in that order. Eight distinct modifications to the study's criterion weights were performed during the research, and the outcomes varied according on the scenarios that were explored.

To identify other options, the sensitivity of franchisee ranking to criteria weights is investigated. Candidate k_3 is the best choice if the first criterion is given top priority. Candidate k_4 is the best choice if the second criterion is given top priority. Candidate k_2 is the best choice if the third criterion is given top priority, and candidate k_1 is the best choice if the fourth criterion is given top priority. In Section 5, we provided a detailed explanation of the franchisee selection using the CIC-IFFr approach, by determining the CIC-IF evaluations of the candidates according to the criteria. This addresses the uncertainty present in decision-making processes and shows how these confidence intervals assist in selecting a reliable sub-franchisee.

Once an appropriate sub-franchisee is chosen, it is necessary to align the franchisee is goals with the master franchise is growth strategies for more efficient business operations and market penetration.

6. Discussion

The proposed method, which integrates Confidence-Interval Circular Intuitionistic Fuzzy Sets (CIC-IFSs) and Confidence-Interval Intuitionistic Fuzzy Index Matrices (CIC-IFIMs), offers a novel and advanced approach to the decision-making process for master and sub-franchise selection. By embedding confidence intervals within circular intuitionistic fuzzy sets, this model significantly enhances the ability to capture uncertainty, vagueness, and hesitancy in expert evaluations—critical factors often encountered in real-world decision-making scenarios. The inclusion of competence coefficients further refines the process by appropriately weighting expert opinions according to their perceived reliability, ensuring that more credible evaluations exert a stronger influence on the final decision.

The introduction of a dynamic evaluation framework is one of the main contributions of this study. Unlike traditional models, where criteria values are static, the proposed method allows for dynamic ranking by experts, tailored to the specific context and requirements of the investor. This flexibility is particularly valuable in complex decision-making environments like franchise selection, where the importance of different criteria may vary significantly based on the specific circumstances.

Moreover, the CIC-IFFr method provides decision-makers with a spectrum of scenarios, from super pessimistic to super optimistic, enabling a more nuanced analysis. This capability to simulate various outcomes under different levels of uncertainty and optimism adds a robust layer of adaptability to the decision-making process. The use of ten forms of aggregation operations over index matrices allows the model to accommodate different decision-making preferences, making it highly versatile and adaptable to various decision contexts.

The application of this model to Pizza Hut's European market serves as a practical demonstration of its efficacy. The study's findings suggest that the CIE-IFFr approach is well-suited to identifying franchisees that align with the brand's strategic and operational criteria, thereby supporting better-informed, resilient, and sustainable franchise selection decisions. The method's ability to integrate both circular intuitionistic fuzzy data and regular data further underscores its versatility, making it applicable to a wide range of decision-making scenarios beyond franchise selection. Crisp and CIC-IF data can be used with the suggested CIE-IFFr approach. It can be used without limitations and adjusts effectively to the different kinds of MCGDM problems that are present in a fuzzy environment. The proposed approach offers 10 decision scenarios from super pessimistic to super optimistic. The use of the CIC-IFIMs apparatus enables the algorithm used to be extended to be used on multidimensional data.

Experts evaluate franchisees and consider the importance of the criteria while evaluating them in order to determine which is the greatest alternative. For this reason, the recommended CIC-IF optimum franchisor selection challenge takes into account the preferences of both experts and decision-makers while maintaining a social perspective. The CIC-IFTs data utilized in the optimum franchising problem study represent the uncertain fuzzy environment more than the C-IFTs ones, and describe the data's uncertainty with a varied probability β, depending on the chosen confidence level from the decision-maker.

7. Conclusions

This study presents a pioneering decision-making framework that leverages confidence-interval circular intuitionistic fuzzy sets (CIC-IFSs) and confidence-interval intuitionistic fuzzy index matrices (CIC-IFIMs) to enhance the selection process for master and sub-franchises. By effectively capturing and incorporating uncertainty, vagueness, and hesitancy—along with the integration of competence coefficients—our model offers a more refined and reliable decision-making process. The dynamic criteria evaluation and the capacity to simulate various decision-making scenarios further enhance the model's robustness and adaptability.

Our method has demonstrated several key advantages.

- Introduction of a novel method: The study introduces a unique method that leverages CIC-IFSs for the first time. This new framework is designed to improve the decision-making process specifically for master and sub-franchise selection.
- Enhanced capturing of uncertainty, vagueness, and hesitancy: by embedding confidence intervals within the circular intuitionistic fuzzy sets, the proposed model effectively captures not only the uncertainty and vagueness, but also the hesitancy in expert evaluations.
- Incorporation of competence coefficients: The model refines the decision-making process by integrating competence coefficients, which weight expert opinions based on their perceived reliability. This ensures that more reliable expert judgments have a greater influence on the final decision.
- Robust evaluation framework: the CIC-IFFr method combines the robustness of confidence intervals with the advantages of C-IFSs, leading to a more comprehensive and trustworthy evaluation framework for franchise selection.

- Dynamic criteria evaluation: Criteria values are expressed as CIC-IF numbers and established by experts with dynamic ranks. The significance of each condition is assessed by the investor, adding a layer of adaptability to the model.
- Scenarios for decision-making: the model allows decision-makers to choose from various scenarios, ranging from super pessimistic to super optimistic, by using ten forms of aggregation operations over index matrices.
- Application to real-world case: the study focuses on Pizza Hut's European market, demonstrating the efficacy of the CIE-IFFr approach in selecting franchisees that meet the brand's strategic and operational criteria.
- Improved decision-making framework: the CIC-IFFr technique outperforms previous multi-criteria decision-making methods by integrating probabilistic information, enhancing the quality and integrity of the data used in the evaluation process.
- Versatility of the model: The model is versatile, as it can be applied to both confidence interval circular IF data and regular data, broadening its applicability. Using the IMs as a means of storing large amounts of data allows the algorithm to be easily extended so that it can be used on multidimensional data.

The CIC-IFFr approach exhibits several key advantages.

It provides a nuanced and comprehensive evaluation framework that captures the varying degrees of membership, non-membership, and hesitancy associated with potential franchisees. The integration of confidence intervals strengthens the robustness of the decision-making process by accounting for variability and imprecision in expert judgments. The circular membership function offers greater flexibility and adaptability than traditional IFSs and their extensions, allowing for a more precise representation of criteria values. The application of this method to the European market of Pizza Hut demonstrates its practical relevance and effectiveness, showing that the CIC-IFFr approach can significantly enhance the quality and integrity of franchise selection decisions. The model's versatility, with the ability to handle both circular intuitionistic fuzzy data and regular data, broadens its applicability across various domains.

In conclusion, the proposed CIC-IFFr method represents a substantial advancement in multi-criteria decision-making frameworks, particularly in contexts requiring careful consideration of expert evaluations under uncertainty. Future research could explore its application to other industries and decision-making scenarios, potentially expanding its utility and further validating its effectiveness.

Author Contributions: Conceptualization, V.N.T. and S.T.T.; methodology, V.N.T.; validation, V.N.T., S.T.T., V.T. and I.D.; formal analysis, V.N.T., V.T. and S.T.T.; investigation, V.N.T. and S.T.T.; resources, V.N.T., V.T., S.T.T. and I.D.; data curation, V.N.T. and V.T.; writing—original draft preparation, V.N.T. and S.T.T.; writing—review and editing, V.N.T.; supervision, I.D., S.T.T. and V.T.; project administration, S.T.T.; funding acquisition, I.D. All authors have read and agreed to the published version of the manuscript.

Funding: Work on Sections 2 and 3 has been supported by the Assen Zlatarov University through project Ref. No. NIX-486/2023 "Application of Intuitionistic Fuzzy Logic in Decision Making", work on Sections 1 and 4 has been supported by the Assen Zlatarov University through the project Ref. No. NIX-482/2023 "Modeling Management Decisions with New Analysis Tools in a Fuzzy Environment". Section 5 is supported by the Bulgarian National Science Fund under Project KP-06-N52/5 "Efficient methods for modeling, optimization and decision making".

Institutional Review Board Statement: Not applicable.

Informed Consent Statement: Not applicable.

Data Availability Statement: Data are contained within the article.

Conflicts of Interest: The authors declare no conflicts of interest.

References

1. Alon, I. The organizational determinants of master international franchising. *J. Bus. Entrep.* **2000**, *12*, 1–18.
2. Atanassov, K. Circular Intuitionistic Fuzzy Sets. *J. Intell. Fuzzy Syst.* **2020**, *39*, 5981–5986. [CrossRef]
3. Zadeh, L. Fuzzy Sets. *Inf. Control* **1965**, *8*, 338–353. [CrossRef]
4. Wang, S.; Wen, J.; Li, H.; Rao, C.; Zhao, X. A novel fuzzy comprehensive evaluation model for application effect of connected vehicle system in a tunnel scenario. *Int. J. Fuzzy Syst.* **2022**, *24*, 1986–2004. [CrossRef]
5. Gundogdu, F.K.; Kahraman, C. Spherical fuzzy sets and spherical fuzzy TOPSIS method. *J. Intell. Fuzzy Syst.* **2019**, *36*, 337–352. [CrossRef]
6. Alcantud, J.C.R. Complemental fuzzy sets: A semantic justification of q-rung orthopair fuzzy sets. *IEEE Trans. Fuzzy Syst. Publ. IEEE Neural Netw. Counc.* **2023**, *31*, 4262–4270. [CrossRef]
7. Xiao, Q.; Gao, M.; Chen, L.; Jiang, J. Dynamic multi-attribute evaluation of digital economy development in China: A perspective from interaction effect. *Technol. Econ. Dev. Econ.* **2023**, *29*, 1728–1752. [CrossRef]
8. Atanassov, K.T. Intuitionistic Fuzzy Sets. VII ITKR Session, Sofia, 20-23 June 1983 (Deposed in Centr. Sci.-Techn. Library of the Bulg. Acad. of Sci., 1697/84) (in Bulgarian). *Int. J. Bioautom.* **2013**, *20*, S1–S6.
9. Davvaz, B.; Sadrabadi, E.H. An application of intuitionistic fuzzy sets in medicine. *Int. J. Biomath.* **2016**, *9*, 81–95. [CrossRef]
10. Ejegwa, P.A.; Anum, M.T.; Isife, K.I. A new method of distance measure between intuitionistic fuzzy sets and its application in admission procedure. *J. Uncertain Syst.* **2024**, *17*, 2440005. [CrossRef]
11. Chen, T.-Y. A circular intuitionistic fuzzy assignment model with a parameterized scoring rule for multiple criteria assessment methodology. *Adv. Eng. Inform.* **2024**, *61*, 102479. [CrossRef]
12. Traneva, V.; Tranev, S. Intuitionistic Fuzzy Model for Franchisee Selection. In *Intelligent and Fuzzy Systems*; Kahraman, C., Tolga, A.C., Cevik, O.S., Cebi, S., Oztaysi, B., Sari, I.U., Eds.; INFUS 2022; Lecture Notes in Networks and Systems; Springer: Cham, Swizerland, 2022; Volume 504, pp. 632–640.
13. Gupta, R.; Kumar, S. Novel similarity measure between hesitant fuzzy set and their applications in pattern recognition and clustering analysis. *J. Eng. Appl. Sci.* **2024**, *71*, 1–26. [CrossRef]
14. Peng, J.J.; Wang, J.Q.; Wu, X.H. Novel multi-criteria decision-making approaches based on hesitant fuzzy sets and prospect theory. *Int. J. Inf. Technol. Decis. Mak.* **2016**, *15*, 621–643. [CrossRef]
15. Sindhu, M.S.; Rashid, T. Selection of alternative based on linear programming and the extended fuzzy TOPSIS under the frame-work of dual hesitant fuzzy sets. *Soft Comput.* **2023**, *27*, 1985–1996. [CrossRef]
16. Torra, V. Hesitant fuzzy sets. *Int. J. Intell. Syst.* **2010**, *25*, 529–539. [CrossRef]
17. Li, R.; Ejegwa, P.A.; Li, K.; Agaji, I.; Feng, Y.; Onyeke, I.C. A new similarity function for Pythagorean fuzzy sets with application in football analysis. *AIMS Math.* **2024**, *9*, 4990–5014. [CrossRef]
18. Yager, R.R. Pythagorean fuzzy subsets. In Proceedings of the 2013 Joint IFSA World Congress and NAFIPS Annual Meeting (IFSA/NAFIPS), Edmonton, AB, Canada, 24–28 June 2013; pp. 57–61.
19. Ejegwa, P.A.; Wanzenke, T.D.; Ogwuche, I.O. A robust correlation coefficient for Fermatean fuzzy sets based on spearman's correlation measure with application to clustering and selection process. *J. Appl. Math. Comput.* **2024**, *70*, 1747–1770. [CrossRef]
20. Senapati, T.; Yager, R.R. Fermatean fuzzy sets. *J. Ambient. Intell. Humaniz. Comput.* **2020**, *11*, 663–674. [CrossRef]
21. Wang, H.; Tuo, C.; Wang, Z.; Feng, G.; Li, C. Enhancing similarity and distance measurements in Fermatean fuzzy sets: Tanimoto-Inspired measures and decision-making applications. *Symmetry* **2024**, *16*, 277. [CrossRef]
22. Atanassov, K.; Gargov, G. Interval valued intuitionistic fuzzy sets. *Fuzzy Sets Syst.* **1989**, *31*, 343–349. [CrossRef]
23. Cuong, C.B.; Kreinovich, V. Picture fuzzy sets-a new concept for computational intelligence problems. In Proceedings of the Third World Congress on Information and Communication Technologies WICT'2013, Hanoi, Vietnam, 15–18 December 2013; pp. 1–6.
24. Kadian, R.; Kumar, S. A new picture fuzzy divergence measure based on Jensen–Tsallis information measure and its application to multicriteria decision making. *Granul. Comput.* **2022**, *7*, 113–126. [CrossRef] [PubMed]
25. Long, H.F.; Luo, M.X. Picture fuzzy aggregation operators and their application to multi-attribute decision making. *J. China Jiliang Univ.* **2021**, *031*, 524–530.
26. Peng, J.J.; Chen, X.G.; Tian, C.; Zhang, Z.Q.; Song, H.Y.; Dong, F. Picture fuzzy large-scale group decision-making in a trust-relationship-based social network environment. *Inf. Sci.* **2022**, *608*, 1675–1701. [CrossRef]
27. Tian, C.; Peng, J.J.; Zhang, S.; Zhang, W.Y.; Wang, J.Q. Weighted picture fuzzy aggregation operators and their applications to multi-criteria decision-making problems. *Comput. Ind. Eng.* **2019**, *137*, 106037. [CrossRef]
28. Ali, Z.; Yang, M.S. On circular q-rung orthopair fuzzy sets with Dombi aggregation operators and application to symmetry analysis in artificial intelligence. *Symmetry* **2024**, *16*, 260. [CrossRef]
29. Yager, R.R. Generalized Orthopair Fuzzy Sets. *IEEE Trans. Fuzzy Syst.* **2017**, *25*, 1222–1230. [CrossRef]
30. Çakır, E.; Taş, M.A. Circular Intuitionistic Fuzzy Decision Making and Its Application. *Expert Syst. Appl.* **2023**, *225*, 120076. [CrossRef]
31. Traneva, V.; Tranev, S. Petrol Station Franchisor Selection Through Circular Intuitionistic Fuzzy Multicriteria Analysis. In *Intelligent and Fuzzy Systems*; Kahraman, C., Sari, I.U., Oztaysi, B., Cebi, S., Cevik Onar, S., Tolga, A.Ç., Eds.; INFUS 2023. Lecture Notes in Networks and Systems; Springer: Cham, Switzerland, 2023; Volume 758, pp. 194–203.

32. Traneva, V.; Tranev, S. An Elliptic Intuitionistic Fuzzy Model for Franchisor Selection. In Proceedings of the 18th Conference on Computer Science and Intelligence Systems, Warsaw, Poland, 17–20 September 2023; Ganzha, M., Maciaszek, L., Paprzycki, M., Slezak, D., Eds.; Annals of Computer Science and Information Systems: Warsaw, Poland, 2023; Volume 37, pp. 337–343. [CrossRef]
33. Vassilev, P.; Atanassov, K. *Modifications and Extensions of Intuitionistic Fuzzy Sets*; "Prof. Marin Drinov" Academic Publishing House: Sofia, Bulgaria, 2019.
34. Mahmood, T.; Abdullah, S.; Bilal, M. Multicriteria decision making based on a cubic set. *J. New Theory* **2017** *16*, 1–9
35. Smarandache, F. *Neutrosophy. Neutrosophic Probability, Set, and Logic*; American Research Press: Rehoboth, DE, USA, 1998.
36. Nguyen, X.T.; Nguyen, V.D. Support-Intuitionistic Fuzzy Set: A New Concept for Soft Computing. *Int. J. Intell. Syst. Appl.* **2015**, *04*, 11–16. [CrossRef]
37. Atanassov, K. Elliptic Intuitionistic Fuzzy Sets. *Comptes Rendus L'AcadÉmie Bulg. Des Sci.* **2021**, *39*, 812–819.
38. Chen, T.-Y. An advanced approach to multiple criteria optimization and compromise solutions under circular intuitionistic fuzzy uncertainty. *Adv. Eng. Inf.* **2023**, *57*, 102112. [CrossRef]
39. Firouzkouhi, N.; Amini, A.; Nazari, M.; Alkhatib, F.; Bordbar, H.; Cheng, C.; Davvaz, B.; Rashidi,M. Advanced artificial intelligence system by intuitionistic fuzzy G-subring for automotive robotic manufacturing. *Artif. Intell. Rev.* **2023**, *56*, 9639–9664. [CrossRef]
40. Çakır, E.; Tas, M.A. Circular intuitionistic fuzzy multi-criteria decision making methodology. *Eur. J. Sci. Technol. Spec. Issue* **2021** *28*, 900–905. [CrossRef]
41. Çakır, E.; Taş, M.A. Circular intuitionistic fuzzy analytic hierarchy process for remote working assessment in COVID-19. In *Intelligent and Fuzzy Systems, INFUS 2022, Lecture Notes in Networks and Systems*; Kahraman, C., Tolga, A.C., Cevik Onar, S., Cebi, S., Oztaysi, B., Sari, I.U., Eds.; Springer: Cham, Switzerland, 2022; Volume 504, pp. 589–597.
42. Kahraman, C; Otay, I. Extension of VIKOR method using circular intuitionistic fuzzy sets. In *Intelligent and Fuzzy Techniques for Emerging Conditions and Digital Transformation, INFUS 2021. Lecture Notes in Networks and Systems*; Kahraman, C., Cebi, S., Onar, S.C., Oztaysi, B., Tolga, A.C., Sari, I.U., Eds.; Springer: Cham, Switzerland, 2022; Volume 308, pp. 48–57.
43. Otay, İ., Kahraman, C. A novel circular intuitionistic fuzzy AHP & VIKOR methodology: An application to a multi-expert supplier evaluation problem. *Pamukkale Univ. J. Eng. Sci.* **2021**, *28*, 194–207.
44. Xu, C.; Wen, Y. New measure of circular intuitionistic fuzzy sets and its application in decision making. *AIMS Math.* **2023**, *8*, 24053–24074. [CrossRef]
45. Chen, T.-Y. A circular intuitionistic fuzzy evaluation method based on distances from the average solution to support multiple criteria intelligent decisions. involving uncertainty. *Eng. Appl. Artif. Intell.* **2023**, *117*, 105499. [CrossRef]
46. Atanassov, K. Generalized index matrices. *Comptes Rendus L'Academie Bulg. Des Sci.* **1987**, *40*, 15–18.
47. Pizza Hut Franchise. Available online: https://franchise.pizzahut.com/faqs (accessed on 15 July 2024).
48. Mieszkowicz-Rolka, A.; Rolka, L. Multi-Criteria Decision-Making with Linguistic Labels. In Proceedings of the 17th Conference FedCSIS, ACSIS, Sofia, Bulgaria, 4–7 September 2022; Ganzha, M., Maciaszek, L., Paprzycki, M., Slezak, D., Eds.; Volume 30, pp. 263–267.
49. Hsu, P.; Chen, B. Developing and Implementing a Selection Model for Bedding Chain Retail Store Franchisee Using Delphi and Fuzzy AHP. *Qual. Quant.* **2007**, *41*, 275–290. [CrossRef]
50. Kuo, R.J.; Chi, S.C.; Kao, S.S. A decision support system for selecting convenience store location through integration of FAHP and artificial neural network. *Comput. Ind.* **2002**, *47*, 199–214. [CrossRef]
51. Traneva, V.; Mavrov, D.; Tranev, S. Software Implementation of the Optimal Temporal Intuitionistic Fuzzy Algorithm for Franchisee Selection. In Proceedings of the 17th Conference on Computer Science and Intelligence Systems (FedCSIS), Sofia, Bulgaria, 4–7 September 2022; pp. 387–390. [CrossRef]
52. Atanassov, K. Index Matrices: Towards an Augmented Matrix Calculus. In *Studies in Computational Intelligence*; Springer: Cham, Switzerland, 2014; Volume 573. [CrossRef]
53. Traneva, V.; Tranev, S. Confidence-Interval Elliptic Intuitionistic Fuzzy Sets to Franchisor Selection. *Stud. Comput. Intell.* 2024, *in press*.
54. Atanassov, K. On Intuitionistic Fuzzy Sets Theory. In *Studfuzz*; Springer: Berlin/Heidelberg, Germany, 2012; Volume 283.
55. Atanassov, K. Remark on an intuitionistic fuzzy operation "division". *Annu. Inform. Sect. Union Sci. Bulg.* **2019**, *10*, 113–116.
56. De, S.K.; Bisvas, R.; Roy, R. Some operations on IFSs. *Fuzzy Sets Syst.* **2000**, *114*, 477–484. [CrossRef]
57. Riecan, B.; Atanassov, A. Operation division by n over intuitionistic fuzzy sets. *NIFS* **2010**, *16*, 1–4.
58. Atanassov, K.; Marinov, E. Four Distances for Circular Intuitionistic Fuzzy Sets. *Mathematics* **2021**, *9*, 1121. [CrossRef]
59. Doane, D.; Seward L. *Applied Statistics in Business and Economics*; McGraw-Hill Education: New York, NY, USA, 2016.
60. Kahraman, C.; Otay, I.; Oztaysi, B. Fuzzy extensions of confidence intervals: Estimation for μ, σ^2, and p. In *Fuzzy Statistical Decision-Making Theory and Applications*; Kahraman, C., Kabak, O., Eds.; Springer: Cham, Switzerland, 2016; Volume 343.
61. Chen, X.; Li, J.; Qian, L.; Hu, X. Distance and similarity measures for intuitionistic hesitant fuzzy sets. In Proceedings of the 2016 International Conference on Artificial Intelligence: Technologies and Applications, Bangkok, Thailand, 24–25 January 2016; Advances in Intelligent Systems Research; Atlantis Press: Amsterdam, The Netherlands, 2016; Volume 127.
62. Traneva, V.; Petrov, P.; Tranev, S. Circular IF Knapsack problem. In *Large-Scale Scientific Computations. LSSC 2023. Lecture Notes in Computer Science*; Lirkov, I., Margenov, S., Eds.; Springer: Cham, Switzerland, 2023; Volume 13952, pp. 279–287.

63. Traneva, V.; Tranev, S. *Index Matrices as a Tool for Managerial Decision Making*; Publishing House of the Union of Scientists: Plovdiv, Bulgaria, 2017. (In Bulgarian)
64. Traneva, V.; Tranev, S.; Stoenchev, M.; Atanassov, K. Scaled aggregation operations over two- and three-dimensional index matrices. *Soft Comput.* **2019**, *22*, 5115–5120. [CrossRef]
65. Atanassov, K.; Szmidt, E.; Kacprzyk, J.; Atanassova, V. An approach to a constructive simplication of multiagent multicriteria decision making problems via ICrA. *Comptes Rendus L'AcadÉmie Bulg. Des Sci.* **2017**, *70*, 1147–1156.
66. Atanassova, V.; Roeva, O. Computational complexity and influence of numerical precision on the results of intercriteria analysis in the decision making process. *Notes Intuitionistic Fuzzy Sets* **2018**, *24*, 53–63. [CrossRef]
67. Todorov, V.; Dimov, I.; Ostromsky, T.; Zlatev, Z.; Georgieva, R.; Poryazov, S. Optimized Quasi-Monte Carlo Methods Based on Van der Corput Sequence for Sensitivity Analysis in Air Pollution Modelling. In *Recent Advances in Computational Optimization. WCO 2020*; Fidanova, S., Ed.; Studies in Comp. Intelligence; Springer: Cham, Switzerland, 2021; Volume 986, pp. 389–405.

axioms

MDPI

Article

Hamiltonian Formulation for Continuous Systems with Second-Order Derivatives: A Study of Podolsky Generalized Electrodynamics

Yazen M. Alawaideh [1,*], Alina Alb Lupas [2,*], Bashar M. Al-khamiseh [1], Majeed A. Yousif [3], Pshtiwan Othman Mohammed [4] and Y. S. Hamed [5]

1 MEU Research Unit, Middle East University, Amman 11118, Jordan
2 Department of Mathematics and Computer Science, University of Oradea, 410087 Oradea, Romania
3 Department of Mathematics, College of Education, University Zakho, Duhok 42001, Iraq; majeed.yousif@uoz.edu.krd
4 Department of Mathematics, College of Education, University of Sulaimani, Sulaymaniyah 46001, Iraq; pshtiwan.muhammad@univsul.edu.iq
5 Department of Mathematics and Statistics, College of Science, Taif University, P. O. Box 11099, Taif 21944, Saudi Arabia
* Correspondence: yazen_awaida@yahoo.com (Y.M.A.); dalb@uoradea.ro (A.A.L.)

Abstract: This paper presents an analysis of the Hamiltonian formulation for continuous systems with second-order derivatives derived from Dirac's theory. This approach offers a unique perspective on the equations of motion compared to the traditional Euler–Lagrange formulation. Focusing on Podolsky's generalized electrodynamics, the Hamiltonian and corresponding equations of motion are derived. The findings demonstrate that both Hamiltonian and Euler–Lagrange formulations yield equivalent results. This study highlights the Hamiltonian approach as a valuable alternative for understanding the dynamics of second-order systems, validated through a specific application within generalized electrodynamics. The novelty of the research lies in developing advanced theoretical models through Hamiltonian formalism for continuous systems with second-order derivatives. The research employs an alternative method to the Euler–Lagrange formulas by applying Dirac's theory to study the generalized Podolsky electrodynamics, contributing to a better understanding of complex continuous systems.

Keywords: Podolsky Lagrangian; Hamiltonian formulation; classical fields variables; Euler–Lagrange equations

MSC: 34C25; 92C60; 92D25

1. Introduction

In the context of a deep understanding of theoretical physics, quantum theories have emerged as a crucial theoretical framework. These are theories that aim to provide an accurate mathematical description of natural phenomena and interactions between particles and fields. We can envision these theories as carefully crafted mathematical tools that enable us to better understand the surrounding world through the interpretation of multiple experiments and measurements. The Podolsky equation exemplifies a type of higher derivative gauge theory within the realm of quantum theories, where a kinetic term is integrated into the Maxwell Lagrangian. This category of theories has prompted extensive scholarly discussion [1–8]. Researchers are currently exploring the potential of achieving enhanced organization of interactions at close distances by incorporating higher-order derivatives akin to the framework employed in Podolsky's electromagnetic dynamics. This approach presents an exciting opportunity to formulate specific theories that surpass the indeterminacies and difficulties associated with traditional gauge theory formulations.

Moreover, systems governed by higher-order Lagrangians have gained increasing significance in investigating physical phenomena. The prominent examples encompass the organization of theories in the field of quantum measurement, in addition to the behaviors of solid strings. In the realm of theoretical physics, the behavior of solid strings is studied as vibrational patterns in space and time. Solid strings are considered theoretical models used to comprehend the behavior of particles at the quantum level, where this theory relies on the interaction of strings with variables like energy and intensity. As such, it can contribute to interpreting phenomena at the particle level [9,10]. These examples also include the study of solid particles [11,12] and relativistic particles in three-dimensional spacetime with curvature and twisting. This concept is part of the general theory of relativity, which posits that spacetime interacts as a single unit called spacetime. In the presence of mass or energy, this leads to the curvature of spacetime around it, affecting the trajectory of moving particles in the curved region [13]. Podolsky's proposal to extend electrodynamics with third-order derivatives [14] has further fueled interest in these system types.

Additionally, the effective Lagrangian in gauge theories was initially pioneered by Ostrogradski [2,15,16]. It provides a valuable framework for deducing Hamiltonian equations of motion and Euler–Lagrange equations. Exploration of systems characterized by fractional higher-order derivatives has been extensively researched in recent years. Building upon this context, Ref. [17] introduces a novel approach to address such systems, specifically those featuring third-order fractional derivatives. This method is then applied to Lee–Wick's generalized electrodynamics, illuminating the behaviors of these intricate systems. Ref. [18] further builds on this foundation, delving into advancements for systems featuring even higher-order derivatives. Drawing from this context, Awaideh et al. have effectively computed high-level fractional order derivatives using the Atangana–Baleanu fractional derivative, allowing them to determine conserved variables such as energy density, momentum, and Poynting's vector [19].

The electromagnetic potentials, φ and A_i, play a crucial role as mathematical constructs intricately connected to electric and magnetic fields through Maxwell's equations. These potentials simplify the understanding of fields, especially those that vary with time, and are essential in deriving the electric field. They effectively embody the electromagnetic field that originates from charged particles, providing an internal view of field distributions within specific spatial regions. In the past, the description relied solely on electric and magnetic fields to portray the electromagnetic field. However, the integration of electromagnetic potentials introduced a precise framework for portraying electromagnetic phenomena with greater comprehensiveness. Everyone contributes to providing an accurate framework for depicting electromagnetic phenomena. The electromagnetic potentials serve as mathematical tools to visualize the distributions of electric and magnetic fields in space, with complete integration into the traditional description of the electromagnetic field.

Higher-order variational theory includes functions that depend on higher-order derivatives. There are two forms: the dependent form that involves derivatives and the independent form that covers the function and its derivatives from the first order up to the $(n - 1)$ th order. The dependent form is helpful in calculating partial derivatives in mathematical physics and for analyzing functions that rely on higher-order derivatives. On the other hand, the independent form is valuable for solving boundary problems and for studying functions that require control over super functions, as demonstrated in the optimal endpoint problem in thermodynamics. Inspired by these discussions, researchers have extended these formulations to encompass broader applications to continuous systems with second-order derivatives. This methodology has also been expanded to include Podolsky's generalized electrodynamics. As a practical application of second-order derivatives in rotational dynamics and stability, several studies [20–23] have examined topics such as rigid body motion with gyrostatic moments, the dynamics of charged solid bodies, and periodic solutions in two degrees-of-freedom systems. The main contributions of this study can be summarized as follows:

i. Second-order Hamiltonian analysis: The study presents a comprehensive analysis of systems using Second-Order Lagrangian and Generalized Dirac's derivatives. Researchers gain insights into how the proposed methodology aligns with expected theories. Subsequently, these results can be compared with the findings of other researchers to verify alignment and attain a more generalized formulation.
ii. Enhanced understanding of Hamiltonian formalism: By applying Dirac's method to second-order Lagrangians, the research sheds light on a deeper understanding of Hamiltonian formalism. This facilitates a more comprehensive analysis of physical systems with intricate dynamics.
iii. Systems governed by higher-order Lagrangians:
    1- These systems have gained increasing significance in investigating physical phenomena, such as the organization of theories in the field of quantum measurement and the behaviors of solid strings.
    2- Other examples include the study of solid particles and relativistic particles in three-dimensional spacetime with curvature and twisting.
iv. Higher-order variational theory: This theory includes functions that depend on higher-order derivatives and is useful for calculating partial derivatives in mathematical physics and analyzing functions that rely on higher-order derivatives.

This research aims to achieve two main objectives. Firstly, it aims to explore the analysis of systems using generalized Dirac's derivatives and second-order Lagrangian. Secondly, it aims to illustrate how Podolsky's generalized electrodynamics can be enhanced through a more comprehensive approach, enabling its application to continuous systems that involve second-order derivatives.

This work is structured as follows: Section 2 provides a concise overview of the Euler–Lagrange equations of motion. Section 3 delves into the examination of the Hamiltonian formulation of continuous systems. The equations of motion, expressed in terms of (ϕ, A_i), are presented in Section 4 through Hamilton's equations. Moving on to Section 5, we explore a classical field example leading to the Podolsky equation in the second-order form. Section 5 will introduce various applications of fractional calculus and provide research recommendations. Lastly, Section 7 encompasses the conclusion of this study.

2. Classical Field Theories: Lagrangians of Second Order

We can discuss a continuous system described by a Lagrangian density, dependent on dynamic field variables and their second-order derivatives. A Lagrangian density is a function that describes a physical system's dynamics, defined as the difference between kinetic and potential energies. In our case, the Lagrangian density captures both the system's current state and its changing behavior over time. The term "continuous system" implies smooth changes in field variables over time and space, contrasting with discrete changes in other systems.

$$\mathcal{L} = \mathcal{L}(\psi_\rho, \partial_\eta \psi_\rho, \partial_\eta \partial_\sigma \psi_p).$$

Now L can be expressed as:

$$L = \int \mathcal{L}(\psi_p, \partial_\eta \psi_\rho, \partial_\eta \partial_\sigma \psi_p) d^3r. \tag{1}$$

The variational principle and the classical variants of Lagrangian of the second order are closely related. The Lagrangian function represents the difference between the kinetic and potential energies of a physical system, and the classical variants of Lagrangian of the second order are a set of mathematical equations used to describe the system's motion based on this function. To derive these equations, the principle of least action is applied to the Lagrangian function, which is a specific form of the variational principle. Therefore, the classical variants of Lagrangian of the second order provide an example of how the variational principle can be used to determine the motion of physical systems.

$$\delta \int Ldt = \int \int \delta \mathcal{L}\, d^3rdt = 0, \tag{2}$$

Equation (1) allows us to calculate the variation of the Lagrangian function in Lagrangian mechanics. The variation of L is denoted by δL and can be written as:

$$\delta \mathcal{L} = \frac{\partial \mathcal{L}}{\partial \psi_\rho} \delta \psi_\rho + \frac{\partial \mathcal{L}}{\partial(\partial_\eta \psi_\rho)} \delta(\partial_\eta \psi_\rho) + \frac{\partial \mathcal{L}}{\partial(\partial_\eta \partial_\sigma \psi_p)} \delta(\partial_\eta \partial_\sigma \psi_p), \tag{3}$$

where $\mathcal{L}$ is the Lagrangian function, ψ_ρ represents the generalized coordinates that describe the configuration of the system, δ is a small parameter, and $\delta\psi_\rho$ is the corresponding variation in the generalized coordinate.

Substituting Equation (3) in Equation (2), and using the following commutation relationship [20],

$$\left. \begin{array}{c} \delta(\partial_\eta \psi_\rho) = \partial_\eta(\delta \psi_\rho) \\ \delta(\partial_\eta \partial_\sigma \psi_p) = \partial_\eta \partial_\sigma(\delta \psi_p) \end{array} \right]. \tag{4}$$

We obtain,

$$\delta L = \int \int \left(\frac{\partial \mathcal{L}}{\partial \psi_\rho} \delta \psi_\rho + \underbrace{\frac{\partial \mathcal{L}}{\partial(\partial_\mu \psi_\rho)} \partial_\mu(\delta \psi_\rho)}_{second} + \underbrace{\frac{\partial \mathcal{L}}{\partial(\partial_\mu \partial_\nu \psi_p)} \partial_\mu \partial_\nu(\psi_p)}_{third} \right) d^3rdt = 0.$$

Integrating the second and third terms by parts we obtain:

$$\delta L = \int \left(\frac{\partial \mathcal{L}}{\partial \psi_\rho} \delta \psi_\rho - \partial_\mu \frac{\partial \mathcal{L}}{\partial(\partial_\mu \psi_\rho)} \delta(\psi_\rho) + \partial_\eta \partial_\sigma \frac{\partial \mathcal{L}}{\partial(\partial_\eta \partial_\sigma \psi_p)} \delta(\psi_\rho) \right) d^3rdt = 0.$$

This leads to Euler–Lagrange equation:

$$\frac{\partial \mathcal{L}}{\partial \psi_\rho} - \partial_\mu \frac{\partial \mathcal{L}}{\partial(\partial_\mu \psi_\rho)} + \partial_\mu \partial_\nu \frac{\partial \mathcal{L}}{\partial(\partial_\mu \partial_\nu \psi_p)} = 0.$$

The equations of motion for a given physical system can be derived from the Euler–Lagrange equation, which relates to the fields involved in the system. In the case of a system with fields (ϕ and A_i), the equations of motion can be constructed using the Euler–Lagrange equation with these fields as variables. This will result in a set of equations that describe the motion of the system under consideration.

$$\frac{\partial \mathcal{L}}{\partial A_0} - \partial_\mu \frac{\partial \mathcal{L}}{\partial(\partial_\mu A_0)} + \partial_\mu \partial_\nu \frac{\partial \mathcal{L}}{\partial(\partial_\mu \partial_\nu A_0)} = 0,$$

$$\frac{\partial \mathcal{L}}{\partial A_i} - \partial_\mu \frac{\partial \mathcal{L}}{\partial(\partial_\mu A_i)} + \partial_\mu \partial_\nu \frac{\partial \mathcal{L}}{\partial(\partial_\mu \partial_\nu A_i)} = 0.$$

To simplify the Euler–Lagrange relations, we can use the notation $(\partial_\mu = \partial_v = \partial_0, \partial_i)$, as an example. With this notation, we can express the Euler–Lagrange relations in their the first of all forms in the following manner:

$$\left(\begin{array}{c} \frac{\partial \mathcal{L}}{\partial A_0} - \partial_0 \frac{\partial \mathcal{L}}{\partial(\partial_0 A_0)} - \partial_i \frac{\partial \mathcal{L}}{\partial(\partial_i A_0)} + \partial_0 \partial_0 \frac{\partial \mathcal{L}}{\partial(\partial_0 \partial_0 A_0)} \\ + \partial_i \partial_0 \frac{\partial \mathcal{L}}{\partial(\partial_i \partial_0 A_0)} + \partial_i \partial_j \frac{\partial \mathcal{L}}{\partial(\partial_i \partial_i A_0)} \end{array} \right) = 0, \tag{5}$$

$$\left(\begin{array}{c} \frac{\partial \mathcal{L}}{\partial A_i} - \partial_0 \frac{\partial \mathcal{L}}{\partial(\partial_0 A_i)} - \partial_i \frac{\partial \mathcal{L}}{\partial(\partial_i A_i)} + \partial_0 \partial_0 \frac{\partial \mathcal{L}}{\partial(\partial_0 \partial_0 A_i)} \\ + \partial_i \partial_0 \frac{\partial \mathcal{L}}{\partial(\partial_i \partial_0 A_i)} + \partial_i \partial_j \frac{\partial \mathcal{L}}{\partial(\partial_i \partial_i A_i)} \end{array} \right) = 0. \tag{6}$$

3. Analysis of Hamiltonian Formalism for Second-Order Lagrangians Using Dirac Method

In that section, we analyzed the Hamiltonian formalism using the Dirac method to adapt it to second-order Lagrangians. We focused on explaining the concepts of "independent variables" and "dependent variables" in detail.

Independent variables are those that are determined independently and are not connected to any other variables in the system. For example, when studying the motion of an object on a flat surface, time can be an independent variable as it is determined separately from the position or velocity. On the other hand, dependent variables are those that depend on independent variables and change based on their values. For instance, if we have a rectangle's length and width, the rectangle's area depends on these variables and represents a dependent variable. Let us clarify this with a simple mathematical example: Let us assume we have an equation for the motion of an object influenced by force and acceleration. In this context, the independent variables are time and distance. The dependent variables are velocity and acceleration, where velocity depends on distance and time, and acceleration depends on the change in velocity over time. Using this example, we can clearly understand the distinction between independent and dependent variables in the context of Hamiltonian analysis. It is important to note that this formalism can be universally applied to any second-order Lagrangian.

We analyze the Lagrangian by utilizing time derivatives of coordinates of the specified type, $\mathcal{L} = \mathcal{L}(\psi_\rho, \partial_\eta \psi_\rho, \partial_\eta \partial_\sigma \psi_p)$. The generalized momenta π_1 and π_2 corresponding to $\dot{\psi}_p = \partial_0 \psi_p$ and $\ddot{\psi}_p = \partial_0^2 \psi_p$ can be defined as follows [21]:

$$\pi_1 = \frac{\partial L}{\partial \dot{\psi}_\rho} - \partial_0 \left(\frac{\partial L}{\partial \ddot{\psi}_\rho} \right),$$

$$\pi_2 = \frac{\partial L}{\partial \ddot{\psi}_\rho}.$$

The Hamiltonian, depending on the time derivatives, reads as:

$$\mathcal{H} = \pi_1 \dot{\psi}_\rho + \pi_2 \ddot{\psi}_\rho - \mathcal{L}(\psi_\rho, \partial_\eta \psi_\rho, \partial_\eta \partial_\sigma \psi_p). \tag{7}$$

Based on the equation provided earlier, the total differential corresponding to this specific function can be articulated in the subsequent manner:

$$d\mathcal{H} = \left\{ \begin{array}{c} \dot{\psi}_\rho d\pi_1 + \pi_1 d\dot{\psi}_\rho + \ddot{\psi}_\rho d\pi_2 + \pi_2 d\ddot{\psi}_\rho \\ -\frac{d\mathcal{L}}{d\psi_\rho} d\psi_\rho - \frac{d\mathcal{L}}{d(\partial_0 \psi_p)} d(\partial_0 \psi_p) - \frac{d\mathcal{L}}{d(\partial_i \psi_p)} d(\partial_i \psi_p) \\ -\frac{d\mathcal{L}}{d(\partial_0^2 \psi_p)} d(\partial_0^2 \psi_p) - \frac{d\mathcal{L}}{d(\partial_i \partial_i \psi_p)} d(\partial_i \partial_i \psi_p) \end{array} \right\}.$$

Now, we can rewrite equations of Hamiltonian's derivative of the above equation in terms of Lagrangian density using the defined values of the momenta given as follows:

$$d\mathcal{H} = \left\{ \begin{array}{c} \dot{\psi}_\rho d\pi_1 + \pi_1 d\dot{\psi}_\rho + \ddot{\psi}_\rho d\pi_2 + \pi_2 d\ddot{\psi}_\rho \\ -\frac{d\mathcal{L}}{d\psi_\rho} d\psi_\rho - \pi_1 d\dot{\psi}_\rho - \pi_2 d\ddot{\psi}_\rho \\ -\frac{d\mathcal{L}}{d(\partial_i \psi_p)} d(\partial_i \psi_p) - \frac{d\mathcal{L}}{d(\partial_i \partial_i \psi_p)} d(\partial_i \partial_i \psi_p) \\ -\frac{d\mathcal{L}}{d(\partial_i \partial_0 \psi_p)} d(\partial_i \partial_0 \psi_p) \end{array} \right\}. \tag{8}$$

This means that the Hamiltonian can be expressed as a mathematical function in the following manner:

$$\mathcal{H} = \mathcal{H}[(\psi_\rho,\ \pi_1,\ \partial_i \psi_p, \pi_2, \partial_0 \partial_i \psi_p)].$$

Given the equation above, the complete differential for this specific function can be formulated as follows:

$$d\mathcal{H} = \left\{ \begin{array}{c} \frac{\partial \mathcal{H}}{\partial(\psi_p)} d(\psi_p) + \frac{\partial \mathcal{H}}{\partial(\partial_g \psi_p)} d(\partial_g \psi_p) + \frac{\partial \mathcal{H}}{\partial \pi_1} d\pi_1 + \frac{\partial \mathcal{H}}{\partial(\pi_2)} d(\pi_2) \\ + \frac{\partial \mathcal{H}}{\partial(\partial_0 \partial_j \psi_p)} d(\partial_0 \partial_j \psi_p) + \frac{\partial \mathcal{H}}{\partial(\partial_i \partial_0 \psi_p)} d(\partial_i \partial_0 \psi_p) \\ + \frac{\partial \mathcal{H}}{\partial(\partial_i \partial_j \psi_p)} d(\partial_i \partial_j \psi_p) \end{array} \right\}. \tag{9}$$

In cases 1 and 2, we can express the variation of the Hamiltonian resulting from changes in the independent variables as a second-order derivative, similar to how we define the variation in the Lagrangian.

Case 1: All variables are independent $(\psi_\rho, \pi_1, \pi_2)$:

$$dH = \left(\frac{\partial H}{\partial \psi_\rho} d\psi_\rho + \frac{\partial H}{\partial \pi_1} d\pi_1 + \frac{\partial H}{\partial \pi_2} d\pi_2 \right). \tag{10}$$

We can rewrite Hamilton's equations of motion by comparing Equations (8) and (9) as outlined below.

$$\left\{ \frac{\partial \mathcal{H}}{\partial \psi_\rho} = -\frac{\partial \mathcal{L}}{\partial_\rho \psi_p}, \right. \tag{11}$$

$$\left\{ \frac{\partial \mathcal{H}}{\partial(\partial_i \psi_p)} = -\frac{d\mathcal{L}}{\partial(\partial_i \psi_p)}, \right.$$

$$\left\{ \begin{array}{l} \frac{\partial \mathcal{H}}{\partial \pi_1} = \dot{\psi}_\rho, \\ \frac{\partial \mathcal{H}}{\partial \pi_2} = \ddot{\psi}_\rho, \end{array} \right.$$

$$\left\{ \frac{\partial \mathcal{H}}{\partial(\partial_i \partial_i \psi_p)} = -\frac{\partial \mathcal{L}}{\partial(\partial_i \partial_i \psi_p)}. \right.$$

The Euler–Lagrange equation may be used to rewrite Equation (10). This equation has the following form:

$$\frac{\partial \mathcal{H}}{\partial \psi_\rho} = -\left(\partial_\mu \frac{\partial \mathcal{L}}{\partial(\partial_\mu \psi_\rho)} - \partial_\mu \partial_\nu \frac{\partial \mathcal{L}}{\partial(\partial_\mu \partial_\nu \psi_\rho)} \right). \tag{12}$$

Extending $\partial_\mu \partial_\nu$ in terms of $(0, i)$, we obtain:

$$\frac{\partial \mathcal{H}}{\partial \psi_\rho} = \left(\begin{array}{c} -\partial_0 \frac{\partial \mathcal{L}}{\partial(\partial_0 \psi_\rho)} - \partial_i \frac{\partial \mathcal{L}}{\partial(\partial_i \psi_\rho)} + \partial_i \partial_0 \frac{\partial \mathcal{L}}{\partial(\partial_i \partial_i \psi_\rho)} \\ + \partial_0 \partial_0 \frac{\partial \mathcal{L}}{\partial(\partial_0 \partial_0 \psi_\rho)} + \partial_i \partial_i \psi_p \frac{\partial \mathcal{L}}{\partial(\partial_i \partial_i \psi_p)} \end{array} \right). \tag{13}$$

Case 2: The value of π_1 depends on the variable (ψ_ρ), while the value of π_2 depends on the variable $(\partial_0 \psi_\rho)$. Therefore, when taking a variation, we only need to consider variations in the independent variables ψ_ρ and $\partial_0 \psi_\rho$. This approach allows us to simplify the calculation and focus only on the variables that have a direct impact on the values of π_1 and π_2.

$$dH = \frac{\partial H}{\partial \psi_\rho} d\psi_\rho + \frac{\partial H}{\partial(\partial_0 \psi_\rho)} d(\partial_0 \psi_\rho). \tag{14}$$

To represent the equations of motion obtained from Equation (14), write π_1 and π_2 in the general case $\pi_1 = R(\psi_\rho)$ and $\pi_2 = f(\partial_0 \psi_\rho)$. As a result, their derivative can be expressed as follows:

$$d\pi_1 = \frac{\partial R}{\partial \psi_\rho} d\psi_\rho, \tag{15}$$

$$d\pi_2 = \frac{\partial f}{\partial(\partial_0 \psi_\rho)} d(\partial_0 \psi_\rho). \tag{16}$$

As a consequence of substituting Equations (15) and (16) for Equation (10) and comparing the results with Equation (14), the following Hamiltonian density formulas are obtained:

$$\frac{\partial \mathcal{H}}{\partial \psi_\rho} = -\left(\partial_\mu \frac{\partial \mathcal{L}}{\partial(\partial_\mu \psi_\rho)} - \partial_\mu \partial_\nu \frac{\partial \mathcal{L}}{\partial(\partial_\mu \partial_\nu \psi_\rho)}\right) + \left(\frac{\partial R}{\partial \psi_\rho} + \frac{\partial f}{\partial\left(\partial_0 \psi_\rho\right)}\right) \partial_0 \psi_\rho. \quad (17)$$

Equations (13) and (15) are powerful tools for analyzing dynamic systems that are constrained by explicit or implicit limitations. In order to incorporate these constraints, Lagrange multipliers are introduced. The Hamiltonian Dirac approach utilizes generalized variables and their conjugate momenta as independent variables while emphasizing the Hamiltonian as the dependent variable. This method is particularly useful for studying complex systems that have constraints.

4. Hamilton Formalism in Form (ϕ, A_i) for Second-Order Lagrangians

Hamiltonian mechanics and classical field theory use the Lagrangian density and field variables in the Hamiltonian formalism to derive equations of motion. This process gives rise to two distinct scenarios: When all variables are independent, the equations derive directly from the Euler–Lagrange equations. This results in a set of coupled partial differential equations that effectively depict the evolution of the field. On the other hand, when certain variables depend on others, a heightened level of complexity emerges. In such cases, the equations of motion must account for these interdependencies. This intricate consideration is achieved by implementing constrained variations, a method that expresses changes in dependent variables (ϕ, A_i) with respect to independent ones. Consequently, this approach leads to the emergence of modified Euler–Lagrange equations.

4.1. In the First Case

All variables $(\psi_\rho, \pi_1, \pi_2)$ are independent, and we can use the definition given in Equation (12) to rewrite the equations of motion (i.e., Equation (13)) in terms of Lagrangian density. Specifically, we can express the Hamiltonian H as a function of the field variables (ϕ, A_i) and their conjugate momenta (π_ϕ, π_{A_i}), and take partial derivatives, with respect to ϕ and A_i, to obtain Equations (16) and (17), respectively.

$$\frac{\partial \mathcal{H}}{\partial A_0} = \left(\begin{array}{c} -\partial_0 \frac{\partial \mathcal{L}}{\partial(\partial_0 A_0)} - \partial_i \frac{\partial \mathcal{L}}{\partial(\partial_i A_0)} + \partial_i \partial_0 \frac{\partial \mathcal{L}}{\partial(\partial_i \partial_i A_0)} \\ +\partial_0 \partial_0 \frac{\partial \mathcal{L}}{\partial(\partial_0 \partial_0 A_0)} \end{array}\right), \quad (18)$$

$$\frac{\partial \mathcal{H}}{\partial A_i} = \left(\begin{array}{c} -\partial_0 \frac{\partial \mathcal{L}}{\partial(\partial_0 A_i)} - \partial_i \frac{\partial \mathcal{L}}{\partial(\partial_i A_i)} + \partial_i \partial_0 \frac{\partial \mathcal{L}}{\partial(\partial_i \partial_i A_i)} \\ +\partial_0 \partial_0 \frac{\partial \mathcal{L}}{\partial(\partial_0 \partial_0 A_i)} \end{array}\right). \quad (19)$$

These equations give us the rate of change of the Hamiltonian with respect to changes in the field variables ϕ and A_i.

4.2. In the Second Case

The variables are dependent on one other; π_1 depends on ψ_ρ, and π_2 depends on $(\partial_0 \psi_\rho)$. To generate equations of motion in terms of Lagrangian density in this scenario, we can still follow the same steps as in the previous one, but we also need to add some more terms. Specifically, we need to add terms related to the variation of the dependent variables with respect to ϕ and A_i. These terms are given by $\frac{\partial R}{\partial(A_0,\, A_i)}$ and $\frac{\partial f}{\partial(A_0,\, A_i)}$:

$$\frac{\partial \mathcal{H}}{\partial A_0} = \left(\begin{array}{c} -\partial_0 \frac{\partial \mathcal{L}}{\partial(\partial_0 A_0)} - \partial_i \frac{\partial \mathcal{L}}{\partial(\partial_i A_0)} + \partial_i \partial_0 \frac{\partial \mathcal{L}}{\partial(\partial_i \partial_i A_0)} \\ +\partial_0 \partial_0 \frac{\partial \mathcal{L}}{\partial(\partial_0 \partial_0 A_0)} \end{array}\right) + \left(\frac{\partial R}{\partial A_0} + \frac{\partial f}{\partial(\partial_0 A_0)}\right) \partial_0 A_0, \quad (20)$$

$$\frac{\partial \mathcal{H}}{\partial A_i} = \begin{pmatrix} -\partial_0 \frac{\partial \mathcal{L}}{\partial(\partial_0 A_i)} - \partial_i \frac{\partial \mathcal{L}}{\partial(\partial_i A_i)} + \partial_i \partial_0 \frac{\partial \mathcal{L}}{\partial(\partial_i \partial_i A_i)} \\ +\partial_0 \partial_0 \frac{\partial \mathcal{L}}{\partial(\partial_0 \partial_0 A_i)} \end{pmatrix} + \left(\frac{\partial R}{\partial A_i} + \frac{\partial f}{\partial(\partial_0 A_i)} \right) \partial_0 A_i. \quad (21)$$

5. Utilizing Euler and Hamiltonian Methods for Modeling the Podolsky Equation

In this section, we investigate the practical implementation of the aforementioned methodology, focusing on the Podolsky Equation. This equation involves a Lagrangian density featuring second-order derivatives [22]. The Lagrangian can be expressed as follows:

$$\mathcal{L} = -\frac{1}{4} F_{\mu\nu} F^{\mu\nu} + a^2 \partial_\lambda F^{\alpha\lambda} \partial_\rho F_{\rho\alpha},$$

where $F_{\mu\nu}$ is defined as $\partial_\mu A_v - \partial_v A_m$.

Expanding L with respect to $(0, i)$, we can rewrite the Lagrangian as:

$$\mathcal{L} = \frac{1}{2} (\partial_0 A_i - \partial_i A_0)^2 - a^2 \left(\partial_i \left(\partial^0 A^i - \partial^i A^0 \right)^2 - \partial_0 \left(\partial^0 A^i - \partial^i A^0 \right)^2 \right).$$

To obtain the conjugated momenta, we use the Euler–Lagrange Equations (5) and (6) separately for the variables $(\phi,\ A_i)$. We then apply derivatives to each variable, which allows us to obtain distinct outcomes for each variable.

$$\left(1 + 2a^2 \left(\partial_0{}^2 - \partial_i{}^2 \right) \right) (\partial_0 + \partial_i) \left(\partial^0 A^i - \partial^i A^0 \right) = 0. \quad (22)$$

The result in (22) is the same as the result in [24–26].

To obtain conjugated momenta, we introduce the generalized momenta with respect to the variables (ϕ, A_i).

$$\pi_1^1 = \frac{\partial \mathcal{L}}{\partial(\partial_0 A_0)} - \partial_0 \left(\frac{\partial \mathcal{L}}{\partial(\partial_0^2 A_0)} \right) = 0, \quad (23)$$

$$\pi_1^2 = \left(\frac{\partial \mathcal{L}}{\partial(\partial_0 A_i)} - \partial_0 \left(\frac{\partial \mathcal{L}}{\partial(\partial_0^2 A_i)} \right) = F_{0i} - a^2 \left(2\partial_0^2 A_i - \partial_0 \partial_i A_0 \right) \right), \quad (24)$$

$$\pi_2^1 = \frac{\partial \mathcal{L}}{\partial(\partial_0^2 A_0)} = 0, \quad (25)$$

$$\pi_2^2 = \frac{\partial \mathcal{L}}{\partial(\partial_0^2 A_i)} = -2a^2 \partial_0 F_{0i}. \quad (26)$$

By using the canonical Hamiltonian, which is defined as:

$$\mathcal{H} = \pi_1^1 \partial_0 A_0 + \pi_1^2 \partial_0 A_i + \pi_2^1 \partial_0^2 A_0 + \pi_2^2 \partial_0^2 A_i - \mathcal{L}.$$

Substituting the Lagrangian, we obtain:

$$\mathcal{H} = \begin{pmatrix} \left[F_{0i} - a^2 \left(2\partial_0^2 A_i - \partial_0 \partial_i A_0 \right) \right] \partial_0 A_i \\ -\left[2a^2 \partial_0 F_{0i} \right] \partial_0^2 A_i - \frac{1}{2} (\partial_0 A_i - \partial_i A_0)^2 \\ a^2 \left(\partial_i (\partial^0 A^i - \partial^i A^0)^2 - \partial_0 (\partial^0 A^i - \partial^i A^0)^2 \right) \end{pmatrix}. \quad (27)$$

Let us use Equations (16) and (17) to represent the dependent variables (ϕ, A_i). In case one, we obtain:

$$\left(1 + 2a^2 \left(\partial_0{}^2 - \partial_i{}^2 \right) \right) (\partial_0 + \partial_i) \left(\partial^0 A^i - \partial^i A^0 \right) = 0. \quad (28)$$

The equation obtained above is equivalent in form to the equation obtained from Equation (20). This equivalence is achieved by taking into account the relationship: $\eta^{\mu\nu}\partial_\mu\partial_\nu = \Box = (\partial_0^2 - \nabla^2)$,

$$\left[1 - 2a^2\Box\right]\partial_\mu F_{\mu\nu} = 0. \tag{29}$$

Here, ($\Box$) represents the Dellembrian operator. The equations presented in this study can be used to describe the motion of fourth-order systems, and the result obtained from Equation (28) is in perfect agreement with the result presented in [25,26]. This result shows how the mathematical analysis used in this study was accurate and consistent.

To obtain the derivative with respect to the independent variables (ϕ, A_i), we use the Hamiltonian Equations (20) and (21).

$$\left(1 + 2a^2\left({\partial_0}^2 - {\partial_i}^2\right)\right)(\partial_0 + \partial_i)\left(\partial^0 A^i - \partial^i A^0\right) = 0. \tag{30}$$

The Hamilton–Dirac method and second-order differential equations show a striking similarity in the equations of motion for both independent and dependent variables, as seen in Equations (17)–(20), respectively. This similarity indicates that the equations of motion derived from both approaches are equivalent, giving researchers confidence in using either method when studying constrained systems. Understanding the mathematical foundations of physical systems, especially those with constraints, is crucial for accurately modeling and analyzing their behavior.

6. Applications of Second-Order Podolsky Lagrangians and Suggestions for Further Research

Using the innovative Dirac theory, the generalized electric dynamics fields proposed by Podolsky stands out as one of the most actively researched areas. These fields primarily focus on exploring second-order derivatives within Podolsky's equations for electrical dynamics, playing a pivotal role in developing the quantum theory for electrical dynamics. These advancements within the Hamiltonian model for continuous second-order systems have the potential to trigger a profound transformation in our understanding of physical phenomena, including Coulomb's law and the principle of superposition. Efforts by physicists have effectively demonstrated the possibility of extending the electrostatic laws derived from the principle of superposition and Coulomb's law to encompass second-order derivatives. Additionally, researchers have conducted thorough examinations of the first-order relativistic model alongside interaction fields. Their precise analyses delve into scenarios characterized by unique momentum-energy projections based on the fractional-order Podolsky equation. Currently, exploration is underway to formulate novel arrangements for individual systems, introducing new methods for investigating these complex setups.

In a broader context, this research builds on classical dynamics frameworks, including Lagrangian equations, Hamiltonians, and Euler equations. Each method has its own strengths and limitations in solving complex problems. For example, additional constraints may arise for second-order derivatives when dealing with exponential and Mittag-Leffler factors that introduce singularities. The Hamiltonian approach with second-order derivatives adds mathematical complexity compared to traditional methods like Euler–Lagrange, especially in scenarios with numerous interactions. Furthermore, applying this approach to specific systems often requires additional controls or assumptions. Challenges also include handling non-physical solutions and analyzing intricate models with implicit electronics, which complicates numerical applications. Such constraints might pave the way for the emergence of a new and distinctive realm of research.

7. Conclusions

We have devised a novel methodology for investigating continuous systems characterized by second-order derivatives. Our approach employs a Hamiltonian formulation, which has enabled us to deduce the Euler–Lagrange equations governing the dynamics of such systems. We also obtained the Hamiltonian for these systems and used it to derive the Hamiltonian equation of motion, which involves second-order derivatives. It is worth noting that our results are consistent with those obtained using the conventional Euler–Lagrange approach. To illustrate the utility of our approach, we have applied it to a specific example of a system with second-order derivatives. This exercise allowed us to validate our framework and obtain a deeper understanding of the physical behavior of such systems. Our study has presented a comprehensive Hamiltonian formulation for continuous systems with second-order derivatives. The novelty of the research lies in an alternative and complementary perspective to the traditional Euler–Lagrange framework. The results obtained through our approach have been verified through a specific example, indicating the potential utility of this framework in investigating a variety of physical systems.

The results confirm the effectiveness of the proposed approach in analyzing continuous systems with second-order derivatives. These findings enhance the understanding of complex physical systems, paving the way for practical applications in electrodynamics and developing advanced control systems. The paper presents a comprehensive mathematical framework that can be applied to a wide range of physical phenomena.

Author Contributions: Conceptualization and data curation, Y.M.A.; funding acquisition, A.A.L. and Y.S.H.; investigation, B.M.A.-k. and M.A.Y.; methodology, Y.M.A.; resources, M.A.Y.; software, P.O.M.; supervision, Y.M.A. and A.A.L.; validation, P.O.M. and Y.S.H.; visualization, B.M.A.-k.; writing—original draft, Y.M.A., B.M.A.-k. and M.A.Y.; writing—review and editing, Y.S.H., A.A.L. and P.O.M. All authors have read and agreed to the published version of the manuscript.

Funding: This research was funded by Taif University, Saudi Arabia, Project No. (TU-DSPP-2024-47). Also, the publication of this research was supported by the University of Oradea, Romania.

Data Availability Statement: Data are contained within the article.

Acknowledgments: The authors extend their appreciation to Taif University, Saudi Arabia, for supporting this work through project number (TU-DSPP-2024-47).

Conflicts of Interest: The authors declare that they have no conflicts interests.

References

1. West, P. Higher derivative regulation of supersymmetric theories. *Nucl. Phys. B* **1986**, *268*, 113–124. [CrossRef]
2. Alekseev, A.I.; Arbuzov, B.A.; Baikov, V.A. Infrared asymptotic behavior of gluon Green's functions in quantum chromodynamics. *Theor. Math. Phys.* **1982**, *52*, 739–746. [CrossRef]
3. Podolsky, B. A Generalized Electrodynamics Part I-Non-Quantum. *Phys. Rev.* **1942**, *62*, 68. [CrossRef]
4. Podolsky, B.; Kikuchi, C. A Generalized Electrodynamics Part II-Quantum. *Phys. Rev.* **1944**, *65*, 228. [CrossRef]
5. Lobo, J.Z. Group analysis of a Hamilton–Jacobi type equation. *J. Interdiscip. Math.* **2023**, *26*, 51–66. [CrossRef]
6. Almalki, A.; Alawaideh, Y.M.; Al-Khamiseh, B.M.; Alawaideh, S.E. Hamilton formulation for the electrodynamics of generalized Maxwell using fractional derivatives. *J. Interdiscip. Math.* **2023**, *26*, 795–808. [CrossRef]
7. Lee, T.D.; Wick, G.C. Finite Theory of Quantum Electrodynamics. *Phys. Rev. D* **1972**, *6*, 2721.
8. Cuzinatto, R.R.; de Melo, C.A.M.; Pompeia, P.J. Second order gauge theory. *Ann. Phys.* **2007**, *322*, 1211–1232. [CrossRef]
9. Pazarci, A.; Turhan, U.C.; Ghazanfari, N.; Gahramanov, I. Hamiltonian formalism for nonlinear Schrödinger equations. *Commun. Nonlinear Sci. Numer. Simul.* **2023**, *121*, 107191. [CrossRef]
10. Kleinert, H. The membrane properties of condensing strings. *Phys. Lett. B* **1986**, *174*, 335–338. [CrossRef]
11. Govaerts, J. A quantum anomaly for rigid particles. *Phys. Lett. B* **1992**, *293*, 327–334. [CrossRef]
12. Sato, N. Generalization of Hamiltonian mechanics to a three-dimensional phase space. *Prog. Theor. Exp. Phys.* **2021**, *2021*, 063A01. [CrossRef]
13. Nesterenko, V.V. On squaring the primary constraints in a generalized Hamiltonian dynamic. *Phys. Lett. B* **1994**, *327*, 50–55. [CrossRef]
14. Galvão, C.A.P.; Pimentel, B.M. The canonical structure of Podolsky generalized electrodynamics. *Can. J. Phys.* **1988**, *66*, 639–654. [CrossRef]
15. Gümral, H. Dirac's analysis and Ostrogradskii's theorem for a class of second-order degenerate Lagrangians. *Int. J. Geom. Methods Mod. Phys.* **2022**, *19*, 2250008. [CrossRef]
16. Ostrogradsky, M. *Memories Sur les Equations Differentials, Relatives au Problem des Isoperimetries*; Académie impériale des sciences: St.-Pétersbourg, Russia, 1850; Volume 6, pp. 385–517.

17. Alawaideh, Y.M.; Hijjawi, R.S.; Khalifeh, J.M. Reformulation of Degasperis-Procesi field by functional derivatives. *Jordan J. Phys.* **2020**, *13*, 67–72.
18. Simon, J.Z. Higher-derivative Lagrangians, nonlocality, problems, and solutions. *Phys. Rev. D* **1990**, *41*, 3720. [CrossRef]
19. Alkhamiseh, B.M.; Alawaideh, Y.M. Electromagnetic Interaction into the Lagrangian Density Fermi Field: Fractional Formulation. *Jordan J. Phys.* **2023**, *16*, 299–304.
20. Amer, T.S.; Farag, A.M.; Amer, W.S. The dynamical motion of a rigid body for the case of ellipsoid inertia close to ellipsoid of rotation. *Mech. Res. Commun.* **2020**, *108*, 103583. [CrossRef]
21. Amer, T.S.; El-Sabaa, F.M.; Sallam, A.A.; Abady, I.M. Studying the vibrational motion of a rotating symmetrically charged solid body subjected to external forces and moments. *Math. Comput. Simul.* **2023**, *210*, 120–146. [CrossRef]
22. Ismail, A.I.; Amer, T.S.; Amer, W.S. Modification of the Large Parameter Approach for the Periodic Solutions of Nonlinear Dynamical Systems. *Mathematics* **2023**, *11*, 3159. [CrossRef]
23. Amer, T.S.; El-Kafly, H.F.; Elneklawy, A.H.; Galal, A.A. Analyzing the spatial motion of a rigid body subjected to constant body-fixed torques and gyrostatic moment. *Sci. Rep.* **2024**, *14*, 5390. [CrossRef]
24. Diab, A.A.; Hijjawi, R.S.; Asad, J.H.; Khalife, J.M. Hamiltonian formulation of classical fields with fractional derivatives: Revisited. *Meccanica* **2013**, *48*, 323–330. [CrossRef]
25. Alawaideh, Y.M.; Al-Khamiseh, B.M. The new formulation of Hamiltonian second order continuous systems of Riemann-Liouville fractional derivatives. *Phys. Scr.* **2022**, *97*, 125210. [CrossRef]
26. Muslih, S.I.; El-Zalan, H.A. Hamiltonian formulation of systems with higher order derivatives. *Int. J. Theor. Phys.* **2007**, *46*, 3150–3158. [CrossRef]

axiomS

MDPI

Article

Local Influence for the Thin-Plate Spline Generalized Linear Model

Germán Ibacache-Pulgar [1,2,*], Pablo Pacheco [3], Orietta Nicolis [4] and Miguel Angel Uribe-Opazo [5]

1 Institute of Statistics, Universidad de Valparaíso, Av. Gran Bretaña 1111, Valparaíso 2360102, Chile
2 Centro de Estudios Atmosféricos y Cambio Climático (CEACC), Universidad de Valparaíso, Valparaíso 2360102, Chile
3 Dirección de Educación Virtual, Universidad de Playa Ancha, Avenida Guillermo González de Hontaneda 855, Playa Ancha, Valparaíso 2360072, Chile; ppachecog@upla.cl
4 Facultad de Ingenieria, Universidad Andres Bello, Calle Quillota 980, Viña del Mar 2520000, Chile; orietta.nicolis@unab.cl
5 Centro de Ciências Exatas e Tecnológicas, Western Paraná State University (UNIOESTE), Cascavel 85819-110, Paraná, Brazil; miguel.opazo@unioeste.br
* Correspondence: german.ibacache@uv.cl

Abstract: Thin-Plate Spline Generalized Linear Models (TPS-GLMs) are an extension of Semiparametric Generalized Linear Models (SGLMs), because they allow a smoothing spline to be extended to two or more dimensions. This class of models allows modeling a set of data in which it is desired to incorporate the non-linear joint effects of some covariates to explain the variability of a certain variable of interest. In the spatial context, these models are quite useful, since they allow the effects of locations to be included, both in trend and dispersion, using a smooth surface. In this work, we extend the local influence technique for the TPS-GLM model in order to evaluate the sensitivity of the maximum penalized likelihood estimators against small perturbations in the model and data. We fit our model through a joint iterative process based on Fisher Scoring and weighted backfitting algorithms. In addition, we obtained the normal curvature for the case-weight perturbation and response variable additive perturbation schemes, in order to detect influential observations on the model fit. Finally, two data sets from different areas (agronomy and environment) were used to illustrate the methodology proposed here.

Keywords: exponential family; smoothing spline; penalized likelihood function; weighted backfitting algorithm; diagnostics measures

MSC: 62P12; 62J20; 62G05

1. Introduction

Thin-Plate Spline Generalized Linear Models (TPS-GLMs) represent an extension of semiparametric generalized linear models (SGLMs) by enabling the application of smoothing splines in multiple dimensions. These models have the same characteristics of the generalized linear model (GLM), as described by McCullagh and Nelder [1]. Like GLMs, TPS-GLMs can assume a variety of distribution families for the response variable. They also allow for a non-linear relationship between the response variable's mean and the linear predictor via a link function, and they account for non constant variance in the data. Furthermore, the TPS-GLM allow modeling non-linear joint interaction effects due to some covariates, as well as the effects of coordinates in spatial data, making them a useful tool to model dynamic pattern in different scientific areas, such as environment, agronomy, ecology, and so on. Some of the main works related to thin-plate spline technique are Duchon [2,3], Bookstein [4], and Chen et al. [5], while in the context of statistical modeling, Wahba [6], Green and Silverman [7], Wood [8], and Moraga et al. [9], can be mentioned, among others.

However, it is well known that diagnostic analysis is a fundamental process in all statistical modeling for any data set. This analysis allows us to validate the assumptions established about the model in question and identify discrepant observations, and eventually influential ones on the fit of the model. One of the main diagnostic techniques used in GLM and SGLM is local influence. In general, the idea of the local influence technique introduced by Cook [10] is to evaluate the sensitivity of the MLEs when small perturbations are introduced in the assumptions of the model or in the data, both in the response variable and in the explanatory variables. This technique has the advantage, regarding the case elimination technique, that it is not necessary to calculate the estimates of the parameters for each case excluded. In our case, we are interested in developing the local influence technique in the TPS-GLM, in order to detect observations that may have a disproportionate influence on the estimators of both the parametric (regression coefficient) and non-parametric (surface) part of the linear predictor. Such influence may be due, for example, to the fact that each experimental unit contributes differently to the model or that our variable of interest is exposed to a certain modification. In the context of GLM and SGLM, there is empirical evidence that the maximum likelihood estimators (MLEs) and maximum penalized likelihood estimators (PMLEs) are sensitive to this type of situation, and therefore we believe that this sensitivity is also present in the estimators of the TPS-GLM, in particular, in the surface estimator.

Various studies have expanded upon the technique of local influence within different parametric models. Thomas and Cook [11] applied Cook's method of local influence [10] to generalized linear models to assess the impact of minor data perturbations. Ouwens and Beger [12] obtained the normal curvature under a generalized linear model in order to identify influential subjects and/or individual observations. Zhu and Lee [13] developed the local influence technique for incomplete data, and extended such results to generalized linear mixed models (see also Zhu and Lee [14] for further details). Espinheira et al. [15] extended the local influence analysis to beta regression models considering various perturbation scenarios. Rocha and Simas [16] and Ferrari et al. [17] derived the normal curvature considering a beta regression model whose dispersion parameter varies according to the effect of some covariates. Ferreira and Paula [18] developed the local influence approach to partially linear Skew Normal models under different perturbation schemes, and Emami [19] evaluated the sensitivity of Liu penalized least squares estimators using local influence analysis. Most recently, Liu et al. [20] have reported the implementation of influence diagnostics in AR time series models with Skew Normal (SK) distributions.

Within a semiparametric framework, Thomas [21] developed diagnostics for local influence to assess the sensitivity of estimates for the smoothing parameter, which were determined using the cross-validation criterion. Zhu and Lee [14] and Ibacache-Pulgar and Paula [22] introduced measures of local influence to analyze the sensitivity of maximum penalized likelihood estimates in normal and partially linear Student-t models, respectively. Ibacache-Pulgar et al. [23,24] explored local influence curvature within elliptical semiparametric mixed models and symmetric semiparametric additive models. Subsequently, ref. [25] and Ibacache-Pulgar and Reyes [26] further extended local influence measures to normal and elliptical partially varying-coefficient models, respectively. Ibacache-Pulgar et al. [27] developed the local influence method within the context of semiparametric additive beta regression models. Meanwhile, Cavieres et al. [28] calculated the normal curvature to assess the sensitivity of estimators in a thin-plate spline model that incorporates skew normal random errors. Jeldes et al. [29] applied the partially coefficient-varying model with symmetric random errors to air pollution data from the cities of Santiago, Chile, and Lima, Peru. In this context, they carried out an application of the local influence technique to detect influential observations in the model fit. Saavedra-Nievas et al. [30] extended the local influence technique for the spatio-temporal linear model under normal distribution and with separable covariance. Recently, Sánchez et al. [31] obtained the normal curvature for the varying-coefficient quantile regression model under log-symmetric distributions, and presented an interesting application of such results to an environmental pollution data set.

In this work, we extend the local influence approach in Thin-Plate Spline Generalized Linear Model.

The contents are organized as follows: Section 2 introduces the thin-plate spline generalized linear model. Section 3 details the method for obtaining maximum penalized likelihood estimators and discusses some statistical inferential results. In Section 4, we provide a detailed description of the local influence method and derives normal curvatures for various perturbation schemes. In Section 5, the methodology is illustrated using two datasets. The paper concludes with some final observations in Section 6.

2. The Thin-Plate Spline Generalized Linear Model (TPS-GLM)

In this section, we present the TPS-GLM and the penalized function to carry out the process of estimating the parameters.

2.1. Statistical Model

Let $\{y_i \mid i = 1, \ldots, n\}$ be a data set where each response variable y_i follows a distribution from the exponential family with the following density function:

$$f_y(y_i; \theta_i, \phi) = \exp\left[\frac{y_i\theta_i - \psi(\theta_i)}{a_i(\phi)} + c(y_i, \phi)\right],$$

where θ_i is the canonical form of the location parameter and depends on the mean μ_i. The term $a_i(\phi)$ represents a known function of the unknown dispersion parameter ϕ (or a vector of unknown dispersion parameters). The function c depends on both the dispersion parameter and the responses, while ψ is a known function, such that the mean and variance of y_i are given by: $\mu_i = \mathrm{E}(y_i) = \partial\psi(\theta_i)/\partial\theta_i$ and $\mathrm{Var}(y_i) = a_i(\phi)\,\mathrm{V}_i$, with $\mathrm{V}_i = \mathrm{V}(\mu_i) = \partial^2\psi(\theta_i)/\partial\theta_i^2$, respectively. The TPS-GLM is defined by Equation (1) and the following systematic component:

$$g(\mu_i) = \eta_i = \mathbf{w}_i^\top \boldsymbol{\alpha} + f(\mathbf{t}_i), \tag{1}$$

where $\mathbf{w}_i$ is a $(p \times 1)$ vector of covariables, $\boldsymbol{\alpha} = (\alpha_1, \ldots, \alpha_p)^\top$ corresponds to the vector of regression coefficients, $f(\cdot)$ is unknown smooth arbitrary surface, and $\mathbf{t}_i$ is a two-dimensional covariates vector. To write the model given by Equation (1) in a matrix form, first consider the one-to-one transformation of the vector $\mathbf{f}$ suggested by Green and Silverman [7], stated as

$$\mathbf{f} = \begin{pmatrix} f(\mathbf{t}_1) \\ \vdots \\ f(\mathbf{t}_n) \end{pmatrix} = \mathbf{E}\delta + \mathbf{T}^T\mathbf{a}\,,$$

where $\mathbf{a}$ is a 3×1 vector with components a_i, $\boldsymbol{\delta}$ is a $n \times 1$ vector with components δ_i, $\mathbf{E}$ is a $(n \times n)$ matrix whose elements are given by $E_{ij} = \frac{1}{16\pi}\|\mathbf{t}_i - \mathbf{t}_j\|^2 \log\|\mathbf{t}_i - \mathbf{t}_j\|^2$, with $E_{ii} = 0$ for each i, and $\mathbf{T}$ is a $(3 \times n)$ matrix defined as

$$\mathbf{T} = \begin{pmatrix} 1 & 1 & \ldots & 1 \\ \mathbf{t}_1 & \mathbf{t}_2 & \ldots & \mathbf{t}_n \end{pmatrix}.$$

Thus, the Model (1) can be written in a matrix form as

$$\boldsymbol{\eta} = \boldsymbol{X\beta} + \mathbf{E}\delta,$$

where the regression matrix is structured as $\boldsymbol{X} = \begin{pmatrix}\mathbf{T}^T & \mathbf{W}\end{pmatrix}^T$, with $\mathbf{W} = \begin{pmatrix}\mathbf{w}_1^\top, & \ldots, & \mathbf{w}_n^\top\end{pmatrix}^T$, and the vector of regression coefficients as $\boldsymbol{\beta} = \begin{pmatrix}\mathbf{a}^T & \boldsymbol{\alpha}\end{pmatrix}^T = (\ \beta_1, \ \ldots, \ \beta_{p+3}\ )$, where

$\beta_j = \text{a}_j$ $(j = 1,2,3)$ and $\beta_j = \alpha_{j-3}$ $(j = 4,\ldots,p+3)$; see [9]. Note that this matrix representation of the linear predictor allows us to treat the TPS-GLM as a semiparametric generalized linear model, in which the term $\boldsymbol{X\beta}$ represents the parametric component and $\mathbf{E}\delta$ the nonparametric component. One of the advantages of the TPS-GLM, apart from being able to model both discrete and continuous variables that belong to the exponential family, is its flexibility to model the non-linear joint effect of covariates through the surface f present in the linear predictor η. In the context of spatial data, this models allows the effect of coordinates to the incorporated into the modeling process. It is important to note that when the surface f is not present in the linear predictor η, the model reduces to the classical generalized linear model. However, if the vector $\mathbf{t}$ reduces to a scalar, t, the model reduces to the semiparametric generalized linear model discussed, for instance, by Green and Silverman [7].

2.2. Penalized Function

Under the TPS-GLM, we have that $\boldsymbol{\theta} = (\boldsymbol{\beta}^\top, \boldsymbol{\delta}^\top, \phi)^\top \subseteq \mathcal{R}^{p^*}$, with $p^* = (p+3)+n+1$ parameters. Then, the log-likelihood function is given by

$$L(\boldsymbol{\theta}) = \sum_{i=1}^{n} L_i(\boldsymbol{\theta}), \quad (2)$$

where

$$L_i(\boldsymbol{\theta}) = \left[\frac{y_i\theta_i - \psi(\theta_i)}{a_i(\phi)} + c(y_i,\phi)\right].$$

To ensure the identifiability of the parameter vector $\boldsymbol{\alpha}$, we assume that f belongs to the function space where all partial derivatives of total order m reside within the Hilbert space $\mathcal{L}^2[E^d]$, the space of square-integrable functions on Euclidean d-space. Incorporating a penalty function over f, we have that the penalized log-likelihood function can be expressed as (see, for instance, Green and Silverman [7])

$$L_{\text{p}}(\boldsymbol{\theta},\lambda_f) = L(\boldsymbol{\theta}) + \lambda_f^* J_m^d(f)\,, \quad (3)$$

where $J_m^d(f)$ is a penalty functional measuring the wiggliness of f, and $\lambda_f^*(\lambda_f)$ is a constant that depends on the smoothing parameter $\lambda_f \geq 0$. In general, a measure of the curvature of f corresponds to its squared norm, $\|f\|$, defined as

$$J_m^d(f) = \|f\| = \sum_{v_1+\ldots+v_d=m} \frac{m!}{v_1!\ldots v_d!}\int_{-\infty}^{+\infty}\cdots\int_{-\infty}^{+\infty}\left(\frac{\partial^m f}{\partial \text{t}_1^{\alpha_1}\ldots\partial \text{t}_d^{\alpha_d}}\right)^2\prod_{j=1}^{d}\text{dt}_j\,.$$

For simplicity, in this work, we will consider the case in which $d = 2, m = 2$ and $g = g(\text{t}_1,\text{t}_2)$. Consequently, the penalty function $J_2^2(f)$ is expressed in the form

$$J_2^2(f) = \int\int_{\mathcal{R}^2}\left\{\left(\frac{\partial^2 f}{\partial \text{t}_1^2}\right)^2 + 2\left(\frac{\partial^2 f}{\partial \text{t}_1\partial \text{t}_2}\right)^2 + \left(\frac{\partial^2 f}{\partial \text{t}_2^2}\right)^2\right\}\text{dt}_1\text{dt}_2\,,$$

and measures the rapid variation in f and the departure from local linearity. In this case, the estimation of f leads to a natural thin-plate spline. According to Green and Silverman [7], we may express the penalty functional as $J_2^2(f) = \delta^T\mathbf{E}\delta$. Then, if we consider $\lambda_f^* = -\lambda_f/2$, the penalized log-likelihood function (3) can be expressed as

$$L_{\text{p}}(\boldsymbol{\theta},\lambda_f) = L(\boldsymbol{\theta}) - \frac{\lambda_f}{2}\delta^T\mathbf{E}\delta\,. \quad (4)$$

The first term in the right-hand side of Equation (4) measures the goodness-of-fit, while the second terms penalizes the roughness of f with a fixed parameter λ_f. Selecting appropriate parameters is crucial in the estimation process, as they determine the balance between the goodness-of-fit and the smoothness (or regularity) of the estimated function. It is important to emphasize that selecting appropriate parameters is crucial in the estimation process because they control the trade-off between goodness-of-fit and the smoothness (or regularity) of the estimated function. In this work, the smoothing parameter is selected through the Akaike Criterion (AIC) based on the penalized log-likelihood function given in Equation (3). More details of the method are given in Section 3.7.

3. Estimation and Inference

In this section, we discuss the problem of estimating the parameters under the TPS-GLM. Specifically, we derive a weighted iterative process based on the backfitting algorithm and estimate the variance–covariance matrix of our estimator from the penalized Fisher information matrix (see Green [32] and Green and Silverman [7]). A brief discussion of the smoothing parameter selection is also presented.

3.1. Penalized Score Function

First, we are going to assume that the function $L_{\mathrm{P}}(\boldsymbol{\theta}, \lambda_f)$ is regular in the sense that it admits first and second partial derivatives with respect to the elements of the parameter vector $\boldsymbol{\theta}$. To obtain the score function for $\boldsymbol{\beta}$, we must calculate $\partial L_{\mathrm{P}_i}(\boldsymbol{\theta}, \lambda_f)/\partial \beta_j$ for $i \in \{1, \ldots, n\}$ and $j \in \{1, \ldots, p+2\}$. After performing some partial derivative operations, we have that the score function for $\boldsymbol{\beta}$ can be written in matrix as follows:

$$\mathbf{U}_{\mathrm{P}}^{\beta}(\boldsymbol{\theta}) = \frac{\partial L_{\mathrm{P}}(\boldsymbol{\theta}, \lambda_f)}{\partial \boldsymbol{\beta}} \quad = \quad \mathbf{X}^{\top}\widetilde{\mathbf{T}}(\mathbf{y} - \boldsymbol{\mu}),$$

where $\mathbf{X}$ is an $(n \times 3 + p)$ matrix whose ith row is $\mathbf{x}_i^{\top}$, $\widetilde{\mathbf{T}} = \mathrm{diag}\Big[(\mathrm{a}_i(\phi))^{-1}\Big(\frac{\partial \mu_i}{\partial \eta_i}\Big)V_i^{-1}\Big]$ is a $(n \times 3 + p)$ matrix, with $V_i = V(\mu_i) = \partial^2\psi(\theta_i)/\partial\theta_i^2$ the variance function, $\mathrm{a}_i(\phi)$ a function of ϕ, $\mathbf{y} = (y_1, \ldots, y_n)^{\top}$ and $\boldsymbol{\mu} = (\mu_1, \ldots, \mu_n)^{\top}$ are $(n \times 1)$ vectors.

Conversely, to derive the score function for δ, we need to compute $\partial L_{\mathrm{P}_i}(\boldsymbol{\theta}, \lambda_f)/\partial \delta_\ell$ for $i \in \{1, \ldots, n\}$ and $\ell \in \{1, \ldots, n\}$. Again, after some algebraic operations, the score function for δ can be written in matrix as follows:

$$\mathbf{U}_{\mathrm{P}}^{\delta}(\boldsymbol{\theta}) = \frac{\partial L_{\mathrm{P}}(\boldsymbol{\theta}, \lambda_f)}{\partial \delta} \quad = \quad \mathbf{E}^{\top}\widetilde{\mathbf{T}}(\mathbf{y} - \boldsymbol{\mu}) - \lambda_f \mathbf{E}\delta,$$

where the matrix $\mathbf{E}$ is defined in Section 2.1. Finally, the score function for ϕ is given by

$$\mathbf{U}_{\mathrm{P}}^{\phi}(\boldsymbol{\theta}) = \frac{\partial L_{\mathrm{P}}(\boldsymbol{\theta}, \lambda_f)}{\partial \phi} \quad = \quad -\sum_{i=1}^{n}(\mathrm{a}_i(\phi))^{-2}\{y_i\theta_i - \psi(\theta_i)\} + \sum_{i=1}^{n} c'(y_i, \phi),$$

with $c'(y_i, \phi) = \partial c(y_i, \phi)/\partial\phi$, for $i \in \{1, \ldots, n\}$. Thus, the vector of penalized score functions of $\boldsymbol{\theta}$ can be expressed compactly as

$$\mathbf{U}_{\mathrm{P}}(\boldsymbol{\theta}) = \begin{pmatrix} \mathbf{U}_{\mathrm{P}}^{\beta}(\boldsymbol{\theta}) \\ \mathbf{U}_{\mathrm{P}}^{\delta}(\boldsymbol{\theta}) \\ \mathbf{U}_{\mathrm{P}}^{\phi}(\boldsymbol{\theta}) \end{pmatrix}.$$

Note that if the model under consideration only considers the parametric component in the linear predictor, that is, the nonparametric component is omitted, the expressions of the remaining score functions are reduced to those obtained under the classical generalized linear model.

3.2. Penalized Hessian Matrix

To obtain the penalized Hessian matrix, we must compute the second-derivate of $L_{\rm p}(\boldsymbol{\theta}, \lambda_f)$ with respect to each element of $\boldsymbol{\theta}$, that is, $\partial^2 L_{\rm p}(\boldsymbol{\theta}, \lambda_f)/\partial\theta_{j^*}\theta_{\ell^*}$, for $j^*, \ell^* \in \{1, \ldots, p^*\}$. After some algebraic operations, we have that the diagonal elements (block matrices) of the Hessian matrix are given by

$$\begin{aligned}
\mathbf{L}_{\rm p}^{\beta\beta} = \frac{\partial^2 L_{\rm p}(\boldsymbol{\theta}, \lambda_f)}{\partial\boldsymbol{\beta}\partial\boldsymbol{\alpha}^\top} &= -\mathbf{X}^\top\mathbf{M}^*\mathbf{X}, \\
\mathbf{L}_{\rm p}^{\delta\delta} = \frac{\partial^2 L_{\rm p}(\boldsymbol{\theta}, \lambda_f)}{\partial\boldsymbol{\delta}\partial\boldsymbol{\delta}^\top} &= -\mathbf{E}^\top\mathbf{M}^*\mathbf{E} - \lambda_f\mathbf{E} \qquad \text{and} \\
\mathbf{L}_{\rm p}^{\phi\phi} = \frac{\partial^2 L_{\rm p}(\boldsymbol{\theta}, \lambda_f)}{\partial\phi^2} &= \sum_{i=1}^{n} 2(\mathrm{a}_i(\phi))^{-3}(y_i\theta_i - \psi(\theta_i)) + \sum_{i=1}^{n} c''(y_i, \phi)),
\end{aligned}$$

where $\mathbf{M}^* = \mathrm{diag}_{1\leq i\leq n}\left[(\mathrm{a}_i(\phi))^{-1}(\partial\mu_i/\partial\eta_i)^2 V_i^{-1}\right]$ and $c''(y_i, \phi) = \partial^2 c(y_i, \phi)/\partial\phi^2$, for $1 \leq i \leq n$. The elements outside the main diagonal of the Hessian matrix take the form

$$\begin{aligned}
\mathbf{L}_{\rm p}^{\beta\delta} = \frac{\partial^2 L_{\rm p}(\boldsymbol{\theta}, \lambda_f)}{\partial\boldsymbol{\beta}\partial\boldsymbol{\delta}^\top} &= -\mathbf{X}^\top\mathbf{M}^*\mathbf{E}, \\
\mathbf{L}_{\rm p}^{\beta_j\phi} = \frac{\partial^2 L_{\rm p}(\boldsymbol{\theta}, \lambda_f)}{\partial\alpha_j\partial\phi} &= -\sum_{i=1}^{n}(\mathrm{a}_i(\phi))^{-2}\left\{(y_i - \mu_i)V_i^{-1}\frac{\partial\mu_i}{\partial\eta_i}x_{ij}\right\} \qquad \text{and} \\
\mathbf{L}_{\rm p}^{\delta_\ell\phi} = \frac{\partial^2 L_{\rm p}(\boldsymbol{\theta}, \lambda_f)}{\partial\delta_\ell\partial\phi} &= -\sum_{i=1}^{n}(\mathrm{a}_i(\phi))^{-2}\left\{(y_i - \mu_i)V_i^{-1}\frac{\partial\mu_i}{\partial\eta_i}e_{i\ell}\right\},
\end{aligned}$$

where x_{ij} denotes the (i,j)th element of the matrix $\mathbf{X}$ and e_{ij} denotes the (i,ℓ)th element of the matrix $\mathbf{E}$, for $i \in \{1, \ldots, n\}$, $j \in \{1, \ldots, p+2\}$ and $\ell \in \{1, \ldots, n\}$. Thus, the penalized Hessian matrix can be represented as

$$\mathbf{L}_{\rm P}(\boldsymbol{\theta}) = \begin{pmatrix} \mathbf{L}_{\rm p}^{\beta\beta} & \mathbf{L}_{\rm p}^{\beta\delta} & \mathbf{L}_{\rm p}^{\beta\phi} \\ \mathbf{L}_{\rm p}^{\beta\delta^\top} & \mathbf{L}_{\rm p}^{\delta\delta} & \mathbf{L}_{\rm p}^{\delta\phi} \\ \mathbf{L}_{\rm p}^{\beta\phi^\top} & \mathbf{L}_{\rm p}^{\delta\phi^\top} & \mathbf{L}_{\rm p}^{\phi\phi} \end{pmatrix}.$$

It is noteworthy that this matrix simplifies to the Hessian matrix used in generalized linear models when the nonparametric component is absent. The primary application of this matrix lies in the normal curvature, which is essential for developing the local influence technique. This will be discussed in the following section.

3.3. Penalized Expected Information Matrix

By taking the expectation of the matrix $-\mathbf{L}_{\rm P}(\boldsymbol{\theta})$, we derive the penalized expected information matrix, which is of dimension $(p^* \times p^*)$, as follows:

$$\mathfrak{J}_{\rm P}(\boldsymbol{\theta}) = -\mathrm{E}\left[\frac{\partial^2 L_{\rm P}(\boldsymbol{\theta}, \boldsymbol{\lambda})}{\partial\boldsymbol{\theta}\partial\boldsymbol{\theta}^T}\right].$$

This matrix assumes the following diagonal structure in blocks:

$$\mathfrak{J}_{\rm P}(\boldsymbol{\theta}) = \begin{pmatrix} \mathfrak{J}_{\rm p}^{\beta\delta}(\boldsymbol{\theta}) & \mathbf{0} \\ \mathbf{0} & \mathfrak{J}_{\rm p}^{\phi\phi}(\boldsymbol{\theta}) \end{pmatrix},$$

where

$$\mathfrak{J}_{\mathrm{p}}^{\beta\delta}(\boldsymbol{\theta}) = \begin{pmatrix} \mathbf{X}^\top\mathbf{M}^*\mathbf{X} & \mathbf{X}^\top\mathbf{M}^*\mathbf{E} \\ \mathbf{E}^\top\mathbf{M}^*\mathbf{X} & \mathbf{E}^\top\mathbf{M}^*\mathbf{E}+\lambda_f\mathbf{E} \end{pmatrix}$$

and

$$\mathfrak{J}_{\mathrm{p}}^{\phi\phi}(\boldsymbol{\theta}) = \sum_{i=1}^{n} -2(\mathrm{a}_i(\phi))^{-3}(\mu_i\theta_i - \psi(\theta_i)) - \sum_{i=1}^{n} \mathrm{E}(c''(y_i,\phi)),$$

with $c''(y_i,\phi) = \partial^2 c(y_i,\phi)/\partial\phi^2$ for $i \in \{1,\dots,n\}$.

3.4. Derivation of the Iterative Process

The value of $\boldsymbol{\theta}$ that maximizes $L_{\mathrm{p}}(\boldsymbol{\theta},\lambda_f)$, called maximum penalized likelihood estimate (MPLE) and denoted by $\widehat{\boldsymbol{\theta}}$, is carried out by solving the corresponding estimation equations. Let $\boldsymbol{\theta} = (\boldsymbol{\theta}_1^\top \quad \theta_2)^\top$, where $\boldsymbol{\theta}_1 = \left(\boldsymbol{\beta}^\top \quad \boldsymbol{\delta}^\top\right)^\top$ and $\theta_2 = \phi$. In addition, consider the partition of the score function vector $\mathbf{U}_{\mathrm{P}}(\boldsymbol{\theta}) = \left(\mathbf{U}_{\mathrm{p}}^{1^\top}(\boldsymbol{\theta}) \quad \mathbf{U}_{\mathrm{p}}^{2^\top}(\boldsymbol{\theta})\right)^\top$, where $\mathbf{U}_{\mathrm{p}}^{1^\top}(\boldsymbol{\theta}) = \left(\mathbf{U}_{\mathrm{p}}^{\beta^\top}(\boldsymbol{\theta}) \quad \mathbf{U}_{\mathrm{p}}^{\delta^\top}(\boldsymbol{\theta})\right)$ and $\mathbf{U}_{\mathrm{p}}^{2}(\boldsymbol{\theta}) = \mathbf{U}_{\mathrm{p}}^{\phi}(\boldsymbol{\theta})$. In order to estimate $\boldsymbol{\theta}$ based on penalized likelihood function given by Equation (4), we have to solve the equations

$$\begin{cases} \mathbf{U}_{\mathrm{p}}^{1}(\boldsymbol{\theta}) = \mathbf{0} \\ \mathbf{U}_{\mathrm{p}}^{2}(\boldsymbol{\theta}) = \mathbf{0}\,. \end{cases}$$

These estimating equations are nonlinear, and necessitate an iterative approach for their solution. An alternative frequently proposed in the context of generalized linear models is the Fisher scoring algorithm (Nelder and Wedderburn, [33]), considering the fact that in some situations the matrix $-\mathbf{L}_{\mathrm{P}}(\boldsymbol{\theta})$ can be non-positive definite. Then, the algorithm for estimating $\boldsymbol{\theta}_1$, with ϕ fixed, is given by

$$\boldsymbol{\theta}_1^{\mathrm{new}} = \boldsymbol{\theta}_1^{\mathrm{old}} + (\mathfrak{J}_{\mathrm{p}}^{\beta\delta}(\boldsymbol{\theta})^{-1})^{\mathrm{old}}\mathbf{U}_{\mathrm{p}}^{1^{\mathrm{old}}}(\boldsymbol{\theta}),$$

which is equivalent to solving the matrix equation

$$\begin{pmatrix} \mathbf{I} & \mathbf{S}_{\beta}^{\mathrm{old}}\mathbf{E} \\ \mathbf{S}_{\delta}^{\mathrm{old}}\mathbf{X} & \mathbf{I} \end{pmatrix}\begin{pmatrix} \boldsymbol{\beta}^{\mathrm{new}} \\ \boldsymbol{\delta}^{\mathrm{new}} \end{pmatrix} = \begin{pmatrix} \mathbf{S}_{0}^{\mathrm{old}}\mathbf{z}^{\mathrm{old}} \\ \mathbf{S}_{1}^{\mathrm{old}}\mathbf{z}^{\mathrm{old}} \end{pmatrix}, \tag{5}$$

where $\mathbf{z}^{\mathrm{old}} = (\mathbf{y}-\boldsymbol{\mu}^{\mathrm{old}}) + \boldsymbol{\eta}^{\mathrm{old}}$, with $\mathbf{S}_{\vartheta}^{\mathrm{old}}$ defined as

$$\mathbf{S}_{\vartheta} = \begin{cases} (\mathbf{X}^\top\mathbf{M}^{*^{\mathrm{old}}}\mathbf{X})^{-1}\mathbf{X}^\top\mathbf{M}^{*^{\mathrm{old}}} & \vartheta = \beta \\ (\mathbf{E}^\top\mathbf{M}^{*^{\mathrm{old}}}\mathbf{E}+\lambda_f\mathbf{E})^{-1}\mathbf{E}^\top\mathbf{M}^{*^{\mathrm{old}}} & \vartheta = \delta\,. \end{cases}$$

Consequently, the weighted back-fitting (Gauss–Seidel) iterations for simultaneously updating $\boldsymbol{\beta}$ and $\boldsymbol{\delta}$ are given by

$$\boldsymbol{\beta}^{\mathrm{new}} = \mathbf{S}_{\beta}^{\mathrm{old}}(\mathbf{z}^{\mathrm{old}} - \mathbf{E}\boldsymbol{\delta}^{\mathrm{old}}), \tag{6}$$

$$\boldsymbol{\delta}^{\mathrm{new}} = \mathbf{S}_{\delta}^{\mathrm{old}}(\mathbf{z}^{\mathrm{old}} - \mathbf{X}\boldsymbol{\beta}^{\mathrm{old}}), \tag{7}$$

It is crucial to note that the system of Equations (5) is consistent, and the back-fitting algorithm converges to a solution for any initial values, provided that the weight matrix

$\mathbf{M}^*$ is symmetric and positive definite. Additionally, if the parametric component $\mathbf{w}_i^\top \boldsymbol{\beta}$ is absent in the linear predictor, the estimator of δ is given by:

$$\delta^{\text{new}} = \mathbf{S}_\delta^{\text{old}} \mathbf{z}^{\text{old}} .$$

The MPLE of the dispersion parameter, $\widehat{\theta}_2 = \widehat{\phi}$, can be determined through the following iterative procedure:

$$\theta_2^{\text{new}} = \theta_2^{\text{old}} - (\mathcal{J}_{\text{p}}^{\phi\phi}(\boldsymbol{\theta})^{-1})^{\text{old}} \mathbf{U}_{\text{p}}^{2\text{old}}(\boldsymbol{\theta}) .$$

Summarizing, each iteration of the Fisher scoring algorithm updates $\boldsymbol{\beta}$ and δ using Equations (6) and (7), and evaluating matrices $\mathbf{S}_\theta$ and $\mathbf{M}^*$ at the MPLE of $\boldsymbol{\theta}$ obtained in the previous iteration, that is, $\boldsymbol{\theta}^{\text{old}}$, until convergence is obtained. The joint iterative process that resolves $\mathbf{U}_{\text{P}}(\boldsymbol{\theta}) = \mathbf{0}$ is presented below.

3.5. Estimation of Surface

To obtain the MPLE of $\mathbf{f}$, we must consider its one-to-one representation given in Equation (2) and MPLE obtained from the iterative process described above. Indeed, we have that $\widehat{\mathbf{f}}$ can be obtained as

$$\widehat{\mathbf{f}} = \mathbf{E}\widehat{\delta} + \mathbf{T}^T\widehat{\mathbf{a}}, \ ,$$

where $\widehat{\delta}$ and $\widehat{\mathbf{a}}$ are the MPLE of δ and $\widehat{\mathbf{a}}$, respectively. Note that vector $\widehat{\mathbf{a}}$ corresponds to the first three elements of vector $\widehat{\boldsymbol{\beta}}$. Consequently, $\widehat{\mathbf{f}}$ is a natural thin-plate spline. Details of the conditions that guarantee this result are given, for example, in Green and Silverman [7] and Wood [34].

3.6. Approximate Standard Errors

In this study, we propose approximating the variance–covariance matrix of $\widehat{\boldsymbol{\theta}}$ by using the inverse of the penalized Fisher information matrix. Specifically, we have that

$$\widehat{\text{Cov}}(\widehat{\boldsymbol{\theta}}) \approx \mathcal{J}_{\text{p}}^{-1}(\boldsymbol{\theta})\big|_{\widehat{\boldsymbol{\theta}}} .$$

If we are interested in drawing inferences for $\boldsymbol{\beta}$, the approximate variance–covariance matrix can be estimated by using the corresponding block-diagonal matrix obtained from $\mathcal{J}_{\text{p}}^{-1}(\boldsymbol{\theta})$, similarly for $\mathbf{f}$ and ϕ.

3.7. On Degrees of Freedom and Smoothing Parameter

For the TPS-GLM, the degree of freedom (df) associated with the smooth surface is given by (see, for instance Green and Silverman [7])

$$df(\lambda_f) = \text{tr}(\mathbf{E}^\top \mathbf{S}_\delta),$$

which approximately represents the number of effective parameters used in the modeling process to estimate the smooth surface f.

Regarding the selection of the smoothing parameter, we propose to use the Akaike Information Criterion (AIC) (see, for instance, [24,35]), defined as

$$AIC(\lambda_f) = -2L_p(\boldsymbol{\theta}, \lambda_f)\big|_{\widehat{\boldsymbol{\theta}}} + 2[1 + p + df(\lambda_f)] \ ,$$

where $L_p(\boldsymbol{\theta}, \lambda_f)$ denote the penalized likelihood function evaluated at MPLE of $\boldsymbol{\theta}$, and p denote the number of parameters in $\boldsymbol{\beta}$. As usual, the idea is to select the value of λ_f that minimizes $AIC(\lambda_f)$.

4. Local Influence

In this section, we extend the local influence technique to evaluate the sensitivity of the MPLE under the TPS-GLM. Specifically, we present some theoretical aspects of the method and, subsequently, we derive the normal curvature for three perturbation schemes.

4.1. Local Influence Analysis

Consider $\boldsymbol{\omega} = (\omega_1, \ldots, \omega_n)^\top$, an $n \times 1$ vector of perturbations restricted to some open subset $\Omega \subset \mathbb{R}^n$. Let $L_p(\boldsymbol{\theta}, \lambda_f \mid \boldsymbol{\omega})$ denote the logarithm of the perturbed penalized likelihood function. Assume there exists a vector of non-perturbation $\boldsymbol{\omega}_0 \in \Omega$, such that $L_p(\boldsymbol{\theta}, \lambda_f \mid \boldsymbol{\omega}_0) = L_p(\boldsymbol{\theta}, \lambda_f)$. To evaluate the influence of small perturbations on the MPL estimate $\widehat{\boldsymbol{\theta}}$, we can consider the penalized likelihood displacement given by:

$$2[L_p(\widehat{\boldsymbol{\theta}}, \lambda_f) - L_p(\widehat{\boldsymbol{\theta}}_\omega, \lambda_f)] \geq 0,$$

where $\widehat{\boldsymbol{\theta}}_\omega$ is the MPL estimate under $L_p(\boldsymbol{\theta}, \lambda_f \mid \boldsymbol{\omega})$. The measure $\mathrm{LD}(\boldsymbol{\omega})$ is useful for assessing the distance between $\widehat{\boldsymbol{\theta}}$ and $\widehat{\boldsymbol{\theta}}_\omega$. Cook [10] suggested examining the local behavior of $\mathrm{LD}(\boldsymbol{\omega})$ around $\boldsymbol{\omega}_0$. The procedure involves selecting a unit direction $\boldsymbol{d} \in \Omega$, with $\|\boldsymbol{d}\| = 1$, and then plotting $\mathrm{LD}(\boldsymbol{\omega}_0 + a\boldsymbol{d})$ against a, where $a \in \mathbb{R}$. This plot, called the lifted line, can be characterized by considering the normal curvature $C_d(\boldsymbol{\theta})$ around $a = 0$. The suggestion is to assume the direction $\boldsymbol{d} = \boldsymbol{d}_{\max}$ corresponding to the largest curvature $C_{d_{\max}}(\boldsymbol{\theta})$. The index plot of $\boldsymbol{d}_{\max}$ can identify those cases that, under small perturbations, have a significant potential influence on $\mathrm{LD}(\boldsymbol{\omega})$. According to Cook [10], the normal curvature in the unit direction $\boldsymbol{d}$ is expressed as

$$C_d(\boldsymbol{\theta}) = -2\{\boldsymbol{d}^\top \boldsymbol{\Delta}_\mathrm{p}^\top \mathbf{L}_\mathrm{p}^{-1} \boldsymbol{\Delta}_\mathrm{p} \boldsymbol{d}\},$$

with

$$\mathbf{L}_\mathrm{p} = \left.\frac{\partial^2 L_p(\boldsymbol{\theta}, \lambda_f)}{\partial\boldsymbol{\theta}\partial\boldsymbol{\theta}^\top}\right|_{\boldsymbol{\theta}=\widehat{\boldsymbol{\theta}}} \quad \text{and} \quad \boldsymbol{\Delta}_\mathrm{p} = \left.\frac{\partial^2 L_p(\boldsymbol{\theta}, \lambda_f|\boldsymbol{\omega})}{\partial\boldsymbol{\theta}\partial\boldsymbol{\omega}^\top}\right|_{\boldsymbol{\theta}=\widehat{\boldsymbol{\theta}},\ \boldsymbol{\omega}=\boldsymbol{\omega}_0}.$$

Note that $-\mathbf{L}_\mathrm{p}$ represents the penalized observed information matrix evaluated at $\widehat{\boldsymbol{\theta}}$ (see Section 3.2), and $\boldsymbol{\Delta}_\mathrm{p}$ is the penalized perturbation matrix evaluated at $\widehat{\boldsymbol{\theta}}$ and $\boldsymbol{\omega}_0$. It is essential to highlight that $C_d(\boldsymbol{\theta})$ denotes the local influence on the estimate $\widehat{\boldsymbol{\theta}}$ after perturbing the model or data. Escobar and Meeker [36] suggested examining the normal curvature in the direction $\boldsymbol{d} = \boldsymbol{e}_i$, where $\boldsymbol{e}_i$ is an $n \times 1$ vector with a one at the ith position and zeros elsewhere. Consequently, the normal curvature, referred to as the total local influence of the ith case, takes the form $C_{e_i}(\boldsymbol{\theta}) = 2|c_{ii}|$ for $i \in \{1, \ldots, n\}$, where c_{ii} is the ith principal diagonal element of the matrix $\boldsymbol{C} = \boldsymbol{\Delta}_\mathrm{p}^\top \mathbf{L}_\mathrm{p}^{-1} \boldsymbol{\Delta}_\mathrm{p}$.

4.2. Derivation of the Normal Curvature

Typically, the perturbation schemes used in the analysis of local influence are determined by the structure of the model under consideration, as discussed by Billor and Loynes [37]. These schemes can generally be divided into two main categories: perturbations to the model (to examine changes in assumptions) or perturbations to the data. For instance, we might consider perturbing the response variable or the explanatory variables. The motivation for employing these perturbation schemes often includes addressing issues such as the presence of outliers or the occurrence of measurement errors in the data. Subsequently, we will present the formulas for the matrix $\boldsymbol{\Delta}_\mathrm{p}$ for various perturbation schemes.

Consider the weights assigned to the observations in the penalized log-likelihood function, given by:

$$L_p(\boldsymbol{\theta}, \lambda_f|\boldsymbol{\omega}) \;=\; L(\boldsymbol{\theta}|\boldsymbol{\omega}) - \sum_{i=1}^{n} \frac{\lambda_f}{2} \boldsymbol{\delta}^\top \mathbf{E} \boldsymbol{\delta}\,,$$

where $L(\boldsymbol{\theta}|\omega) = \sum_{i=1}^{n} \omega_i L_i(\boldsymbol{\theta})$, $\boldsymbol{\omega} = (\omega_1, \ldots, \omega_n)^\top$ is the vector of weights, with $0 \leq \omega_i \leq 1$. In this case, the vector of no perturbation is given by $\boldsymbol{\omega}_0 = 1_{(n\times 1)}$. Differentiating $L_p(\boldsymbol{\theta}, \lambda_f|\boldsymbol{\omega})$ with respect to the elements of $\boldsymbol{\theta}$ and $\boldsymbol{\omega}^T$, we have that the matrix $\boldsymbol{\Delta}_\mathrm{p}$ takes the form

$$\boldsymbol{\Delta}_\mathrm{p} = \begin{pmatrix} \mathbf{X}^\top \mathbf{D}_\tau \\ \mathbf{E}^\top \mathbf{D}_\tau \\ \widehat{\mathbf{u}}^\top \end{pmatrix},$$

where the matrix $\mathbf{D}_\tau = \mathrm{diag}_{1\leq i \leq n}(\tau_i)$ and $\mathbf{u} = (u_1, \ldots, u_n)^\top$, with $\tau_i = (\mathrm{a}_i(\phi))^{-1}(y_i - \partial\psi(h(\eta_i))/\partial h(\eta_i))\partial h(\eta_i)/\partial\eta_i$, $h(\eta_i) = \psi^{'-1}(\eta_i)$, $\psi^{'-1}(\cdot)$ denotes the inverse function of $\psi^{'}(\cdot)$, $u_i = -(\mathrm{a}_i(\phi))^{-2}(y_i h(\eta_i) - \psi(h(\eta_i)) + \mathrm{c}'(y_i, \phi)\mathbf{e}_{in}^\top$, and $\mathbf{e}_{in}$ a vector with 1 at the ith position and zero elsewhere.

To perturb the response variable values, we consider $y_{i\omega} = y_i + \omega_i$ for $i \in \{1, \ldots, n\}$, where $\boldsymbol{\omega} = (\omega_1, \ldots, \omega_n)^\top$ is the vector of perturbations. The vector of no perturbation is $\boldsymbol{\omega} = (0, \ldots, 0)^\top$. The perturbed penalized log-likelihood function is constructed from Equation (3) with y_i replaced by $y_{i\omega}$, as follows:

$$L_p(\boldsymbol{\theta}, \lambda_g|\boldsymbol{\omega}) = L(\boldsymbol{\theta}|\boldsymbol{\omega}) - \sum_{i=1}^{n} \frac{\lambda_f}{2} \delta^\top \mathbf{E} \delta\,,$$

where $L(\cdot)$ is defined in Equation (2) with $y_{i\omega}$ replacing y_i. By differentiating $L_p(\boldsymbol{\theta}, \boldsymbol{\lambda} \mid \boldsymbol{\omega})$ with respect to the elements of $\boldsymbol{\theta}$ and ω_i, and after some algebraic manipulation, we obtain:

$$\boldsymbol{\Delta}_\mathrm{p} = \begin{pmatrix} \mathbf{X}^\top \mathbf{D}_c \\ \mathbf{E}^\top \mathbf{D}_c \\ \widehat{\mathbf{d}}^\top \end{pmatrix},$$

where the matrix $\mathbf{D}_c = \mathrm{diag}_{1\leq i \leq n}(c_i)$ and $\mathbf{d} = (d_1, \ldots, d_n)^\top$, with $c_i = \partial h(\eta_i)/\partial\eta_i$ and $d_i = -(\mathrm{a}_i(\phi))^{-2}(h(\eta_i)\mathbf{e}_{in}^\top + c'(y_{i\omega}, \phi)/\partial\omega_i)$, with $\mathbf{e}_{in}$ denoting a vector with 1 at the ith position and zero elsewhere.

5. Applications

In this section, we show the applicability of the TPS-GLM and the local influence method with two real data applications. The model estimation and diagnostics have been implemented using `MatLab` 9.13.0 (R2022b) software [38] (the developed code is available on request by the authors).

5.1. Wypych Data

The first dataset we use to illustrate the applicability of the TPS-GLM consists of 83 sample points within a 46.6-hectare agricultural area in Wypych, located at latitude 24°50′24″ S and longitude 53°36′36″ W, with an average altitude ranging from 589 to 660 m. The data were collected during the 2006/2007 agricultural year in the western region of Paraná State, Brazil (see [39], Appendix 4). The soil is classified as Dystroferric Red Latosol with a clayey texture. The region's climate is mesothermal, super-humid temperate, classified as Cfa according to (Köeppen), with a mean annual temperature of 21 °C. The 83 georeferenced points were determined by a regular grid of 75 × 75 m using a global positioning system (GPS). The collected variables were as follows:

- Soya: average of soybean yield (t/ha).
- Height: average height (cm)of plants at the end of the production process.
- Pods: average number of pods.
- Lat: latitude (UTM).
- Long: longitude (UTM).

The original objective was to investigate the spatial variability of soybean yield (Soya) in the studied area based on the covariates: average plant height, average number of pods per plant, latitude, and longitude. Figure 1 shows the scatterplots between the response variable Soya and the explanatory variables Height and Pods. In addition, the plot of the response variable against the coordinates is shown. Clearly, from Figure 1a,b, it can be seen that the explanatory variables Height (X2) and Pods (X3) are linearly related to the response variable Soya (Z). The spatial effect given by the coordinates (X,Y) will be incorporated into the model through a smooth surface.

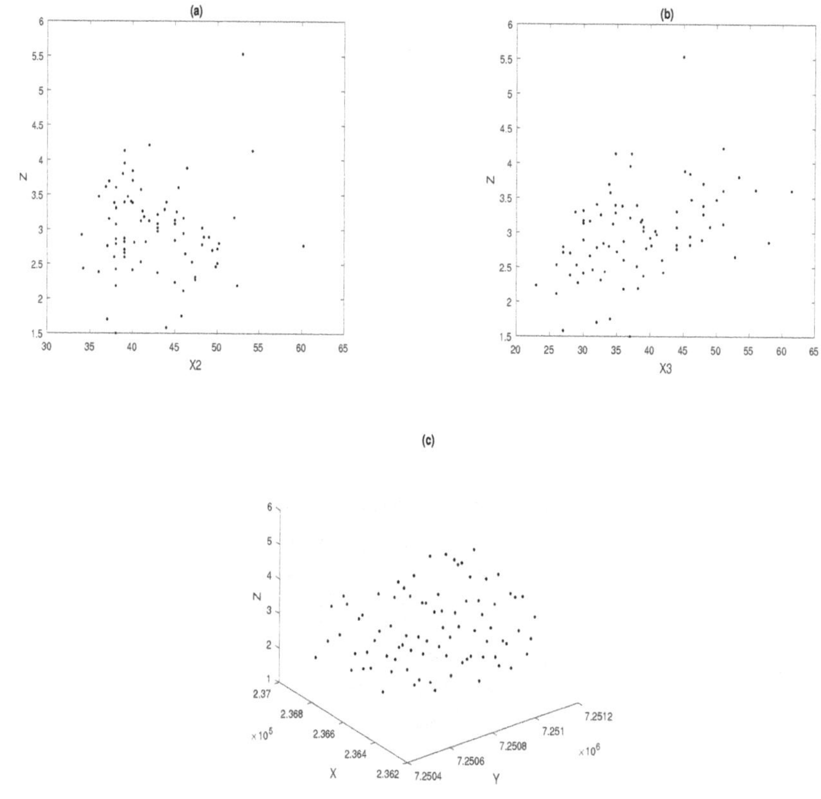

Figure 1. Scatter plots: Soya versus Height (**a**), Soya versus Pods (**b**), and Soya versus coordinates in UTM (**c**).

5.1.1. Fitting the TPS-GLM

Based on the above analysis, we propose the TPS-GLM, introduced in Section 2, to model the trends present in the Wypych data. Specifically, we are going to assume that the response variable Soya belongs to the Gaussian family, and that the link function is the identity. Therefore, the model is expressed as follows:

$$g(\mu_i) = \mu_i = \beta_0 + \beta_1 \text{Height}_i + \beta_2 \text{Pods}_i + f(\text{Lat}_i, \text{Long}_i) \qquad i \in \{1, \ldots, 83\},$$

where $\boldsymbol{\beta} = (\beta_0, \beta_1, \beta_2)^\top$ correspond to the regression coefficients associated with the parametric component of the model, and $f(\cdot)$ is a smooth surface. Table 1 lists the MPLE of $\boldsymbol{\beta}$. The respective asymptotic standard errors are presented in parentheses.

Table 1. MPLEs with their standard errors (within parenthesis), AIC and R^2(Adj).

Parameters	Model	
	Gaussian Linear	**TPS-GLM**
β_0	1.1921 (0.672)	0.497 (0.751)
β_1	0.0116 (0.0128)	0.032 (0.015)
β_2	0.0339 (0.0079)	0.030 (0.008)
AIC	149.99	139.9992
R^2(Adj)	0.168	0.315

The value of the smoothing parameter λ_f was selected in such a way that the AIC criterion was minimized. The adjusted determinant coefficients (R^2(Adj)) are evaluated for assessing the goodness-of-fit of the two models. It is important to note that our model have a lower AIC and an higher R^2(Adj), compared to the multiple regression model that does not consider the spatial effect. Figure 2a shows the QQ-plot for the standardized residuals, whose adjustment to the Gaussian TPS-GLM seems to be reasonable. However, the presence of some atypical observations is observed in one of the tails of the distribution. Figure 2b displays the scatter plot between the observed values, Soya, and their estimated values, $\widehat{\text{Soya}}$. Considering the trend of the points, we conclude that the estimates are good, since they generate consistent adjusted values of the response variable.

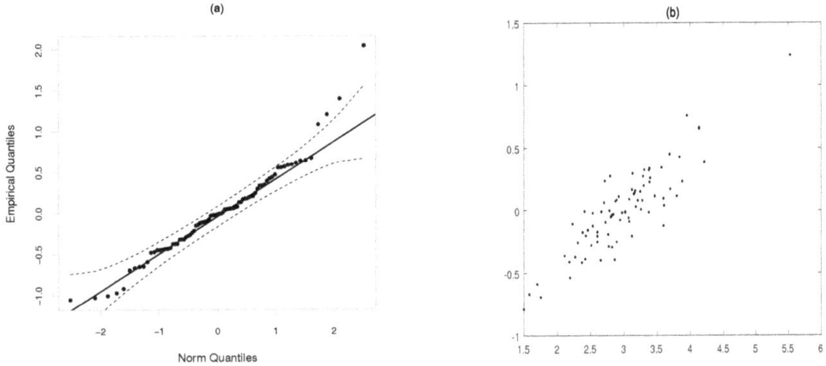

Figure 2. QQ-plots of the standardized residuals for the TPS-GLM with its confidence interval (dashed lines) (**a**) and scatterplot between Soya and $\widehat{\text{Soya}}$ (**b**), under model fitted to Wypych data.

5.1.2. Diagnostic Analysis

To identify potentially influential observations on the MPLE under the fitted Gaussian TPS-GLM for the Wypych data, we present several index plots of $B_i = B_{e_i}(\gamma)$ for $\gamma = \boldsymbol{\beta}, \delta$. Figure 3 shows the index plot B_i for the case-weight perturbation scheme under the fitted model. Figure 3a reveal that the observations #6, #61, #69 and #71 are more influential on $\widehat{\boldsymbol{\beta}}$, whereas the observations #6, #66, #61 and #38 are more influential on $\widehat{\delta}$; see Figure 3b. When we perturb the response variable additively, we have that the observations #80, #32, #75 and #88 are more influential on $\widehat{\boldsymbol{\beta}}$; see Figure 4a. Regarding $\widehat{\delta}$, observations #3, #42 and #80 appear as slightly influential as seem in Figure 4b.

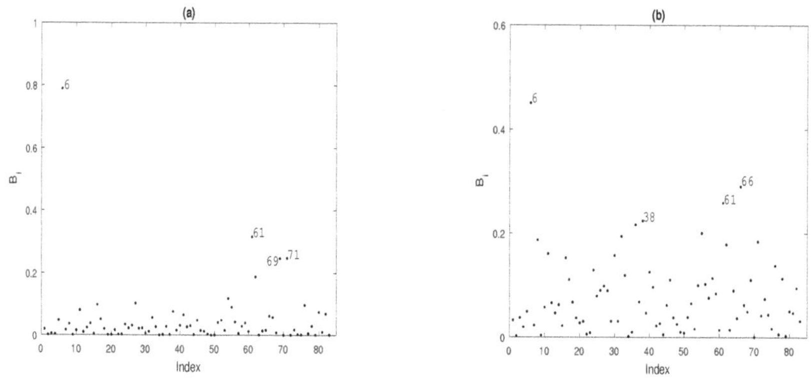

Figure 3. Index plots of B_i for assessing local influence on $\widehat{\beta}$ (**a**) and $\widehat{\delta}$ (**b**), considering case-weight perturbation.

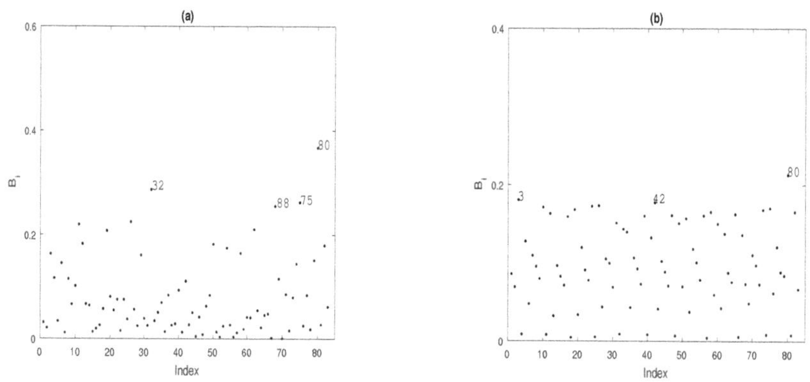

Figure 4. Index plots of B_i for assessing local influence on $\widehat{\beta}$ (**a**) and $\widehat{\delta}$ (**b**), considering response variable additive perturbation.

We conclude that the maximum penalized likelihood estimates (MPLE) of the regression coefficients and the smooth surface exhibit sensitivity to modifications made to the data or the model. This analysis has shown that observations identified as influential for the parametric component do not necessarily exert influence on the non-parametric component, and vice versa. For instance, under the case-weight perturbation scheme, observations #69 and #71 were detected as influential for the parametric component, but not for the nonparametric component.

5.1.3. Confirmatory Analysis

Table 2 displays the relative changes experienced by each element in the vector of regression coefficients. In this analysis, we only consider the three most influential observations under the case-weight perturbation scheme. As can be seen in this table, observations #6, #61 and #69 generate significant changes in the estimates. Still, no relevant inferential changes were noted. However, the AIC and &R^2(Adj) present some differences once the above observations are dropped.

Table 2. Relative changes (RCs) (in %) in the MPL estimates of β_j in cases-weight perturbation under the TPS-GLM. The last two columns indicate the AIC and R^2(Adj) of the model with dropped observations.

	Parameters and Relatives Changes							
Dropped Obs.	β_0	β_1	β_2	**RC$_{\beta_0}$**	**RC$_{\beta_1}$**	**RC$_{\beta_2}$**	**AIC**	**R^2(Adj)**
6	1.696	0.009	0.023	122.59	63.93	27.52	125.50	0.267
61	0.987	0.022	0.027	29.47	15.19	12.23	131.96	0.356
69	0.432	0.035	0.028	43.33	35.04	10.85	138.07	0.326
6-61	1.996	0.002	0.022	161.89	92.06	27.65	116.20	0.218
6-69	1.481	0.014	0.023	94.35	45.61	26.09	124.52	0.268
61-69	0.704	0.029	0.028	7.59	9.58	10.93	131.03	0.358
6-61-69	1.868	0.005	0.023	145.16	81.03	26.90	115.83	0.310

On the other hand, Table 3 shows the relative changes in the vector of regression coefficients under the additive perturbation scheme of the response variable. Here, we consider the four most influential observations. As can be seen in the table, observations #32, #69, #75 and #80 generate important relative changes in the estimates of the parametric component of the model. However, no significant inferential changes were observed. About the AIC and &R^2(Adj), there are not evident differences.

Table 3. Relative changes (RCs) (in %) in the MPL estimates of β_j in response variable perturbation under the TPS-GLM. The last two columns indicate the AIC and R^2(Adj) of the model with dropped observations.

	Parameters and Relatives Changes							
Dropped Obs.	β_0	β_1	β_2	**RC$_{\beta_0}$**	**RC$_{\beta_1}$**	**RC$_{\beta_2}$**	**AIC**	**R^2(Adj)**
32	0.701	0.027	0.029	8.000	4.62	5.23	138.73	0.319
69	0.432	0.034	0.027	43.33	29.0	12.22	138.07	0.326
75	0.760	0.028	0.027	0.24	6.22	12.65	139.44	0.307
80	0.699	0.028	0.029	8.21	7.86	8.16	139.01	0.311
32-69	0.382	0.035	0.030	49.87	32.82	4.00	136.81	0.33
32-75	0.700	0.027	0.030	8.17	4.12	4.90	138.11	0.319
32-80	0.621	0.028	0.031	18.49	6.34	0.16	137.63	0.316
69-75	0.430	0.035	0.028	43.61	34.96	10.96	137.53	0.318
69-80	0.333	0.036	0.029	56.33	38.32	5.39	136.99	0.322
75-80	0.695	0.028	0.029	8.85	7.25	7.90	138.39	0.302
32-69-75	0.381	0.035	0.030	49.98	32.33	3.74	136.22	0.322
32-75-80	0.621	0.028	0.031	18.54	5.23	0.96	136.93	0.308
69-75-80	0.333	0.036	0.029	56.26	37.40	5.09	136.42	0.314
32-69-75-80	0.271	0.035	0.032	64.47	30.15	3.22	134.96	0.320

5.2. Ozone Concentration Data

For our analysis, we utilize data from a study examining the relationship between atmospheric ozone concentration (O3) and various meteorological variables in the Los Angeles Basin for a sample of 330 days in 1976. The data were initially presented by Breiman and Friedman [40], and are available for download from various public repositories. Although the dataset includes several variables, in this application, we will consider only three explanatory variables, which are detailed in the following.

- O3: daily maximum one-hour average ozone concentration in Upland, CA, measured in parts per million (ppm).
- Temp: Sandburg Air Base temperature, in Celsius.
- Vis: visibility, in miles.
- Day: calendar day.

Figure 5 contains the dispersion graphs between the outcome variable (log(O3)) and each one of the explanatory variables Temp, Vis and Day.

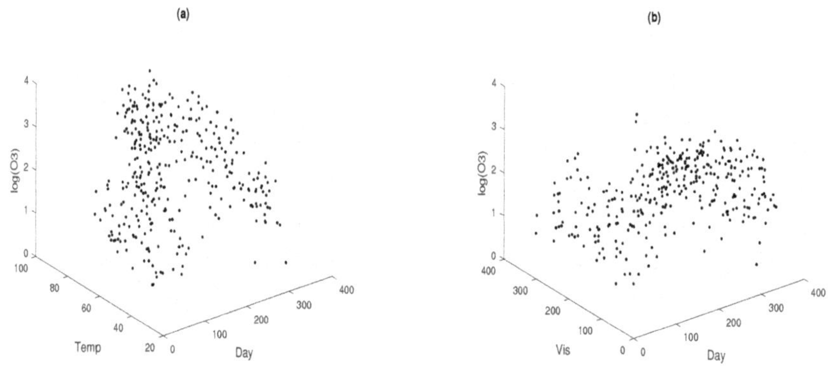

Figure 5. 3D plots between the response variable and the explanatory variables: logarithm of ozone data versus temperature and day variables (**a**), and logarithm of ozone data versus visibility and day variables (**b**).

Figure 5a shows a curved surface in the relationship between the variable log(O3) and the joint effect of the explanatory variables Temp and Day, whereas the relationship between log(O3) and the joint effect of the explanatory variable Vis and Day shows less curve; see Figure 5b. This graphical analysis recommends the inclusion in the model of a nonparametric component, specifically a surface, that can explain the relationship between log(O3) and the combined effect of the explanatory variables Temp and Day. For simplicity, in this work, we will include the effect of the explanatory variable Vis in a linear form. To begin our analysis, we are going to consider the fit of a GLM assuming that the variable of interest O3 is Poisson distributed with mean μ_i and logarithmic link function. Different structures of the linear predictor for the explanatory variables Vis, Temp, and Day will be considered (see Table 4).

Table 4. Four structures of the linear predictor for the explanatory variables Vis, Temp, and Day, assuming that the response variable log(O3) follows a $\text{Poisson}(\mu_i)$ distribution.

Model	$g(\mu_i) = \log(\mu_i)$
I	$\beta_0 + \beta_1 \text{Vis}_i + \beta_2 \text{Temp}_i + \beta_3 \text{Day}_i$
II	$\beta_0 + \beta_1 \text{Vis}_i + \beta_2 \text{Temp}_i + f(\text{Day}_i)$
III	$\beta_0 + \beta_1 \text{Vis}_i + \beta_2 \text{Temp}_i + \beta_3 \text{Day}_i + \beta_4 \text{Temp}_i \times \text{Day}_i$
IV	$\beta_0 + \beta_1 \text{Vis}_i + f(\text{Temp}_i, \text{Day}_i)$

For Model I, we consider only the individual effects of the explanatory variables Vis, Temp and Day. Note that all these effects were incorporated in a linear form in the systematic component of the model. For Model II, we consider the inclusion of a nonparametric term to model the nonlinear effects of the explanatory variable Day; see Ibacache et al. [41]. Model III considers a systematic component that contains the individual effects of the explanatory variables Vis, Temp and Day, in addition to the incorporation of the interaction effect between the explanatory variables Temp and Day. Here, the interaction effect is introduced linearly in the model. Model IV corresponds to a TPS-GLM where the joint effect of the Temp and Day explanatory variables is included nonlinearly by using smooth surface. Table 5 contains the ML and MPL estimates associated with the parametric component for the four fitted models.

It is important to note that both the individual and interaction effects are statistically significant, as the corresponding p-values (not shown here) are less than 0.05. Additionally, the estimates of β_0 are similar across the four models, whereas the estimates of β_1 vary considerably, particularly in Model IV. Concerning the associated standard errors, all the estimators exhibit small values. The last two rows of Table 5 display the Akaike Information Criterion (AIC) and R^2 values, respectively. It is evident that the TPS-GLM, with AIC$(\lambda_f) = 1777.705$, provides the best fit to the Ozone data, followed by Model II with an AIC of 1806.837. This is corroborated by the QQ-plots in Figure 6, specifically Figure 6b,d. Furthermore, the R^2 value associated with our model is higher than those of Models I, II, and III. The smoothing parameter λ_f was chosen such that the effective degrees of freedom were approximately 7. Figure 7 illustrates the 3D plot of the adjusted log(O3) against the explanatory variables Temp and Day, showing an adequate fit of the TPS-GLM.

Table 5. AIC, R^2(Adj), ML and MPL estimates for all four fitted models to the Ozone data.

Parameters	I	II	III	IV
β_0	0.577 (0.104)	0.478 (0.142)	0.787 (0.198)	2.507 (0.040)
β_1	−0.002 (0.0003)	−0.002 (0.0003)	−0.002 (0.0003)	−0.002 (0.0003)
β_2	0.035 (0.001)	0.033 (0.002)	0.032 (0.003)	-
β_3	−0.001 (0.002)	-	−0.002 (0.001)	-
β_4	-	-	0.00002 (0.00002)	-
AIC	1887.312	1806.837	1887.757	1789.92
R^2(Adj)	0.673	0.715	0.670	0.728

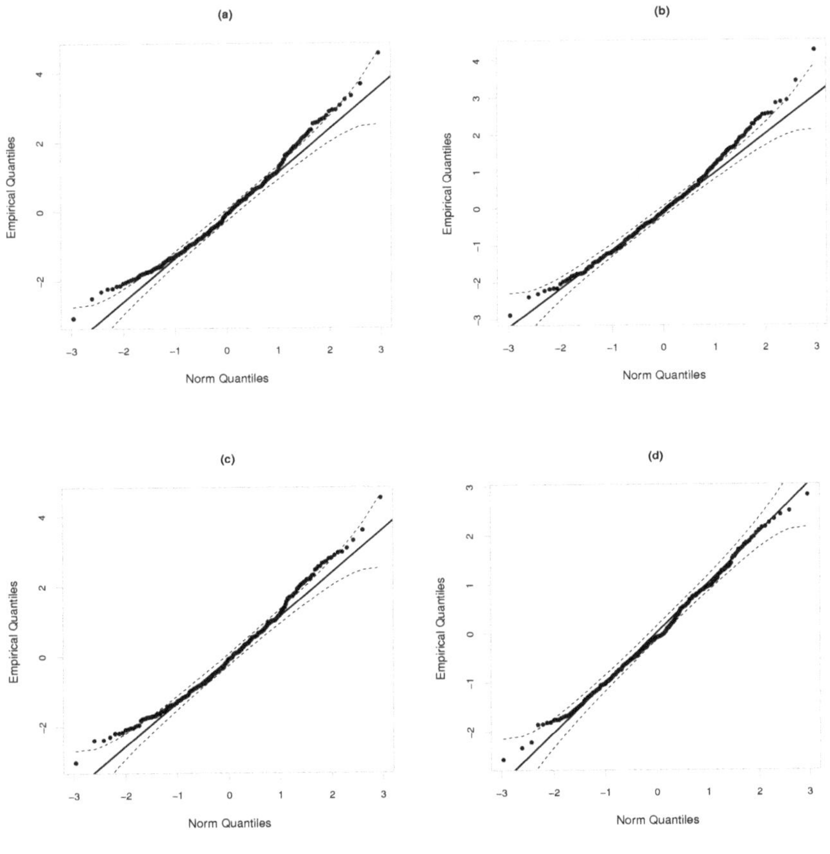

Figure 6. QQ-plot of the standardized residuals for the models described in Table 5: Model I (**a**), Model II (**b**), Model III (**c**) and Model IV (**d**).

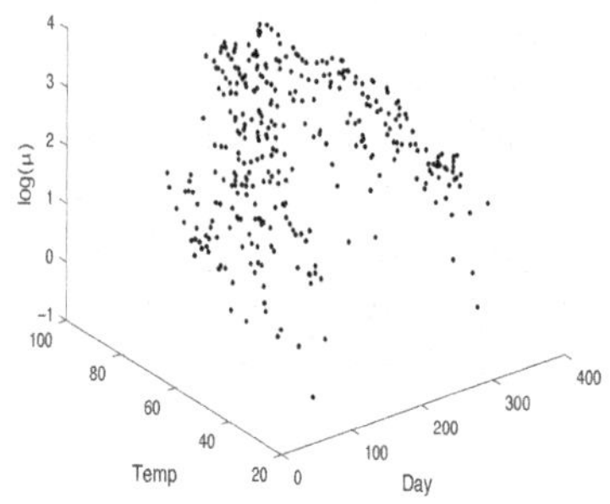

Figure 7. 3D plot between $\widehat{\log(\mu)}$ and explanatory variables Temp and Day.

5.2.1. Diagnostic Analysis

To identify potentially influential observations on the MPL estimators under the fitted TPS-GLM for the Ozone data, we present some index plots of $B_i = B_{e_i}(\gamma)$, for $\gamma = \beta, \delta$. Figure 8 shows the index plot of B_i for the case-weight perturbation scheme under the fitted model. In Figure 8a,b, note that observations #167, #220, #168, and #177 are more influential on $\widehat{\beta}$ and $\widehat{\delta}$, respectively. By perturbing the response variable additively, it becomes clear that observations #125, #175, #218, #219, and #221 are more influential on $\widehat{\beta}$ and $\widehat{\delta}$; see Figure 9a and 9b, respectively.

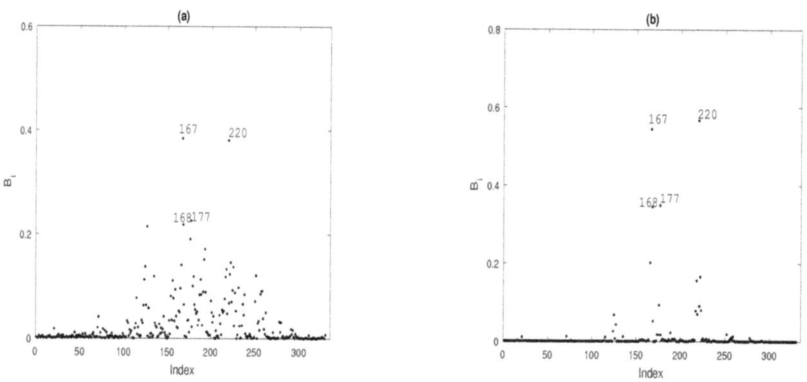

Figure 8. Index plots of B_i for assessing local influence on $\widehat{\beta}$ (**a**) and $\widehat{\delta}$ (**b**), considering case-weight perturbation under model fitted to Ozone data.

From the local influence analysis, we conclude that the MPLE of the regression coefficients and the smooth surface are sensitive to perturbations in the data or the model. Furthermore, this analysis revealed that observations identified as influential for the parametric component are also influential for the nonparametric component, and vice versa. For example, under the case-weight perturbation scheme, observations #167, #220, #168, and #177 were found to be influential for both the parametric and nonparametric components.

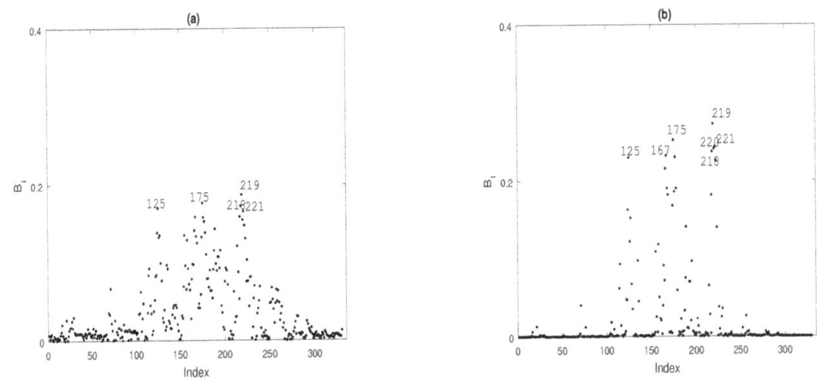

Figure 9. Index plots of B_i for assessing local influence on $\widehat{\boldsymbol{\beta}}$ (**a**) and $\widehat{\boldsymbol{\delta}}$ (**b**), considering response variable additive perturbation.

5.2.2. Confirmatory Analysis

To investigate the impact on model inference when influential potentially observations detected in the diagnostic analysis are removed, we present the relative changes (RCs) in the MPL estimate of β_j for $j \in \{1,2\}$ after removing the influential observations from the dataset (%). The RC is defined as $\mathrm{RC}_{\xi} = \left|\frac{\widehat{\xi}-\widehat{\xi}_{(I)}}{\widehat{\xi}}\right| \times 100\%$, where $\widehat{\xi}_{(I)}$ denotes the MPL estimate of ξ, with $\xi = \beta_j$, after the corresponding observation(s) are removed according to set I. Table 6 presents the RCs in the regression coefficient estimates after removing the observations identified as potentially influential for the parametric component of the model.

Table 6. Relative changes (RCs) (in %) in the MPL estimates of β_j under the TPS-GLM. The last two columns indicate the AIC and R^2(Adj) of the model with dropped observations.

Dropped Obs.	β_0	β_1	RC_{β_0}	RC_{β_1}	AIC	R^2(Adj)
167	2.513	−0.002	0.231	0.378	1777.07	0.737
175	2.506	−0.002	0.051	1.673	1784.58	0.724
219	2.540	−0.002	1.334	7.105	1784.44	0.725
220	2.507	−0.002	0.012	0.263	1777.87	0.728
167-175	2.511	−0.002	0.169	1.052	1771.76	0.734
167-219	2.538	−0.002	1.242	6.853	1771.58	0.735
167-220	2.511	−0.002	0.179	0.884	1765.08	0.738
175-219	2.538	−0.002	1.248	7.368	1779.10	0.722
175-220	2.504	−0.002	0.104	0.684	1772.55	0.725
219-220	2.507	−0.002	0.007	0.289	1772.807	0.725
167-175-219	2.536	−0.002	1.155	7.136	1766.269	0.732
167-175-220	2.512	−0.002	0.215	3.415	1759.79	0.735
175-219-220	2.504	−0.002	0.098	0.678	1767.484	0.721
167-175-219-220	2.534	−0.002	1.072	7.800	1754.761	0.731

6. Concluding Remarks and Future Research

In this work, we study some aspects of the Thin-Plate Spline Generalized Linear Models. Specifically, we derive an iterative process to estimate the parameters and the Fisher information matrix to approximate, through its inverse, the variance–covariance matrix of the estimators. In addition, we extended the local influence method, obtaining closed expressions for the Hessian and perturbation matrices under cases-weight perturbation and additive perturbation of the response variable. We performed a statistical data analysis with two real data sets of the agronomic and environmental area. The study showed the advantage of incorporating a smooth surface to model the joint effect of a pair of explanatory variables or the spatial effect determined by the coordinates. In both applications, it was observed that the adjusted values of the response variable were consistent. In addition, it was observed that our model presented a better fit to model the soybean yield and ozone concentration data, compared to some classic parametric and semiparametric models, respectively. In our analysis, it was found that those observations detected as potentially influential generated important changes in the estimates, but not significant inferential changes. In addition, our study confirms the need to develop the local influence method to evaluate the sensitivity of maximum penalized likelihood estimators and thus determine those observations that can exert an excessive influence on both the parametric and non-parametric components, or on both.

As future work, we propose to incorporate a correlation component in the model and extend the local influence technique to other perturbation schemes, mainly on the non-parametric component of the model.

Author Contributions: Conceptualization, G.I.-P., P.P., M.A.U.-O. and O.N.; methodology, G.I.-P. and O.N.; software, G.I.-P. and P.P.; validation, G.I.-P. and P.P.; formal analysis, P.P.; investigation, G.I.-P., P.P., O.N. and M.A.U.-O.; data curation, P.P. and M.A.U.-O.; writing—original draft preparation, G.I.-P. and P.P.; writing—review and editing, O.N. and M.A.U.-O.; supervision, G.I.-P. and O.N.; project administration, O.N.; funding acquisition, O.N. All authors have read and agreed to the published version of the manuscript.

Funding: This research was funded by ANID-Fondecyt grant number 1201478.

Institutional Review Board Statement: Not applicable.

Informed Consent Statement: Not applicable.

Data Availability Statement: Data cannot be shared openly but are available on request from authors.

Acknowledgments: The third author acknowledges the support of ANID-Fondecyt 1201478.

Conflicts of Interest: The authors declare no conflicts of interest.

References

1. McCullagh, P.; Nelder, J.A. *Generalized Linear Models*, 2nd ed.; Chapman and Hall: London, UK, 1989.
2. Duchon, J. Interpolation des fonctions de deux variables suivant le principe de la flexion des plaques minces. *RAIRO Anal. Numér.* **1976**, *10*, 5–12. [CrossRef]
3. Duchon, J. Splines minimizing rotation-invariant semi-norms in Sobolev spaces. *Lect. Notes Math.* **1977**, *57*, 85–100.
4. Bookstein, F.L. Principal warps: Thin-plate splines and decomposition of deformations. *IEEE Trans. Pattern Anal. Mach. Intell.* **1989**, *11*, 567–585. [CrossRef]
5. Chen, C.; Li, Y.; Yan, C.; Dai, H.; Liu, G. A Thin Plate Spline-Based Feature-Preserving Method for Reducing Elevation Points Derived from LiDAR. *Remote Sens.* **2015**, *7*, 11344–11371. [CrossRef]
6. Wahba, G. *Spline Models for Observational Data*; SIAM: Philadelphia, PA, USA, 1990.
7. Green, P.J.; Silverman, B.W. *Nonparametric Regression and Generalized Linear Models*; Chapman and Hall: Boca Raton, FL, USA, 1994.
8. Wood, S.N. Thin plate regression splines. *J. R. Stat. Soc. Ser. B (Methodol.)* **2003**, *65*, 95–114. [CrossRef]
9. Moraga, M.S.; Ibacache-Pulgar, G.; Nicolis, O. On an elliptical thin-plate spline partially varying-coefficient model. *Chil. J. Stat.* **2021**, *12*, 205–228.
10. Cook, R.D. Assessment of Local Influence. *J. R. Stat. Soc. Ser. B (Methodol.)* **1986**, *48*, 133–169. [CrossRef]
11. Thomas, W.; Cook, R.D. Assessing influence on regression coefficients in generalized linear models. *Biometrika* **1989**, *76*, 741–749. [CrossRef]
12. Ouwens, M.N.M.; Tan, F.E.S.; Berger, M.P.F. Local influence to detect influential data structures for generalized linear mixed models. *Biometrics* **2001**, *57*, 1166–1172. [CrossRef]
13. Zhu, H.; Lee, S. Local influence for incomplete-data models. *J. R. Stat. Soc. Ser. B* **2001**, *63*, 111–126. [CrossRef]
14. Zhu, H.; Lee, S. Local influence for generalized linear mixed models. *Can. J. Stat.* **2003**, *31*, 293–309. [CrossRef]
15. Espinheira, P.L.; Ferrari, P.L.; Cribari-Neto, F. Influence diagnostics in beta regression. *Comput. Stat. Data Anal.* **2008**, *52*, 4417–4431. [CrossRef]
16. Rocha, A.; Simas, A. Influence diagnostics in a general class of beta regression models. *TEST* **2001**, *20*, 95–119. [CrossRef]
17. Ferrari, S.; Spinheira, P.; Cribari-Neto, F. Diagnostic tools in beta regression with varying dispersion. *Stat. Neerl.* **2011**, *65*, 337–351. [CrossRef]
18. Ferreira, C.S.; Paula, G.A. Estimation and diagnostic for skew-normal partially linear models. *J. Appl. Stat.* **2017**, *44*, 3033–3053. [CrossRef]

19. Emami, H. Local influence for Liu estimators in semiparametric linear models. *Stat. Pap.* **2018**, *59*, 529–544. [CrossRef]
20. Liu, Y.; Mao, G.; Leiva, V.; Liu, S.; Tapia, A. Diagnostic Analytics for an Autoregressive Model under the Skew-Normal Distribution. *Mathematics* **2020**, *8*, 693. [CrossRef]
21. Thomas, W. Influence diagnostics for the cross-validated smoothing parameter in spline smoothing. *J. Am. Stat. Assoc.* **1991**, *9*, 693–698. [CrossRef]
22. Ibacache, G.; Paula, G.A. Local Influence for student-t partially linear models. *Comput. Stat. Data Anal.* **2011**, *55*, 1462–1478. [CrossRef]
23. Ibacache-Pulgar, G.; Paula, G.A.; Galea, M. Influence diagnostics for elliptical semiparametric mixed models. *Stat. Model.* **2012**, *12*, 165–193. [CrossRef]
24. Ibacache, G.; Paula, G.A.; Cysneiros, F. Semiparametric additive models under symmetric distributions. *Test* **2013**, *22*, 103–121. [CrossRef]
25. Zhang, J.; Zhang, X.; Ma, H.; Zhiya, C. Local influence analysis of varying coefficient linear model. *J. Interdiscip. Math.* **2015**, *3*, 293–306. [CrossRef]
26. Ibacache-Pulgar, G.; Reyes, S. Local influence for elliptical partially varying coefficient model. *Stat. Model.* **2018**, *18*, 149–174. [CrossRef]
27. Ibacache-Pulgar, G.; Figueroa-Zuñiga, J.; Marchant, C. Semiparametric additive beta regression models: Inference and local influence diagnostics. *REVSTAT-Stat. J.* **2019**, *19*, 255–274.
28. Cavieres, J.; Ibacache-Pulgar, G.; Contreras-Reyes, J. Thin plate spline model under skew-normal random errors: Estimation and diagnostic analysis for spatial data. *J. Stat. Comput. Simul.* **2023**, *93*, 25–45. [CrossRef]
29. Jeldes, N.; Ibacache-Pulgar, G.; Marchant, C.; López-Gonzales, J.L. Modeling Air Pollution Using Partially Varying Coefficient Models with Heavy Tails. *Mathematics* **2022**, *10*, 3677. [CrossRef]
30. Saavedra-Nievas, J.C.; Nicolis, O.; Galea, M.; Ibacache-Pulgar, G. Influence diagnostics in Gaussian spatial—Temporal linear models with separable covariance. *Environ. Ecol. Stat.* **2023**, *30*, 131–155. [CrossRef]
31. Sánchez, L.; Ibacache-Pulgar, G.; Marchant, C.; Riquelme, M. Modeling Environmental Pollution Using Varying-Coefficients Quantile Regression Models under Log-Symmetric Distributions. *Axioms* **2023**, *12*, 976. [CrossRef]
32. Green, P.J. Penalized Likelihood for General Semi-Parametric Regression Models. *Int. Stat. Rev.* **1987**, *55*, 245–259. [CrossRef]
33. Nelder, J.A.; Wedderburn, R.W.M. Generalized Linear Models. *J. R. Stat. Soc. Ser. A (Gen.)* **1972**, *135*, 370–384. [CrossRef]
34. Wood, S.N. *Generalized Additive Models: An Introduction with R*, 2nd ed.; Chapman and Hall/CRC: Boca Raton, FL, USA, 2017.
35. Akaike, H. Information theory as an extension of the maximum likelihood principle. In *Proceedings of the Second International Symposium on Information Theory*; Petrov, B.N., Csaki, F., Eds.; Academiai Kiado: Budapest, Hungary, 1973.
36. Escobar, L.A.; Meeker, W.Q. Assessing Influence in Regression Analysis with Censored Data. *Biometrics* **1992**, *48*, 507–528. [CrossRef] [PubMed]
37. Billor, N.; Loynes, R.M. Local influence: A new approach. *Comm. Statist. Theory Meth.* **1993**, *22*, 1595–1611. [CrossRef]
38. MathWorks Inc. *MATLAB Version: 9.13.0 (R2022b)*; The MathWorks Inc.: Natick, MA, USA, 2022. Available online: https://www.mathworks.com (accessed on 10 October 2022).
39. Uribe-Opazo, M.A.; Borssoi, J.A.; Galea, M. Influence diagnostics in Gaussian spatial linear models. *J. Appl. Stat.* **2012**, *3*, 615–630. [CrossRef]
40. Breiman, L.; Friedman, J.H. Estimating optimal transformations for multiple regression and correlation. *J. Am. Stat. Assoc.* **1985**, *80*, 580–598. [CrossRef]
41. Ibacache-Pulgar, G.; Lira, V.; Villegas, C. Assessing Influence on Partially Varying-coefficient Generalized Linear Model. *REVSTAT-Stat. J.* **2022**. Available online: https://revstat.ine.pt/index.php/REVSTAT/article/view/507 (accessed on 10 October 2022).

axioms

MDPI

Article

On a Stability of Non-Stationary Discrete Schemes with Respect to Interpolation Errors

Raimondas Čiegis [1,*], Olga Suboč [1] and Remigijus Čiegis [2]

1 Mathematical Modelling Department, Faculty of Fundamental Sciences, Vilnius Gediminas Technical University, Saulėtekio al. 11, LT-10223 Vilnius, Lithuania; olga.suboc@vilniustech.lt
2 Kaunas Faculty, Vilnius University, Muitinės St 8, LT-44280 Kaunas, Lithuania; remigijus.ciegis@knf.vu.lt
* Correspondence: raimondas.ciegis@vgtu.lt

Abstract: The aim of this article is to analyze the efficiency and accuracy of finite-difference and finite-element Galerkin schemes for non-stationary hyperbolic and parabolic problems. The main problem solved in this article deals with the construction of accurate and efficient discrete schemes on nonuniform and dynamic grids in time and space. The presented stability and convergence analysis enables improving the existing accuracy estimates. The obtained stability results show explicitly the rate of accumulation of interpolation and projection errors that arise due to the movement of grid points. It is shown that the cases when the time grid steps are doubled or halved have different stability properties. As an additional technique to improve the accuracy of discretizations on non-stationary space grids, it is recommended to use projection operators instead of interpolation operators. This technique is used to solve a test parabolic problem. The results of specially selected computational experiments are also presented, and they confirm the accuracy of all theoretical error estimates obtained in this article.

Keywords: finite-difference schemes; Galerkin schemes; non-uniform grids; adaptive grids; hyperbolic problems; parabolic problems; stability; interpolation errors; projection errors

MSC: 65M06; 65M12; 65M15

1. Introduction

Numerical algorithms that form the basis for recent simulations of various complex processes in engineering, technologies, physics, and medicine are based on two of the most important theoretical topics. The first one is the approximation theory, and the second one is the stability analysis. The general convergence framework states that the stability and approximation properties guarantee the convergence of discrete solutions [1,2]. The deep, broad, and constructive theories of approximation and stability are developed, and they cover various important topics dealing with non-smooth data [3–5], weak solutions [6–8], energy and maximum principle stability estimates [1,2,9,10], ill-posed and inverse problems [11,12], and nonlocal mathematical models including fractional derivatives [13–16].

The topic of the stability of discrete methods for solving non-stationary linear PDEs is very important and actively investigated. In our paper, we restrict ourselves to a specific question dealing with the stability of finite-difference schemes with respect to interpolation and projection errors. In addition, here, we note the impact of A.V. Gulin on this field of research [17]. Again, in the presented review, we mainly restricted ourselves to Gulin's works connected to a research topic that is close to our paper, when second-order PDEs are solved with non-classical nonlocal boundary conditions [18,19].

Adaptive grids in both space and time are used to fit the grid points to the dynamics of the solution and to minimize the approximation error [1,20,21]. At the same time, in many cases, uniform grids have been used in recent big data projects due to two important properties: high-order approximations can be constructed directly on uniform grids, and the obtained structure of the grids is well suited for parallel computing techniques [22,23]. Thus, different modifications of the algorithms are proposed that try to preserve the uniformity of the grid as close as possible [24].

There are a huge number of different methods for solving linear second-order partial differential equations of parabolic and hyperbolic types. Still, we are not proposing new methods in this article. Our goal is to analyze the efficiency of the scheme that is constructed in [25]. It uses the interpolation technique to define initial conditions on the previous time level. Thus, our aim is to derive stability estimates with respect to this new source of discretization error. It is shown that such errors accumulate undesirably fast. As an alternative, we recall the Discontinuous Galerkin (DG) method, which uses the projection operator instead of the interpolation operator. The results of the computational experiments confirm the theoretical estimates. We note that the presented example of the time grid was selected only as a benchmark to compare the accumulation rates of interpolation and projection errors.

We conclude that, in this article, we present the stability and convergence analysis of a new three-level finite-difference scheme, which is used to solve a hyperbolic problem on a perturbed uniform time grid [25]. At some specific points, the length of the grid steps can be doubled or halved. The error analysis performed in this paper is based on the energy method and state that, in the worst case, changes of step lengths can lead to the estimates of the global error (see also [9]):

$$\|Z^n\|_E \leqslant (M_- + M_+)\big(\|Z^1\|_E + \sum_{k=1}^{n} \tau_k \|\Psi^n\|\big). \tag{1}$$

Here, Ψ^n is the truncation error of the discrete scheme and

$$M_- = 2^{m_-}, \quad M_+ = 2^{m_+},$$

where m_- is the number of times the time step is halved and m_+ is the number of times the time step is doubled. We note once more that our aim is to make a full stability analysis of the interpolation errors introduced by the proposed algorithm. It is proven that the cases of doubling and reducing twice the time steps lead to different error accumulation rates. Our main aim is not to develop the ideas proposed in [25], but to explain why this new finite-difference scheme is not working as good as can be expected from schemes constructed on a uniform grid. The estimates derived in our analysis agree well with the results of extensive computational experiments.

We also investigate the difference in the stability of the backward Euler (BE) finite-difference scheme and the DG finite-element scheme when both schemes are used to solve one-dimensional parabolic problems on dynamically shifted uniform space grids. A good review on the DG method is given in [20,21,26], and applications for parabolic and hyperbolic problems are described in [4,5,27] Our analysis also proves that the accumulation of interpolation and projection approximation errors is quite different. The stability of the DG scheme with respect to the projection error has much better properties. Numerical examples illustrate these theoretical results.

In Section 2, the semi-discrete hyperbolic problem is formulated, and a standard three-level finite difference scheme is constructed on the uniform time grid. The stability of this scheme is investigated by using the energy and spectral methods. Note that the spectral method will be the main tool in our theoretical analysis.

In Section 3, the three-level finite-difference scheme from [25] is considered. It is defined on modified uniform time grids when, at some points, the lengths of the grid steps are doubled or halved. The most valuable property of this scheme is that the approximation is performed on uniformly distributed grid points; thus, the basic advantages of such discrete schemes are preserved. In Section 3.1, the case when the sizes of the grid are doubled is considered. We prove that, in this case, the finite- difference scheme remains unconditionally stable and the second-order accuracy in time is valid. This estimate improves the result presented in [25]. The new global error estimate is connected to the fact that no additional approximation errors, such as an interpolation error, are introduced, and it is sufficient to analyze the stability of the scheme on uniform sub-grids only.

In Section 3.2, the case when the sizes of the grid are halved is considered. The obtained stability estimates give a possibility to define the convergence rate for different asymptotics of the number of times the time step is halved. In particular, it is proven that, due to the accumulation of interpolation errors, the convergence order of the global error is reduced to the first-order if the grid sizes are halved only at a finite number of points and the discrete solution is not converging at all if this number is proportional to $O(1/\tau)$. The results of the computational experiments agree well with these theoretical conclusions.

In Section 4, the accumulation of interpolation errors is demonstrated also for parabolic problems. It is proven that, if the space grid depends on time (in a discontinuous fashion), then the stability of the implicit backward Euler (BE) finite-difference scheme with respect to the interpolation error leads only to conditional convergence rates. As a possibility to avoid this negative effect, it is recommended to use DG schemes, when the interpolation operator is changed to the projection operator. The DG scheme is stable with respect to the projection error. The results of the computational experiments agree well with these conclusions.

Some final conclusions are given in Section 5.

2. Problem Formulation

Let $\Omega = (0,1)^d$ be an open and bounded domain $\Omega \subset \mathbb{R}^d$, $d \geqslant 1$. Define a self-adjoint linear elliptic diffusion operator:

$$\mathcal{A}u = -\text{div}(\mathcal{K}\nabla u) \quad \text{in } \Omega \tag{2}$$

with $\mathcal{K}(x) \in \mathbb{R}^{d\times d}$ symmetric and the uniformly positive definite $d \times d$ matrix. Operator $\mathcal{A}$ is supplemented with homogeneous Dirichlet boundary conditions on $\partial\Omega$.

Next, by using the finite-volume or finite-element methods, we approximate operator $\mathcal{A}$ by discrete operator A_h, which is defined in a real finite-dimensional Hilbert space H:

$$A_h = A_h^* \geqslant \alpha_A I, \quad \alpha_A > 0, \tag{3}$$

where I is the identity operator in H. In order to simplify the notation for discrete operators, we restrict ourselves to $d = 1$.

Consider a semi-discrete hyperbolic problem for the function $u(t) \in H$:

$$\frac{d^2u}{dt^2} + \beta\frac{du}{dt} + A_h u = f(t), \quad t > 0 \tag{4}$$

$$u(0) = u_0, \quad \frac{du}{dt}(0) = v_0, \quad u_0, v_0 \in H, \tag{5}$$

where $\beta > 0$. Then, the following a priori estimate of the solution of (4) can be proven directly by using the energy method (see also [1,9,25]):

$$\left\|\frac{du}{dt}(t)\right\|^2 + \|u(t)\|_{A_h} \leqslant \|v_0\|^2 + \|u_0\|_{A_h}^2 + \frac{1}{2\beta}\int_0^t \|f(s)\|^2 ds, \tag{6}$$

where, for any self-adjoint positive definite operator B, a Hilbert space H_B is defined with the inner product and the norm:

$$(u,v)_B = (Bu, v), \quad \|u\|_B = (u,u)_B^{1/2}.$$

First, let us define a uniform time grid

$$\omega_t = \{t^n : \ t^n = t^{n-1} + \tau, \ \ n = 1, \dots, N, \ \ t^0 = 0, \ t^N = T\}.$$

The discrete function $U^n = U(t^n)$ gives an approximation of the exact solution $u(t^n)$. The differential problem (4) is approximated by the following standard implicit symmetrical three-level scheme:

$$\frac{U^{n+1} - 2U^n + U^{n-1}}{\tau^2} + \beta \frac{U^{n+1} - U^{n-1}}{2\tau} + A_h \frac{U^{n+1} + U^{n-1}}{2} = F^n, \tag{7}$$
$$U^0 = u_0, \quad U^1 = u_0 + \tau v_0.$$

The unconditional stability of this scheme can be proven by using the energy and spectral methods. They give similar general information on the stability of the discrete solution, but still can give estimates of the accumulation of truncation and interpolation errors in different norms. This possibility enables us to follow the dynamics of the interpolation errors in more detail.

Let us start from the application of the standard energy method [9]. If $\beta > 0$, then it is easy to obtain the following stability estimate:

$$\begin{aligned} &\left\| \frac{U^{n+1} - U^n}{\tau} \right\|^2 + \frac{1}{2}\|U^{n+1}\|^2_{A_h} + \frac{1}{2}\|U^n\|^2_{A_h} \\ &\quad \leqslant \left\| \frac{U^n - U^{n-1}}{\tau} \right\|^2 + \frac{1}{2}\|U^n\|^2_{A_h} + \frac{1}{2}\|U^{n-1}\|^2_{A_h} + \frac{\tau}{2\beta}\|F^n\|^2. \end{aligned} \tag{8}$$

First, the uniform space grid is used:

$$\omega_x = \{x_j : \ x_0 = 0, \ x_J = 1, \ \ x_j = jh\}.$$

Then, discrete functions $U_j = U(x_j)$, $x_j \in \omega_x$ can be defined. Let us assume that functions U satisfy the homogeneous boundary conditions:

$$U_0 = 0, \quad U_J = 0.$$

The inner product in the Hilbert space H is defined in a standard way:

$$(U, V) = \sum_{j=1}^{J-1} U_j V_j h.$$

Then, the second-order derivative $-\frac{\partial^2 u}{\partial x^2}$ is approximated by the discrete operator:

$$A_h U = -\frac{U_{j+1} - 2U_j + U_{j-1}}{h^2}.$$

The eigenvectors $\{\varphi_k(x_j) = \sqrt{2}\sin(\pi k x_j)\}$ of A_h make a full basis set of orthonormal vectors [1,9]:

$$A_h \sin(\pi k x_j) = \lambda_k \sin(\pi k x_j), \quad \lambda_j = \frac{4\sin^2(\pi k h/2)}{h^2}, \ \ k = 1, \dots, J-1.$$

It follows that A_h is a self-adjoint and positive definite operator in H.

We also consider a general nonuniform space grid:

$$\omega_x = \{x_j : \ \ x_0 = 0, \ \ x_{J_n} = 1, \ \ x_j = x_{j-1} + h_{j-0.5}, \ j = 1, \dots, J-1\}.$$

By using the finite-volume method [1,9], the following operator A_h can be defined on this grid:

$$A_h U = -\frac{1}{h_j}\left(\frac{U_{j+1} - U_j}{h_{j+0.5}} - \frac{U_j - U_{j-1}}{h_{j-0.5}}\right),$$

where $h_j = (h_{j+0.5} + h_{j-0.5})/2$. The inner product in the Hilbert space H is defined by

$$(U, V) = \sum_{j=1}^{J-1} U_j V_j h_j.$$

Again, it easy to prove that A_h is a self-adjoint and positive definite operator in H, i.e., the estimates (3) are valid.

As a basic technique for the stability analysis of discrete schemes proposed in this paper, we use the spectral method. It was efficiently used for non-stationary problems with nonlocal fractional-order elliptic operators [16,28,29].

Functions $U^n \in H$ can be written as

$$U_j^n = \sum_{k=1}^{J-1} c_k^n \varphi_k(x_j), \quad j = 1, \dots, J-1,$$

where $c_k^n = (U^n, \varphi_k)$.

By using the Fourier method, we write discrete problems for each coefficient c_k^n:

$$\begin{aligned} &\frac{c_k^{n+1} - 2c_k^n + c_k^{n-1}}{\tau^2} + \beta\frac{c_k^{n+1} - c_k^{n-1}}{2\tau} + \lambda_k \frac{c_k^{n+1} + c_k^{n-1}}{2} = f_k^n, \\ &c_k^0 = \widetilde{u}_k, \quad c_k^1 = \widetilde{u}_k + \tau\widetilde{v}_k, \end{aligned} \tag{9}$$

where

$$\begin{aligned} F_j^n &= \sum_{k=1}^{J-1} f_k^n \varphi_k(x_j), \quad j = 1, \dots, J-1, \\ u_j^0 &= \sum_{k=1}^{J-1} \widetilde{u}_k \varphi_k(x_j), \quad v_j^0 = \sum_{k=1}^{J-1} \widetilde{v}_k \varphi_k(x_j). \end{aligned}$$

Lemma 1. *Let us assume that* $\beta \geqslant 0$, *then the discrete scheme* (9) *is unconditionally stable.*

Proof. The solution of the homogeneous version of Equation (9) can be written as

$$c_k^n = \gamma_{k1} q_1^n + \gamma_{k2} q_2^n,$$

where q_1 and q_2 are solutions of the characteristic equations:

$$\Big(1 + \frac{\tau}{2}\beta + \frac{\tau^2}{2}\lambda_k\Big) q^2 - 2q + \Big(1 - \frac{\tau}{2}\beta + \frac{\tau^2}{2}\lambda_k\Big) = 0.$$

Next, we write this equation in a standard form:

$$q^2 - \frac{2}{1 + \frac{\tau}{2}\beta + \frac{\tau^2}{2}\lambda_k} q + \frac{1 - \frac{\tau}{2}\beta + \frac{\tau^2}{2}\lambda_k}{1 + \frac{\tau}{2}\beta + \frac{\tau^2}{2}\lambda_k} = 0. \tag{10}$$

It follows from the Hurwitz criterion that $|q_{1,2}| \leqslant 1$ if and only if

$$\frac{1 - \frac{\tau}{2}\beta + \frac{\tau^2}{2}\lambda_k}{1 + \frac{\tau}{2}\beta + \frac{\tau^2}{2}\lambda_k} \leqslant 1, \quad \frac{2}{1 + \frac{\tau}{2}\beta + \frac{\tau^2}{2}\lambda_k} \leqslant \frac{2 + \tau^2\lambda_k}{1 + \frac{\tau}{2}\beta + \frac{\tau^2}{2}\lambda_k}.$$

Both inequalities are unconditionally satisfied. The proof is finished. □

3. Nonuniform Grids

Let us consider a general nonuniform grid:

$$\omega_t = \{t^n : \ t^n = t^{n-1} + \tau_{n-1/2}, \ \ n = 1, \dots, N, \ \ t^0 = 0, \ t^N = T\} \tag{11}$$

and denote $t^{n-1/2} = t^{n-1} + 0.5\tau_{n-1/2}$.

3.1. The Time Steps Are Doubled at Some Grid Points.

In [25], special weakly nonuniform grids are considered, when the step size of the grid can be doubled or halved at a finite number of points. Let us consider the case that, when starting at time $t = t^n$, the grid step is doubled $\tau_{n+1} = 2\tau_n$. Here, τ_n denotes the length of the discrete step till the grid point t^n, and τ_{n+1} is a modified step for the following sequence of uniformly distributed grid points.

The original algorithm is defined by

$$\begin{aligned}
&\frac{U^{n+1/2} - 2U^n + U^{n-1}}{\tau_n^2} + \beta\frac{U^{n+1/2} - U^{n-1}}{2\tau_n} + A_h\frac{U^{n+1/2} + U^{n-1}}{2} = F^n, \\
&\frac{U^{n+1} - 2U^{n+1/2} + U^n}{\tau_n^2} + \beta\frac{U^{n+1} - U^n}{2\tau_n} + A_h\frac{U^{n+1} + U^n}{2} = F^{n+1/2};
\end{aligned}$$

next, U^{n+2} is computed using the standard three-level scheme on the uniform grid with the step τ_{n+1}:

$$\frac{U^{n+2} - 2U^{n+1} + U^n}{\tau_{n+1}^2} + \beta\frac{U^{n+2} - U^n}{2\tau_{n+1}} + A_h\frac{U^{n+2} + U^n}{2} = F^{n+1}. \tag{12}$$

We present a slightly modified version of the original discrete scheme when temporary grid points are not used. First, the solution U^{n+1} is computed

$$\frac{U^{n+1} - 2U^n + U^{n-2}}{\tau_{n+1}^2} + \beta\frac{U^{n+1} - U^{n-2}}{2\tau_{n+1}} + A_h\frac{U^{n+1} + U^{n-2}}{2} = F^n \tag{13}$$

Next, the uniform grid version of the discrete scheme (12) is used to compute U^{n+2}.

The stability and convergence analysis is based on the results of Lemma 1.

Theorem 1. *The solution of the finite-difference scheme* (12) *and* (13) *converges to order* $O(\tau^2)$.

Proof. We restrict ourselves to the analysis of one time moment where the time step is doubled. First, starting at time point t^n, the discrete scheme is again defined as a three-level scheme on a uniform grid with a doubled time step $\tau_{n+1} = 2\tau_n$. Thus, the scheme remains unconditionally stable.

Second, the initial conditions, i.e., discrete solutions on layers t^n and t^{n-2}, are calculated by using solutions derived by a more accurate scheme with the time step τ_n. As a conclusion, we obtain that the discrete solution converges to order $O(\tau^2)$. In the case of more time moments, when the step size of the grid ω_t is doubled, the same arguments are iteratively applied. □

In the computational experiments, we compared the accuracy of the constructed combined discrete scheme (12) and (13) with a popular benchmark scheme. This three-level finite-difference scheme is constructed on a general non-uniform time grid (11):

$$\begin{aligned}
&\frac{1}{\tau_n}\Big(\frac{U^{n+1} - U^n}{\tau_{n+1/2}} - \frac{U^n - U^{n-1}}{\tau_{n-1/2}}\Big) + \beta\frac{U^{n+1} - U^{n-1}}{2\tau_n} \\
&\quad + A_h\Big[U^n + \frac{1}{2}\tau_n\Big(\frac{U^{n+1} - U^n}{\tau_{n+1/2}} - \frac{U^n - U^{n-1}}{\tau_{n-1/2}}\Big)\Big] = F^n.
\end{aligned} \tag{14}$$

Here, $\tau_n = \frac{1}{2}(\tau_{n+1/2} + \tau_{n-1/2})$.

We present the results of the computational experiments. The differential problem (4) is solved for $\beta = 1$ till the final time moment $T = 1$. The initial and boundary data and $f(x,t)$ are chosen so that the solution $u(x,t)$ is the function:

$$u(x,t) = e^t \sin(\pi x).$$

The space grid ω_x is uniform, and the number of points is equal to $J = 20$. The time grid is generated by dividing the time interval $[0,1]$ into five subintervals:

$$[(k-1)/5,\ k/5], \quad k = 1,\ldots,5.$$

In each subinterval, uniform grids are generated with time step sizes of

$$\tau(k) = 2^{k-5}/N, \quad k = 1,\ldots,5.$$

Let us denote $Z_j^n = u(x_j, t^n) - U_j^n$ as the global error of the discrete solution. The maximum norm of a discrete function Z^n is defined as

$$\|Z(t^n)\|_\infty = \max_{0<j<J} |Z_j^n|.$$

The experimental convergence rate $\rho(\tau)$ is defined as

$$\rho(\tau) = \log_2\left(\frac{\|Z(2\tau)\|_\infty}{\|Z(\tau)\|_\infty}\right).$$

In order to show that the constructed three-level discrete scheme on this special non-uniform time grid ω_t is stable and additional grid points really reduce the global error of the discrete solution, we give also the errors Z_3 of the classical three-level discrete scheme (14) when the time grid is uniform and it has N discrete points. The results of the computational experiments are presented in Table 1, where Z_1 is the error for the discrete solution of the scheme (12) and (13), Z_2 is the error for the discrete solution of the classical finite-difference scheme (14) on non-uniform time grids, and Z_3 is the error of the solution of the symmetrical scheme (7) when the time grid is uniform in $[0,1]$ and it has N points.

Table 1. Errors $\|Z_1\|_\infty$ and experimental convergence rates $\rho(\tau)$ at $T = 1$ for the discrete solution of the scheme (12) and (13) and errors $\|Z_2\|_\infty$ and experimental convergence rates $\rho(\tau)$ for the discrete solution of the finite-difference scheme (14) for a sequence of time steps τ. $\|Z_3\|_\infty$ is the error of the discrete solution of the the symmetrical scheme (7) when the time grid is uniform and it has N points.

N	$\|Z_1\|_\infty$	$\rho_1(\tau)$	$\|Z_2\|_\infty$	$\rho_2(\tau)$	$\|Z_3\|_\infty$
20	1.018×10^{-3}	—	1.279×10^{-3}	—	3.611×10^{-3}
40	2.429×10^{-4}	2.067	3.255×10^{-4}	1.974	9.042×10^{-4}
80	5.914×10^{-5}	2.038	8.204×10^{-5}	1.988	2.261×10^{-4}
160	1.458×10^{-5}	2.020	2.052×10^{-5}	1.999	5.654×10^{-5}
320	3.620×10^{-6}	2.010	5.131×10^{-6}	2.000	1.414×10^{-5}

As expected, the new three-level discrete scheme is stable and preserves the second order of convergence. We also note that additional grid points decrease the error; thus, the application of such a modified time grid is justified.

3.2. The Time Steps Are Halved at Some Grid Points

For the case when the time step size is halved $\tau_{n+1} = \frac{1}{2}\tau_n$, the following algorithm is proposed in [25]. The auxiliary solution $\widetilde{U}^{n+2}$ is computed using the standard three-level scheme:

$$\frac{\widetilde{U}^{n+2} - 2U^n + U^{n-1}}{\tau_n^2} + \beta \frac{\widetilde{U}^{n+2} - U^{n-1}}{2\tau_n} + A_h \frac{\widetilde{U}^{n+2} + U^{n-1}}{2} = F^n. \quad (15)$$

Then, solution U^{n+1} is computed by using the linear interpolation algorithm:

$$U^{n+1} = \frac{\widetilde{U}^{n+2} + U^n}{2}. \quad (16)$$

The final value of the solution U^{n+2} is obtained on the uniform grid with time step τ_{n+1}:

$$\frac{U^{n+2} - 2U^{n+1} + U^n}{\tau_{n+1}^2} + \beta \frac{U^{n+2} - U^n}{2\tau_{n+1}} + A_h \frac{U^{n+2} + U^n}{2} = F^{n+1}. \quad (17)$$

Again, we propose a modification of this algorithm when an auxiliary solution is not required. It is sufficient to use $U^{n-1/2}$, which is obtained by the linear interpolation:

$$\frac{U^{n+1} - 2U^n + U^{n-1/2}}{\tau_{n+1}^2} + \beta \frac{U^{n+1} - U^{n-1/2}}{2\tau_{n+1}} + A_h \frac{U^{n+1} + U^{n-1/2}}{2} = F^n. \quad (18)$$

In order to simplify the stability analysis, we take $\beta = 0$. Note, that it follows from the results given above that the real part of the solutions of characteristic Equation (10) is decreased for $\beta > 0$.

Theorem 2. *Let us assume that the interpolation error of* (16) *can be bounded by*

$$|\Psi_I| \leqslant C\tau^2.$$

If M is the number of times the time step of grid ω_t is halved, then the following estimate of the global error of scheme (18) *is valid:*

$$\|Z^n\| \leqslant M\tau. \quad (19)$$

In particular, if M is finite, then the error of the solution of discrete scheme (18) *is estimated by*

$$\|Z^n\| \leqslant C\tau. \quad (20)$$

If $M = C/\sqrt{\tau}$, then we have the estimate:

$$\|Z^n\| \leqslant C\sqrt{\tau}. \quad (21)$$

If $M = C/\tau$, then the discrete solution of (18) *is not converging at all:*

$$\|Z^n\| \leqslant O(1). \quad (22)$$

Proof. It is sufficient to consider the following problem for the Fourier coefficients of the error vector:

$$z_k^n = \gamma_{k1} q_{k1}^n + \gamma_{k2} q_{k2}^n, \quad k = 1, \dots, J-1,$$
$$z_k^0 = 0, \quad z_k^1 = d, \quad |d| = C\tau^2,$$

where q_{k1} and q_{k2} are solutions of the characteristic equation:

$$\left(1+\frac{\tau^2}{2}\lambda_k\right)(q_k^{n+1})^2 - 2q_k^n + \left(1+\frac{\tau^2}{2}\lambda_k\right) = 0.$$

Let us denote

$$b = \frac{1}{1+\frac{\tau^2}{2}\lambda_k}.$$

Simple computations give

$$q_{k,1,2} = b \pm i\sqrt{1-b^2},$$

$$z_k^n = \frac{d}{\sqrt{1-b^2}}\sin(\varphi n),$$

where

$$b \pm i\sqrt{1-b^2} = \cos(\varphi) \pm i\sin(\varphi).$$

Then, it follows that

$$\sqrt{1-b^2} = \sqrt{1-1/\left(1+\frac{\tau^2}{2}\lambda_k\right)^2}$$
$$= \frac{\tau\sqrt{\lambda_k}\sqrt{1+\tau^2\lambda_k}}{1+\tau^2\lambda_k/2}. = C\tau.$$

Thus, taking into account the estimate of the interpolation error and the bound for $\sqrt{1-b^2}$, we obtain that the global error estimate (19) is valid. The remaining error estimates (20)–(22) follow directly. □

Next, we present the results of computational experiments. The time grid is generated by dividing the time interval $[0,1]$ into five subintervals:

$$[(k-1)/5,\ k/5], \quad k = 1,\ldots,5.$$

In each subinterval, uniform grids are generated with step sizes

$$\tau(k) = 2^{1-k}/N, \quad k = 1,\ldots,5,$$

where N is the selected number of time points in the first subinterval. The results of the computational experiments are given in Table 2, where Z_1 is the error for the discrete solution of the scheme (18), Z_2 is the error for the discrete solution of the classical finite-difference scheme (14) on non-uniform time grids, and $\rho_{1,2}(\tau)$ are experimental convergence rates.

Table 2. Errors $\|Z_1\|_\infty$ and experimental convergence rates $\rho(\tau)$ at $T=1$ for the discrete solution of the scheme (18) and errors $\|Z_2\|_\infty$ and experimental convergence rates $\rho(\tau)$ for the discrete solution of the finite-difference scheme (14) for a sequence of time steps τ.

N	$\|Z_1\|_\infty$	$\rho_1(\tau)$	$\|Z_2\|_\infty$	$\rho_2(\tau)$
20	6.600×10^{-3}	—	2.205×10^{-4}	—
40	3.200×10^{-3}	1.044	5.787×10^{-5}	1.930
80	1.573×10^{-3}	1.025	1.481×10^{-5}	1.966
160	7.798×10^{-4}	1.012	3.743×10^{-6}	1.984
320	3.881×10^{-4}	1.007	0.941×10^{-7}	1.991

The presented results agree well with the theoretical convergence rate $O(\tau)$ given in Theorem 2.

In the final computational experiment, the length of the time grid steps was allowed to be doubled or halved. The length of sub-blocks is equal to 4τ, $\tau = 1/N$, and the grid points are distributed as

$$\begin{aligned} &n = 12m, \quad m = 0, 1, \ldots \\ &t^{n+k} = t^{n+k-1} + \tau, \quad k = 1, 2, 3, 4, \\ &t^{n+4+k} = t^{n+4+k-1} + \tau/2, \quad k = 1, \ldots, 8. \end{aligned}$$

The results of the computational experiments are given in Table 3, and they agree well with the theoretical estimates.

It follows from the presented results that, as is stated in Theorem 2, the discrete solution is not converging at all for such a modified time grid. Still the solution of the finite-difference scheme (14) is converging to quadratic order.

Table 3. Errors $\|Z_1\|_\infty$ and experimental convergence rates $\rho(\tau)$ at $T = 1$ for the discrete solution of the scheme (18) and errors $\|Z_2\|_\infty$ and experimental convergence rates $\rho(\tau)$ for the discrete solution of the finite-difference scheme (14) for a sequence of time steps τ.

N	$\|Z_1\|_\infty$	$\rho_1(\tau)$	$\|Z_2\|_\infty$	$\rho_2(\tau)$
20	1.036×10^{-2}	—	1.819×10^{-3}	—
40	9.391×10^{-3}	0.142	4.245×10^{-4}	2.099
80	9.033×10^{-3}	0.056	1.084×10^{-4}	1.969
160	8.964×10^{-3}	0.011	2.737×10^{-5}	1.986
320	8.958×10^{-3}	0.010	6.873×10^{-6}	1.994

4. Parabolic Interpolation

Let us consider one-dimensional parabolic problem:

$$\begin{cases} \dfrac{\partial u}{\partial t} = \dfrac{\partial^2 u}{\partial x^2} + f(x,t), \ (x,t) \in Q, \\ 0 < x < 1, \ 0 < t \leqslant T, \\ u(0,t) = \mu_0(t), \ u(1,t) = \mu_1(t), \\ u(x,0) = u_0(x), \ 0 \leqslant x \leqslant 1, \end{cases} \qquad (23)$$

where $Q = \{(x,t) : \ 0 < x < 1, \ 0 < t \leqslant T\}$ and functions $f(x,t)$, $u_0(x)$, $\mu_0(t)$, and $\mu_1(t)$ are sufficiently smooth.

In addition to the uniform time grid ω_t:

$$\omega_t = \{t^n : \ t^n = n\tau, \ n = 1, 2, \ldots, N\},$$

we define a nonuniform space grid, which can depend on time:

$$\omega_x(t^n) = \{x_j^n : \ x_0^n = 0, \ x_{J_n}^n = 1, \ x_j^n = x_{j-1}^n + h_{j-0.5}^n\}.$$

The grid $\omega_h(t^k)$ is not constant in time; thus, the number of grid points J_n and the position of each point may depend on t^n.

4.1. Finite-Difference Scheme

The main aim of this subsection is to show that the accumulation of the classical truncation error and of the additional interpolation error can be very different [1,9]. Generally, we are interested in investigating the stability of the BE finite difference scheme with respect to different types of local approximation errors.

In order to simplify our analysis, we assume that, at each time level that the space grid $\omega_x(t^n)$ is uniform, only the number of grid points J_n can vary from one step to another. The differential problem (23) is approximated by the implicit backward Euler (BE) scheme:

$$\begin{cases} \dfrac{U_j^n - I_{n-1}^n U_j^{n-1}}{\tau} = U_{\overline{x}x}^n + f(x_j^n, t^n), \quad 0 < j < J_n, \\ U_0^n = \mu_0(t^n), \quad U_{J_n}^n = \mu_1(t^n), \\ U^0(x_j) = U_0(x_j), \quad x_j^0 \in \omega_k(t^0). \end{cases} \tag{24}$$

Here, we denote the discrete solution $U_j^k = U(x_j^k, t^k)$, and the discrete operator:

$$U_{\overline{x}x} = \frac{U_{j+1} - 2U_j + U_{j-1}}{h^2}, \quad j = 1, \ldots, J-1$$

is used to approximate the second-order derivative in space. Then, the linear interpolation operator I_{n-1}^n:

$$I_{n-1}^n U_j^{n-1} = \frac{x_j^n - x_l^{n-1}}{x_{l+1}^{n-1} - x_l^{n-1}} U_{l+1}^{n-1} + \frac{x_{l+1}^{n-1} - x_j^n}{x_{l+1}^{n-1} - x_l^{n-1}} U_l^{n-1}$$

is applied to compute the values of a discrete solution U^{n-1} at grid points $x_j^n \in \omega_x(t^n)$, where $x_l^{n-1} \leqslant x_j^n \leqslant x_{l+1}^{n-1}$.

Let us denote $Z_j^n = u(x_j^n, t^k) - U_j^n$ as the error of the discrete solution; it satisfies the following discrete problem:

$$\begin{cases} \dfrac{Z_j^n - Z_j^{n-1}}{\tau} = Z_{\overline{x}x}^n + \Psi_A^n + \Psi_I^n, \\ Z_0^n = 0, \quad Z_{J_n}^n = 0, \end{cases} \tag{25}$$

where Ψ_A^n is the truncation error of the discrete scheme and Ψ_I^n is the interpolation error.

Lemma 2. *Let us assume that $u(x,t) \in C_4^2(\overline{Q})$. The truncation error Ψ_A^n of the discrete scheme* (24) *and the interpolation error Ψ_I^n can be estimated by*

$$|\Psi_A| \leqslant C(h^2 + \tau), \quad |\Psi_I| \leqslant \frac{Ch^2}{\tau}. \tag{26}$$

The proof of these estimates is based on the Taylor expansion technique and is given in many classical textbooks; see, e.g., [1].

Let us define the maximum norm of a discrete function Z, which satisfies the homogeneous boundary conditions:

$$\|Z\|_\infty = \max_{0<j<J} |Z_j|.$$

Theorem 3. *The solution of the discrete scheme* (24) *converges to the solution of the differential problem* (23), *and the following error estimate is valid:*

$$\|Z^n\|_\infty \leqslant C\Big(\tau + h^2 + \frac{h^2}{\tau}\Big), \quad n = 1, \ldots, N.$$

Proof. By applying the maximum principle to the solution of the problem (25), we obtain the stability estimate:

$$\|Z^n\|_\infty \leqslant \|Z^{n-1}\|_\infty + \tau\Big(\|\Psi_A^n\|_\infty + \|\Psi_I^n\|_\infty.\Big)$$

By applying this stability inequality iteratively, we show that

$$\|Z^n\|_\infty \leqslant \|Z^0\|_\infty + \sum_{k=1}^{n} \tau\Big(\|\Psi_A^k\|_\infty + \|\Psi_I^k\|_\infty.\Big)$$

The required estimates of the global error are obtained by using the estimates of Lemma 2. □

As one interesting conclusion from Theorem 3, we provide the accuracy estimates when the discrete time step τ is asymptotically decreased with respect to the space grid step h:

$$\|Z^n\|_\infty \leqslant C \begin{cases} h, \ if \ \tau = O(h), \\ \sqrt{h}, \ if \ \tau = O(h^{1.5}) \\ O(1), \ if \ \tau = O(h^2). \end{cases}$$

In order to show the accuracy of the obtained theoretical estimates, we present the results of the computational experiments. The data $u_0(x)$, μ_0, μ_1, and $f(x,t)$ were chosen so that the solution $u(x,t)$ is the function:

$$u(x,t) = e^t \sin(\pi x).$$

The given test problem is solved till $T = 1$.

The space grids are defined as a sequence of two uniform/almost uniform grids in the following way:

$$\omega_x(t^n) = \begin{cases} \omega_{x1} = \{x_j: \ x_0 = 0, \ x_J = 1, \ x_j = jh, \ j = 1, \dots, J-1\}, & \text{if } n = 2m, \\ \omega_{x2} = \{x_j: \ x_0 = 0, \ x_{J+1} = 1, \ x_j = (j + \frac{1}{2})h, j = 1, \dots, J\}, & \text{if } n = 2m+1. \end{cases}$$

We see that the lengths of the steps of both grids are equal, but the grid points are shifted by $\frac{1}{2}h$ relative to each other. In the case of odd time layers, the approximation of the second-order derivatives near the boundaries is performed by using the standard discrete operators as was described in the previous section. The second order of the truncation error is preserved also for this modified discrete scheme.

The results of the computational experiments are presented in Table 4, where Z is the error for the discrete solution of the BE scheme (24) and $\rho(h)$ denotes the experimental convergence rate.

Table 4. Errors $\|Z\|_\infty$ and experimental convergence rates $\rho(h)$ at $T = 1$ for the discrete solution of the BE scheme (24) for a sequence of time and space steps τ, h.

	J	τ	$\|Z\|_\infty$	$\rho(h)$
$\tau = 4h$	80	0.05	5.55×10^{-3}	—
	160	0.025	2.71×10^{-3}	1.034
	320	0.0125	1.34×10^{-3}	1.016
	640	0.00625	6.65×10^{-4}	1.011
$\tau = 2h^{1,5}$	160	3.12×10^{-3}	3.37×10^{-3}	—
	320	1.10×10^{-3}	2.56×10^{-3}	0.397
	640	3.91×10^{-4}	1.87×10^{-3}	0.453
	1280	1.38×10^{-4}	1.34×10^{-3}	0.481
$\tau = 40h^2$	80	6.25×10^{-3}	6.65×10^{-3}	—
	160	1.56×10^{-3}	7.41×10^{-3}	−0.156
	320	3.91×10^{-4}	7.62×10^{-3}	−0.040
	640	9.76×10^{-5}	7.67×10^{-3}	−0.009

The presented results of the computational experiments agree well with the theoretical estimates obtained above.

4.2. Discontinuous Galerkin Method

In this subsection, we solve the same parabolic problem by applying the discontinuous Galerkin (DG) method [20,27]. Let us consider the time intervals:

$$I_n = \{t: \quad t^{n-1} \leqslant t \leqslant t^n\}.$$

A space of discrete solutions is defined as

$$W^{(0)} = \{U(x,t): \quad U|_{I_n} \in S^1_{h,n}\},$$

where $S^1_{h,n}$ is a space of piecewise linear in x functions:

$$S^1_{h,n} = \{v(x,t): \; v(x,t) = \sum_{j=0}^{J_n} c_j^n \varphi_j^n(x)\}$$

and the basis functions φ_j are defined as

$$\varphi_j = \begin{cases} \frac{x-x_{j-1}}{h_{j-1/2}}, & x_{j-1} \leqslant x \leqslant x_j, \\ \frac{x_{j+1}-x}{h_{j+1/2}}, & x_j \leqslant x \leqslant x_{j+1}, \end{cases} \quad , \quad 0 \leqslant j \leqslant J.$$

By using the discontinuous Galerkin method, we define a discrete function $U \in W^{(0)}$, which is constant in time t on each time interval I_n and satisfies the equation:

$$\tau\Big(\frac{dU^n}{dx}, \frac{dv}{dx}\Big) + ([U^{n-1}], v^+_{n-1}) = \int_{t^{n-1}}^{t^n} (f, v)dt, \qquad \forall v \in S^1_{h,n}, \tag{27}$$

where

$$[U^{n-1}] = U^n - U^{n-1},$$
$$v_n^\pm = v(t^n \pm 0), \quad v^n = v_n^- = v^+_{n-1},$$
$$U_0^- = u_0.$$

From (27), we obtain the discrete scheme:

$$\frac{U^n - P_h U^{n-1}}{\tau} = U^n_{\bar{x}x} + \frac{1}{\tau}\int_{t^{n-1}}^{t^n} (P_h f)dt, \tag{28}$$

where $P_h f$ defines the L_2 projection:

$$(P_h f, v) = (f, v), \quad \forall v \in S^1_{h,n}.$$

By comparing the DG scheme (27) with the BE finite-difference scheme (24), we see that the main difference is in the way in which the solution values on the previous time level are computed. In the DG scheme, instead of the interpolation operator, the projection operator is used.

By applying the convergence analysis techniques described, e.g., in [20], the following result is proven directly.

Theorem 4. *The solution of the DG scheme* (28) *converges to the solution of the differential problem* (23), *and the error estimate is valid:*

$$\|u(t^k) - U^k\| \leqslant C\Big(2 + \log\Big(\frac{t^k}{\tau}\Big)\Big) \max_{1\leqslant k\leqslant K} \Big(\|h_k^2 f\|_{I_k} + \|\tau f\|_{I_k} + \|[U_{k-1}]\|$$
$$+ \Big\|\frac{h_k^2}{\tau}[U_{k-1}]\Big\|^*\Big) \leqslant C(\tau + h^2).$$

The term $\|\cdot\|^*$ arises only if $S^1_{h,n-1} \not\subseteq S^1_{h,n}$.

Next, in Table 5, we present the results of the computational experiments. The same test problem is solved as for the BE scheme (24). Here, Z is the error for the discrete solution of the DG scheme (27) and $\rho(h)$ denotes the experimental convergence rate.

Table 5. Errors $\|Z\|_\infty$ and experimental convergence rates $\rho(h)$ at $T = 1$ for the discrete solution of the DG scheme (27) for a sequence of time and space steps τ, h.

	J	τ	$\|Z\|_\infty$	$\rho(h)$
$\tau = 4h$	80	0.05	1.12×10^{-2}	—
	160	0.025	6.19×10^{-3}	0.855
	320	0.0125	3.11×10^{-3}	0.993
	640	0.00625	1.55×10^{-3}	0.998
$\tau = 2h^{1.5}$	160	3.12×10^{-3}	3.98×10^{-4}	—
	320	1.10×10^{-3}	1.40×10^{-4}	1.507
	640	3.91×10^{-4}	4.93×10^{-5}	1.506
	1280	1.38×10^{-4}	1.74×10^{-5}	1.503
$\tau = 40h^2$	80	6.25×10^{-3}	8.12×10^{-4}	—
	160	1.56×10^{-3}	2.03×10^{-4}	2.00
	320	3.91×10^{-4}	5.08×10^{-5}	2.00
	640	9.76×10^{-5}	1.27×10^{-5}	2.00

It follows from the presented results that the the solution of the DG scheme (27) is unconditionally converging to order $O(\tau + h^2)$.

5. Conclusions

In this paper, we investigated the stability of two finite-difference and finite-element schemes constructed for the solution of hyperbolic and parabolic problems. The main result shows that the accumulation of the classical truncation errors and the accumulation of the interpolation errors are quite different. The accumulation of the interpolation errors gives only conditional estimates, and the application of the discrete scheme with smaller time steps can lead to not smaller, but larger global errors.

A more accurate stability analysis was performed for the three-level discrete scheme, which was presented in a recent paper [25]. It was proven that, for almost uniform time grids with a possibility to double the step sizes of the grid at some time moments, the second-order convergence rates are preserved. In the case when the time grid step sizes are halved at some time moments, additional interpolation errors are introduced. A detailed spectral stability analysis was used to estimate the asymptotics of the global error in this case.

The results of extensive computational experiments were presented, they confirmed the accuracy of the obtained theoretical convergence estimates.

Author Contributions: R.Č. (Raimondas Čiegis): Conceptualization; Methodology; Writing—Original Draft Preparation; Numerical Algorithms; R.Č. (Remigijus Čiegis): Analysis; Validation; Writing—Editing; O.S.: Software; Computational Experiments, Analysis of Results. All authors have read and agreed to the published version of the manuscript.

Funding: This research received no external funding.

Data Availability Statement: Not applicable.

Conflicts of Interest: The authors declare no conflict of interest.

References

1. Hundsdorfer, W.; Verwer, J. *Numerical Solution of Time-Dependent Advection-Diffusion-Reaction Equations*; Springer Series in Computational Mathematics; Springer: Berlin/Heidelberg, Germany; New York, NY, USA; Tokyo, Japan, 2003; Volume 33. [CrossRef]

2. LeVeque, R.J. *Finite Difference Methods for Ordinary and Partial Differential Equations: Steady-State and Time-Dependent Problems*; SIAM: Philadelphia, PA, USA, 2007.
3. Zunino, P. Discontinuous Galerkin methods based on weighted interior penalties for second order PDEs with non-smooth coefficients. *J. Sci. Comput.* **2009**, *38*, 99–126. [CrossRef]
4. Neilan, M.; Salgado, A.J.; Zhang, W. Numerical analysis of strongly nonlinear PDEs. *Acta Numer.* **2017**, *26*, 137–303. [CrossRef]
5. Hansbo, A. Strong stability and non-smooth data error estimates for discretizations of linear parabolic problems. *Bit Numer. Math.* **2002**, *42*, 351–379. [CrossRef]
6. Ruzhansky, M.; Yessirkegenov, N. Very weak solutions to hypoelliptic wave equations. *Differ. Equ.* **2020**, *268*, 2063–2088. [CrossRef]
7. Pileckas, K.; Ciegis, R. Existence of nonstationary Poiseuille-type solutions under minimal regularity assumptions. *Z. Angew. Math. Phys.* **2020**, *71*, 192. [CrossRef]
8. Corallo, D.; Dörfler, W.; Wieners, C. Space-time discontinuous Galerkin methods for weak solutions of hyperbolic linear symmetric friedrichs systems. *J. Sci. Comput.* **2023**, *94*, 27. [CrossRef]
9. Samarskii, A.A. *The Theory of Difference Schemes*; Marcel Dekker: New York, NY, USA, 2001.
10. Knabner, P.; Angermann L. *Numerical Methods for Elliptic and Parabolic Partial Differential Equations*; Springer Series Texts in Applied Mathematics; Springer: Berlin/Heidelberg, Germany, 2003; Volume 44.
11. Kinash, N.; Janno, J. Inverse problems for generalized subdiffusion equation with final overdetermination. *Math. Model. Anal.* **2019**, *24*, 236–262. [CrossRef]
12. Umbricht, G. Identification of the source for full parabolic equations. *Math. Model. Anal.* **2021**, *26*, 339–357. [CrossRef]
13. Čiegis, R.; Panasenko, G.; Pileckas, K.; Šumskas, V. ADI scheme for partially dimension reduced heat conduction models. *Comput. Math. Appl.* **2020**, *80*, 1275–1286. [CrossRef]
14. Amosov, A.; Panasenko, G. Partial decomposition of a domain containing thin tubes for solving the diffusion equation. *J. Math. Sci.* **2022**, *264*, 25–33. [CrossRef]
15. Hofreither, C. An algorithm for best rational approximation based on barycentric rational interpolation. *Numer. Algorithms* **2021**, *88*, 365–388. [CrossRef]
16. Čiegis, R.; Dapšys, I. On a framework for the stability and convergence analysis of discrete schemes for nonstationary nonlocal problems of parabolic type. *Mathematics* **2022**, *10*, 2155. [CrossRef]
17. Samarskii, A.A.; Gulin, A.V. *Stability of Finite Difference Schemes*; Nauka: Moscow, Russia, 1973. (In Russian)
18. Gulin, A.V.; Ionkin, N.I.; Morozova, V.A. Study of the norm in stability problems for nonlocal difference schemes. *Differ. Equat.* **2006**, *42*, 974–984. [CrossRef]
19. Gulin, A.; Ionkin, N.; Morozova, V. Stability criterion of difference schemes for the heat conduction equation with nonlocal conditions. *Comput. Meth. Appl. Math.* **2006**, *6*, 31–55. [CrossRef]
20. Eriksson, K.; Estep, D.; Hansbo, P.; Johnson, C. *Computational Differential Equations*; Cambridge University Press: Cambridge, UK, 1996.
21. Bangerth, W.; Rannacher, R. *Adaptive Finite Element Methods for Differential Equations*; Birhauser Basel, Book Series Lectures in Mathematics; ETH Zürich: Zürich, Switzerland, 2003. [CrossRef]
22. Zlotnik, A.; Čiegis, R. On construction and properties of compact 4th order finite-difference schemes for the variable coefficient wave equation. *J. Sci. Comput.* **2023**, *95*, 3. [CrossRef]
23. Jiang, Y.; Ge, Y. An explicit high-order compact finite difference scheme for the three-dimensional acoustic wave equation with variable speed of sound. *Int. J. Comp. Math.* **2023**, *100*, 321–341. [CrossRef]
24. Omella, Á.J.; Pardo, D. r-Adaptive deep learning method for solving partial differential equations. *Comput. Math. Appl.* **2024**, *153*, 33–42. [CrossRef]
25. Vabishchevich, P.N. Three-level schemes with double change in the time step. *Comput. Math. Math. Phys.* **2023**, *63*, 1989–1995. [CrossRef]
26. Thomee, V. *Galerkin Finite Element Methods for Parabolic Problems*; Springer Series in Computational Mathematics; Springer: Berlin/Heidelberg, Germany, 1997; Volume 25.
27. Georgoulis, E.H.; Lakkis, O.; Wihler, T.P. A posteriori error bounds for fully-discrete hp-discontinuous Galerkin timestepping methods for parabolic problems. *Numer. Math.* **2021**, *148*, 363–386. [CrossRef]
28. Bonito, A.; Pasciak, J.E. Numerical approximation of fractional powers of elliptic operators. *Math. Comput.* **2015**, *84*, 2083–2110. [CrossRef]
29. Lee, H.G. A second-order operator splitting Fourier spectral method for fractional-in-space reaction–diffusion equations. *J. Comput. Appl. Math.* **2018**, *333*, 395–403. [CrossRef]

MDPI AG
Grosspeteranlage 5
4052 Basel
Switzerland
Tel.: +41 61 683 77 34

Axioms Editorial Office
E-mail: axioms@mdpi.com
www.mdpi.com/journal/axioms

www.ingramcontent.com/pod-product-compliance
Lightning Source LLC
Chambersburg PA
CBHW062048220926
51850CB00010B/2695
* 9 7 8 3 7 2 5 8 6 1 5 1 4 *